Ian Tungatt
A Portsmouth Living Legend

To

My Good Mate chris all the Best

Ian Tungatt
A Portsmouth Living Legend

ISBN 978-1-912821-09-9
A CIP catalogue record for this book is
available from the British Library.

Published 2018 Tricorn Books, Aspex
42 The Vulcan Building Gunwharf Quays
Portsmouth PO1 3BF

A PORTSMOUTH LIVING LEGEND

IAN TUNGATT

Contents

I would like to give praise to Ian, for when I was Lord Mayor of Portsmouth he arranged a charity evening at the dog track which was very enjoyable and for the Lord Mayor's charity, a tidy sum was raised. I have nothing but praise for Ian and always found him to be a very honourable person, offering help whenever I required it.

Jim Patey, former Lord Mayor

I've been in fights and seen many a good fighter over the years and Ian is the best and hardest I have ever seen.

Johnnie Stanley

Although many acquaintances have now passed away, some infamous stories have been left out for fear of incriminating others.

IWT

Chapter 1

I was born Ian Tungatt at home in Station Approach, Gosport, across the water from Portsmouth. I was raised into a family of four brothers and three sisters, and son to George and Dora (or Dot, as many would call her). When I was five months old we moved to the island of Portsea, containing most of Portsmouth. They were very hard times in Portsea and like most post-war families in the Portsea area, we were not well off. We came under the category of a poor family, and we would get free orange juice and vitamins from the health authorities. We would often get the nit-nurse at school; they would comb our hair through with a very close tooth comb on to a piece of white paper, in search of nits. They would proceed to coat your hair with this smelly concoction, which would stay on your hair until you got home, and then it was washed out. It was not very nice, as anyone who saw your hair covered in this smelly stuff, knew you had head lice.

Although there was a community spirit, and everyone would come together in times of trouble, if a person in the road had some stale bread, they would often knock on mum's door and say "Dot, got this bread if you can use it?" Mum would soak it in water to soften it, to make a bread cake with, or if she had the ingredients in the larder, she would do a nice bread pudding. How we loved them – looking back that seemed a luxury.

All the grown-ups would gang up and go in search of a lost child or children, but the real reason was that if the dad had given the missing ones a good hiding they would run away from home just to get away from the beatings. I would often run away by myself or with a brother. Looking back, Dad would be beery and then start on us when he got in. I remember one night hiding in a hole on the bomb site, pulling a sheet of tin over the hole and sleeping there till it got light, then making sure Dad had gone to work before venturing back in doors, then getting ready for school.

Mum stayed at home, Dad did not earn much. He was unskilled, and sometimes he would box for money or even fight on the street or in the fair along Southsea seafront. Although he would drink most of the money he earned away and at times come home violent.

We had no bathrooms; all we had was an outside toilet. We would have newspaper ripped into squares and have a hole bored through the corner, where a piece of string would be placed and made into a loop, and hung on a nail banged into the toilet door frame. So when we did use the toilet, we could pull off the pieces of paper as required. The toilet was quite a way down the garden and was usually very cold outside, especially during winter. Looking back it was a wonder we didn't get hypothermia using it.

There would be a tin bath hanging on the wall at the bottom of the garden, where it would be taken down and placed accordingly, ideally in the sun if it was out. Mum would go through the motions of heating up the gas boiler, tipping hot and cold water into the bath to get the temperature right. It was down to order of age who went in first, usually the four oldest kids. After we got out, the bath would be topped up, and the rest of the water was used for whoever was left.

We were always mucking about; Mum would leave us to wash while she would get on with other things. We would make so much noise and she would come back out ranting and swinging her cane telling us to keep it down because we had neighbours to consider. I remember one time my brothers were ignoring Mum's rants, and they pushed me down into the bath and ran away from Mum swinging her cane. As I came back up I took the full force of it. I put my hands up to stop the swipes but had all the tops of my fingers split as the cane was splintered. With blood pouring down my fingers I ran to the bottom of the garden to follow my brothers over the wall, which had barbed wire at the top to stop intruders. I managed to get caught up in the wire, and still had the cane striking the backs of my lower legs and feet. I fell on to the bomb site, as we called it, and ran across the broken bricks barefooted. Not a pleasant pain, and still to this day from those experiences, I still have trouble walking on stones or on unlevelled surfaces.

There was no social security in those days, so often it was soup and bread, mainly pea and ham on the bone, or stews, when Dad had a bit more income than usual.

As the days and weeks went by the stew would turn to weak soup, as more water was added the longer the period went with Dad bringing in less. When times were really hard we would have bread and OXO, with bread and milk at the end. We would all sit around the table and Mum would put a bowl in front of us giving each an OXO and then put two loaves of bread in the middle of the table, she would bring a large kettle and in turn pour the hot water into each bowl.

We would crumble the OXO into the hot water and break the bread up, dunking it until the OXO had gone and only water remained. We ate fast as my eldest brother Dougie often gladly took the liberty of eating his first and then stealing the rest from our plates, cheeky sod! After we had finished, the bowls were replaced in front of us again, but instead of OXO it was milk poured into the bowl, and in similar fashion we would break the bread into the bowl, sprinkle some sugar onto the bread and soak it into the hot water and milk. There was no way we could have extra OXO or milk, as this could not be afforded, it was very hard, but we survived.

Chapter 2

The main road leading down to the sea, commonly known as The Hard, was Queen Street. It was the centre of all activity in Portsea, as it was also the main road to the dockyard. At the time this is where most of the people in the area were employed. It was the road to all area naval bases, and where most of the sailors were based.

From as young as six my brothers and I had to go out and earn money for the family. We were lucky in some respects living on The Hard close to the sea, which gave us more than one way of making a bob or two. We would get string and tie fish heads to it and dangle them into the water and bait for crabs, or crabbing as we called it, and sell on to the local fishmonger. We had made wooden trolleys, so when the ferries or navy ships came in we used them to offer passengers to carry their luggage. Once there was an American family who made me go all the way up to Edinburgh Road which was about two miles away, and all I got was a thanks and no payment – not much you can do when you're six I guess.

When it was hot and sunny we used to mudlark. We would see the navy ships coming back to port, we would yell at the sailors and wave, giving them a hero's welcome, and while walking on to the mainland they would throw coins into the mud in appreciation. We would have to dive onto the money as there were other kids trying to grab it – it was like gold dust. As I grew older we would collect old newspapers out of bins and knock on household doors. When we collected enough we would bundle it and sell it on to the local waste collection firm. We were given so much by what the bundles weighed, so prior to weighing, we would get a brick and place it in the middle or just wet the middle of the bundle to make it heavier. The staff weighing it would never bother to check! If we were out late at times to get food we would chat up the prostitutes, or that is what I thought I was doing anyway, and they would give us the scraps from the local chip shop as they earned enough to keep by. There was definitely recognition of community back then. There would be asphalt blocks of tarmac on the road side, we would break off bits and chew it like gum. I stopped at 10 years old, not for health reasons but because we stopped seeing it on the streets. They must have changed the way they went about working with it.

One of my friends Johnnie who was a scout showed me how to mix plain flour with water until it was doughy, then you wrapped it around a stick and held it over an open fire which browned the dough off. We let it cool then ate it just to fill our bellies. I was soon stealing the flour from the mill in Portsea and making what I was calling dough rolls, then selling them for two a penny. I didn't make much, but every little helped, at least I could have sweets and crisps more often than any of my chums.

Chapter 3

"IAN!" Shit! Dad is pissed again. I knew what was coming. I could hear the heavy footsteps coming up the stairs tormenting me of the inevitable. I was in bed, the door flung open, the handle smacked the wall where there was already a hole. He stood there with anger in his eyes, fuelled red from the booze. I could smell it strong like vapour, thick and syrupy flowing up into my nostrils, nipping at my sinuses. Here we go I thought. "YOU LITTLE SHIT" he yelled. He marched over to me and grabbed me by the arm and flung me like a rag doll against the wall, bashing the back of my head, nearly knocking me out as I fell to the floor. He raced up with his belt and smacked it hard over my back. The pain was unbearable the first time, I built up some tolerance to it, but you always had to make sure you showed that you could take no more, just in case he would keep going. He walked out, closed the door and went downstairs to my mother, and I heard screams as he beat her too with his belt. My three brothers and my sisters in the other bedroom were crying. I had to calm my brothers down as I did not want him back upstairs hitting them as well, or even me again! If only I was big enough, I used to think, as I would dread my Mum getting hit. Bastard!

I learned to fight just to keep what was mine, like sweets and biscuits, and even a broken packet of crisps, in fact anything that was wanted by whoever wished to take it, even by people other than my family and friends. I retaliated and fought for what I wanted, and I soon found that I was good at this. Due to all the beatings Dad gave me, having a punch-up was second nature, so much so that the local bullies soon left me alone, instead picking on easier prey.

My brother Reg and I went to H.M.S *Vernon*. Dad seemed proud that we were in the naval cadets, but then you wouldn't know for sure as he was very moody, depending on the amount of drink he had taken. But this made no difference to us, as we got tea and cake there, and it was a chance to let off steam. We would hit the punchbag in the gym, and soon learned to box. I found this very rewarding, as it was a way to fight one on one and not as in the street, where often two or three would jump in should you be winning a fight. I would normally find myself fighting more than the one I had the grievance with.

Despite the boxing, fighting carried on throughout my childhood. My ear was always to the ground and I would find out the local bullies then challenge them to a fight. I was very thin and must have been suffering from malnutrition due to our diet or lack of it, and looking at me they would think I would be a push over. Even more so when I would run away, they thought I was scared. The secret was to let them think you were scared of them, and then they would agree to meet me for a fight. The fights were arranged by someone who the bullies thought had nothing to do with me, partly as they would be older. Whoever arranged it would then charge to watch the fight – about one penny. This was quite a lot when you had nothing. The bigger the reputation of the bully, the bigger the fee to watch, to as much as three pence, a tidy sum in those days. Thankfully I never lost. Eventually no one would want to take me on. After all I was just helping the weaker from getting hit by the bullies. So apart from cleaning up the area of this scum I was cut in to some fair money to keep the bullies away. When times got really tough though, like most in Portsea we would often turn to some sort of crime, like stealing milk or bread left outside a house by the milkman. Me and my brother Reg progressed and started breaking into working men's clubs. All we would do was get in through the back windows, go into the bar area and take all the cigarettes, crisps chocolate, baccy, cigars, and break open anything money would be stored in. We then gave it all to our Dad; he in turn gave us some money – only half a crown or may be a bit more – when he sold it on. We did so many clubs we were described in the paper as the club burglars. We had a good long run at this, then one day my brother was at the rear of a club we were getting into when he pushed the glass window so hard his hand went through the glass. The cut on his hand was long and deep, we tried putting toilet roll round it to stem the flow of blood, but it was still pouring out, it was everywhere. There was nothing for it but to visit the royal hospital. We were booked in and waiting to be seen when a couple of police came into the waiting area. This was the end of our little scam, I remember thinking. They waited till Reg was stitched up then proceeded to take us to the police station. We were shown the evening news and the headlines said, "Blood led to hospital" and words to the effect "club burglars caught". We were charged and let go, pending the court case. When Dad got us home he went mad saying we should have made it home and he would have sorted the cut out, obviously thinking of his loss of supplies, not our well-being.

When we did go to court, Reg was 12 and I was 11 years old. They gave him three years in approve school, and me a probation let off. It was strange not having my brother around as we seemed to do everything together, but get over it I did and proceeded to make other friends. The move of house our Mum and Dad made must have helped.

Within a year I was back with a new friend stealing and breaking into places, one of which was called the rope walk. It was off Church Road near Lake Road and near our new school. One day we were running on the roof of the rope walk playing around, I fell through the roof as it was only corrugated tin, and rusted at that. I fell onto a pile of rags, so I called out to a few friends on the roof saying I was OK. I then realised I was on top of a load of expensive rags. These could make us good money judging by the weight. I called to the boys to catch them and commenced throwing them out of the hole I fell in. This was going on for some time as all I could see was money in every handful thrown out. But then the correspondence I was having with my friends stopped. I heard running on the roof, then after a while of silence I heard "OK!" So I started throwing the rags up again, but in fact when a head peered down, I found out I was throwing them up to a police officer, caught bang to rights. He and a colleague took me to the police station, again.

They paid a visit to my house but only Mum was there. She came down to the station. I was put before a judge and sent to a remand centre called Glen House near Sarisbury Green on the way to Southampton. This is where I would stay until the court case. Dad did visit me on one occasion, but just kept on telling me how stupid I was etc. He told me I wouldn't be coming home; the police had told him I was to get locked up, how they knew that was beyond me. I was still only 11 years old so a shock to me.

Chapter 4

There were a few bullies in Glen House, up to the age of about 14 years old, and I was soon being picked on, as I must have looked thin and frail. Never mind, I was now back to fighting, this was one thing I did well at to express myself. I soon was taking big boys round the back of the school and beating them up; at last they were listening to me and not trying to beat me. Eventually a few months had passed and the date of my court case came through. This is where I would learn my fate. On reaching the court I appeared before a judge holding my Mum's hand; Dad didn't even turn up. They said I would be going to approve school for three years, this was a shock, and I was by now nearly 12. I wouldn't be seeing my Mum or family for three years, no it couldn't happen I thought, I was in a world of disbelief!

"Mum" I cried as they pulled me away. "Mum don't let them take me!" I screamed. I was kicking the police and anyone in the way of my hands or feet were getting hit. Mum was crying, that was the last I remembered until being put in a cell and awaiting my lift to start my incarceration.

When sitting in the cell I was at a loss to think my next three years were to be away from my family and friends, the shock of just knowing that at such a tender age was heart wrenching. Still it couldn't be changed now, so I awaited my transport to the next port of call. It was in fact back to Glen House, and then on to Kingswood Classifying School near Bristol. Here I was with youths up to 15 years old, and the bullying was again rife. But not to be deterred I got on with life, getting quite a few kicks in the ankle and digs in the side; the pests here seemed a lot bigger than at Glen House.

So I had to take a lot of the punishment dished out, not for long though, one kid I hit over the head with a broom, another with a shovel. There was one though who seemed bigger and stronger than the others – Big Jock. He would take a swipe at anyone, a big bully. How was I going to deal with him? He had to be hit hard, very hard. So I devised a plan whereby I would hide a cricket bat, then batter him over the head when the time arose. I hid the bat between two walls; I was the only one to know where it was. After our game of cricket, for some time everyone was looking for the lost bat, as it had to be handed in and accounted for. Working on the plan of surprise, when Big Jock walked near to where the bat was hidden, he would get it as hard as I could over his head.

I was sitting on the grass with a Portsea boy who was in there with me. He was about two years older than me, streetwise of course coming from there. His name was Basky Perryman. We had a good chat and he explained that my plan had big complications, and would it stop Big Jock anyway? What if I really hurt him and got more time added on to my sentence? This made me think Basky was right; I had to abandon my plan. I went to where I hid the bat and made out I had just found it, and the members of staff were pleased it was back and had not been stolen.

It was very hard in Kingswood, up at six every morning, we had to get up and run through a freezing cold shower and into the cold swimming pool. The initial shock was heart stopping. The pigs who made us do it were like sadists, that's all you could call them. After a few months, we had to be assessed to determine where we would be sent, to complete our three-year term. During the meeting with the governors I would praise my elder brother Reg making him out to be my guardian angel. "He is the only one who can calm me down and I listen to him at all times," I told them. I had about three interviews with the heads of Kingswood and every time my Reg got more and more a hero in my eyes, all a ploy mind, knowing where he was doing his time I wanted to be with him, my brother. The persistence of keeping Reg on a pedestal for so long had finally worked, he was the only one who could straighten me out and calm me down in their eyes, and now I was off to join him at Winton House School in Andover Road, Winchester. A great result! All the planning had worked.

On the way from the classifying school in Bristol, to the selected approve school Winton House School in Winchester, where I was to spend the next three years, I had time to go over in my mind some of the things that had happened to me family wise, before all this had now materialised. My head was spinning with all that had gone on in the past, it made me feel a lot older than the nearly twelve that I actual was.

First I missed Mum of course, then I would miss my brothers and sisters, of course I would even if it was mainly because of all the arguments and rows we had – we were still a family. That is time served and all going towards a life, a hard one but a life, then Dad would I miss him! Not in the slightest...

All the flashbacks were horrible of him, once he threw me down the stairs when I was about three years old, breaking my right arm; it was so bad it nearly came in two. It was hanging dangling, just about held together by the skin. The hospital thought I might lose it. Anyway, they cast it up as best they could, it was in fact set around the wrong way, and to this day if I straighten my right arm the elbow faces the floor. While I was in plaster I stayed at my Nan's, she would not stand any nonsense, so I knew I was safe and could recuperate without being hit. I stayed until out of plaster and it was set. One time after he returned from a drinking binge, he hung me on a coat hook behind the door and beat me with his buckle belt... I was black and blue.

Another time came to my mind, when near Christmas he gave me a pushbike as a present, it must have been stolen looking back, as it was painted completely red. Fresh paint as well, to cover up any noticeable marks on it. Dad then put two blocks of wood onto the peddles bolted through, as it was a man's bike and that way I could reach them. The wood was about six inches thick, even then I had a job to reach them, after all I was only a child and had a hard time just steering it right. One day I was on it and trying as best I could to manoeuvre it straight, but to no avail I went straight into a lamp post. This resulted in me breaking the front forks. My brother Reg helped me carry it back home. When Dad saw it he went berserk, and with no thought of Christmas cheer he belted me, wherever he could hit me, not thinking I had not wanted to break the bike but that I had done it deliberately... After that hiding I ached all over. So would I miss him? To this, it was a resounding no. I can honestly say no. I can even remember once being in a deep sleep, only to be startlingly awoken by Dad belting me in bed with his thick belt. Not a nice father at all, putting it mildly. Looking back, I can't remember him ever giving me a cuddle, let alone a kiss, not nice.

Chapter 5

The trip down to Winchester from Bristol seemed never-ending, but we did stop on the way and the officers with me brought me a sandwich and a drink. This seemed to calm me down, as cars never went too fast in those days. You would feel a bit sick after so long, so now I felt better, and now looking forward to seeing my brother Reg again. After all it had been some time since we last met.

The officers informed me that we were about to arrive at Winton House, this made me look up and take it all in. My heart was pounding as if out of my chest. What was I to expect, being locked in a cell, or locked in a room? I just could not envisage what to expect the situation to be, all that I did know was that my brother Reg would be there.

We drove down quite a long drive lined with trees; it opened up at the end with an area that you could drive round like a cul de sac, to leave the same way you entered.

The house was just like a large mansion, covered all over with growing ivy, just like one you would see on a poster or Christmas card. A marvellous looking residence, the officer then asked me to get out and take my belongings with me. They led me to a pair of very large front doors and pulled the bell. The door was opened by a maid of some sort and we entered.

We turned left through a door into the actual approve school area. This was separate from the front building and opened up into another world. We were introduced and escorted to the back section by the head master Mr Bottom. He was a very imposing looking man, very smart with a suit and tie. What I could remember was he was very stern looking, his shoes were sparkling, clearly polished to perfection and gleaming in the light.

I was then handed with my belongings to a teacher; I will never forget his name as over time he came to be a nutter. His name was Denis Barry Norman Chin Chin. His name ended up engraved in my brain which will be explained.

He took down all my particulars – age, home address, and Kingswood School where I came directly from. I was weighed and measured and asked a few questions to evaluate me. He took me to a supply room and gave me underwear, clothes plus boots, shoes, wellies. The trousers were in fact shorts made of a heavy tweed material. I also got shirts, jumpers, socks (two pairs one normal and one pair thick woolly ones).

I was then given a number, one that would stay with me all the time I spent at the school. It was number five. I had that number on all my lockers in the school. I guess it was giving you a bit of individuality during your stay. I had one in the living area, washroom area and shower room; there was also one in the quiet room where you would keep all your private things – letters, books, pens, pencils – anything for just yourself and not for other inmates.

I had the clothes put on my arms, and the boots and shoes were placed on the top, just like in the war films you see on TV. I had help from a prefect; he got that title for good behaviour and being near the end of his sentence. He led me through a corridor on my way to the locker in the changing room and wash area. We went passed a lot of pupils gathered around a fight that was going on between two other inmates. There was chanting and shouting "fight, fight, fight!". We stopped to look on. I could see just by looking over the shoulders of the crowd gathered round the fight, where one of the kids was just covering up and taking a lot of punishment. This is one thing I couldn't understand, why he wasn't fighting back; just trying to avoid the punches was beyond me.

Then I saw the face of the kid taking the blows. You can imagine my amazement and shock when I realised it was in fact my brother Reg. I instinctively threw my clothes and shoes down, and then jumped in hitting the attacker, then having a real battle with him. The bastard, hitting my brother, no way, I was thinking. We went at it like hammer and tongs; it seemed to go on for ages, a real hard fight. Soon blood was running down both our faces, pouring out from our noses and mouths. I had a cut eye as well.

I found out later after a master broke us up that he was the school bully and said to be the best fighter in the school as well. His name was Jones, a blond haired and stocky boy of 15. There was a lot of difference in age then, me nearly 12 and him three years older, a hell of an age gap, not when you are older, but then it seemed a ten-year difference was a life time. The teacher who stopped us told me to pick up my clothes and shoes then go to the locker room where the showers were and get cleaned up. While I was changing into my clean clothes, a boy came up to me and said one of the most stupid things you could hear, "Are you the new boy?" No there are hundreds of us you fool I thought. Anyway, he said, "Jones wants to see you in the quiet room." My immediate thoughts were that Jones wanted to see me to make up, as if bygones be bygones. The stupid boy took me to Jones' room. He was smiling and smirking all the way there. The door was opened and I couldn't believe what I saw, all the boys present were sitting on the lockers all around the room, the tables and chairs were all cleared away and there in the middle of the room stood Jones stripped to his waist. Still with blood on his face, and banging his fist into the other hand's palm, "Come on you squirt, you need a hiding now."

This is where my instinct took over. I took my top off, said three hail Marys then jumped in prepared to have a good long and hard fight. It seemed to go on for ages, but this was my comfort zone I was now in, as I never knew how or when to give in.

After what seemed like an hour, but could only had been ten or 15 minutes, Jones cried "Enough!" His face was a real mess, cuts over both eyes which were nearly closed, a bloodied nose and mouth and he looked exhausted. I didn't know how I looked, but I felt like Jones looked.

My face was sore to the touch and I had blood coming from my mouth and nose. Never mind, I was the winner and there were no mirrors in the room, so nothing to get too concerned about. I soon learned that he was supposed to be the best fighter in the school, so some achievement at my tender age. Really all I had done was what I would call naturally defending yourself, and that was something I was very good at.

I went back to the shower room to clean up, and this is where I finally meet our Reg.

Reg helped me wash away the blood, and told me to be careful, as Jones was a sneak and a bully so could jump me any time. I told him not to worry about that as I had until he left to get back at him again. I knew Jones knew, that is a thing I learned in Portsea, that bullies don't come back at you. They know if you're a fighter and don't give in and one that doesn't care as they just keep going.

After all, I never knew how to surrender. I questioned Reg and how he could just let Jones hit him without retaliating; I told him, "If you fight back you won't feel the blows coming at you, so just go into attack mode."

The fight I had with Jones seemed to have done me a lot of good. In fact it gave me good standing with the inmates, and a lot of the boys now wanted to talk and get on with me, knowing I could look after myself. This certainly helped me settle into the new environment.

The way things were done at Winton House were very regimental, just like I assume being in the services. You ran when called, and answered "Sir" when talking to a staff member. Even lining up you would put your right arm out straight and turn your head looking along your arm, and shuffle to form a straight line with your fist on the shoulder of the one next to you, and forming a perfect line. When I look back it was a domineering process! No answering back, no swearing when members of staff were around, and jumping when the head master was around. One of the best things looking back at that time of my life that we had to do, was every morning at wash time you were made to scrub your teeth, then you queued up to have them inspected by whoever was on duty to take morning wash period. That has stayed with me till this day, and it must have kept me in good stead as I have never had one tooth extracted to this day. This is surely a good thing to install in your child or children's heads. Life seemed to go along quite quickly when I had settled in.

I was getting the odd letter from Mum telling me how the family were. Dad even came to see us every few months, depending on his job at the time or whether he could use transport, supplied by the firms that is. He would never be able to afford his own car or van. He would sooner drink his money than spend it on luxuries like transport. Nevertheless, it was still nice to get a visit from him now and then, even if it was just to know how Mum and the family were keeping. The head master loved sport and was said to have played for Yorkshire at cricket. That was what we were lead to believe anyway, at what level we never knew, but he loved us mucking about at it, and playing cricket on the large game field we had in the grounds. He would pick two teams out and arrange games against each other. I really liked the freedom I felt playing the game in the large field – a feeling of freedom. At halftime you had a snack break, and then at fulltime we had sandwiches cakes and fruity drinks. We also had football matches, and had a similar setup within the grounds and a separate football pitch. I was a real sports boy. I would play football, cricket, basketball, rounders and running races. Anything to do with fitness and exercise, but I liked the boxing training the best. I was virtually untouchable sparring. We often had Winchester College in to play us at cricket and football, we even played rugby but now this is a game I could not handle. I remember we played against Winchester College twice at rugby, and twice I was sent off. You would be in a scrum when someone from the college team would screw your ear nearly off or punch and twist your nose nearly off. So naturally I would just hit out hard with anger, which inevitably led to me being sent off. This behaviour put me totally off the game of rugby, whereby I never volunteered to play again. Probably because I didn't feel in control, a bit like Dad beating me and nobody seeing it happen, which enraged me so much. I was a good runner and swimmer, so I would stay as fit as a butcher's dog, whatever that term meant.

I found to be a good chess player, which I learned from my time at Glen House remand home. There was a Hampshire champion chess player that came in regularly. He was also a very good tutor and I learnt it well, playing him on many occasions and coming close to beating him. If you won he would give you a box of chocolates, which no one ever managed to win. Although I was playing him one day, the game was very good and close and then he made a mistake, and I knew I had him. The playtime period was over and the chess set was placed on top of the book case in the rest room to finish later. I couldn't wait till the next break to beat the champ I thought. Alas when I looked at the board after our interval, the chess pieces were not in the same place as before the break. The master had changed a piece, and on resumption of the game he won. He knew he had changed the board, and in fact gave me a box of chocolates, and this said it all.

Most of my time at Winton House School, I would be receiving challenges to fight. Some stupid pupils must have thought all my wins were flukes so would like to prove it. They were obviously not the full shilling. The hardest thing was to arrange these fights away from members of staff so not to get caught. My favourite place for this was what I called the coal hole, a place at the side of the playground and just above the boiler room. This was going all the time, and a noisy place, just right to drown the shouting and screaming. Unless you were in my clique whereby you could watch, no one would know what was going on. The coal hole was a nice place to sort someone out, I would say a gifted one for a good fight, and I would visit this place many times while doing my time at Winton House School.

We were training in the gym one day and sparring at boxing when the head came in with a principal from Winchester College. Unbeknown to us they were going to arrange a boxing tournament against the college to be held at our school. Good job they never saw me or our Reg sparring with anyone as I'm sure they would have cried off. Inside the ring our Reg really came into his own, he was so tall for his weight and with a very long reach, so no one could get near him, and my god could he hit. He would tell anyone if he caught them clean he was so gifted in that department. I used to be bewildered, why he wouldn't fight outside the ring. There again being between the ropes was his comfort zone and he was very good in it.

So the matches with the college were to be arranged, and the stipulation being the Winchester College boys had to have a few weeks to get ready, thinking that would be giving them the edge over our lot.

The day of the tournament had arrived, we had the ring in our hall erected and very imposing it looked. All the competitors from Winchester College were arriving with quite a large entourage of parents and friends and were shown to their seats. There were many seats but the Winchester lot had been shown to all the best seats in the front rows around the ring apron. The head loved to think he was one of what I would call snobs. They were talking with plums in their mouths, so their boxers were their little rich boys and not rough and ready like we were.

There were to be six bouts. We were crammed into a small changing room close to the wash house, but the visitors were given the whole changing room adjacent to the showers, so they had plenty of space to change and relax, then unwind while waiting for their bout in peace and quiet. We were gloved up then sent out of our small dressing room with no room to warm up, but we did manage to get some shadow boxing in the dining room, unbeknown to the head. Ding! Ding! The first bout was on. Our boy easily well out-boxed the Winchester boy, yet he only got a draw which was disgraceful. The second bout was the same, our boy well beat the Winchester boy again and winning every round, yet they gave the decision to the college boy. As far as I was concerned it was very one sided. I glanced across at the head, he was sitting there cheering and clapping, and having a good chinwag with a college representative and seeming well happy with himself. That was it, I had decided us next four boxers together, having a good chat at how we could get the results we unreservedly deserved. We would go at them right from the first bell, don't stop punching forget the rules, just get the college boys out of their stride. This advice was to work to perfection. The next one in just kept punching, giving his opponent a very bad bloody nose, the boy just covered up and stopped fighting back. The referee had no choice than to step in and stop the bout. The cheers from our inmates were at fever pitch and a load of clapping which was great to hear, and then I was on. I opened up on my opponent, hitting him with everything in my armoury. He sank to one knee and the ref started a very slow count giving him plenty of time to recover, but on his rise I was straight back on him again, feeling every punch sinking into his body. He just could not last with this barrage of punches. Sure enough he went down again this time not to rise, my hand was held aloft, the noise from the inmates was now deafening. I could not wait to rub down, take my gloves off and return to watch the next fight.

In this fight our boy cut the college boy's eye quite badly, and unbelievably the boy stopped boxing and started to cry. I have never seen anything like this before. The wimp! Our boys were again chanting "Easy! Easy!" and clapping loudly. This sounded great, and glancing at our head, he appeared red faced and very quiet. Now our Reg was on next and he looked a lot taller than their boy, but also a lot thinner. The one he was fighting must have been their best boxer as the reception he got from the college mob was twice as much as any of these other competitors, the Winchester college's number one. I thought looking at Reg he seemed quiet and fully focused on the job in hand. They were both announced, and on this the chanting and clapping seemed louder than ever. With a lot of the visitors standing up to give this boy a really good clap, well Reg just went at him on the sound of the bell, measured him with his right hand then let his left hand go. It hit him with such a thud the boy's head was knocked upwards as if looking at the ceiling and down he went like a sack of spuds. It looked a very bad fall and he was out cold. The cheers and clapping started but this stopped quickly when it was obvious the boy was really hurt. He never moved at all, and for one minute I thought he had died it was that bad. The head master went straight to the ring to assist the doctor who was already there. The poor boy was out for the count. It took some time to bring him around, having been doused with cold water from a wet sponge, he was still very groggy but rose and was ushered out of the ring, and he was taken straight to Winchester hospital. What happened next was hard to believe, Reg was told to shower and get changed. He was going with the head master to the hospital to say sorry, yes sorry, and to give the boy a box of chocolates supplied by the head himself. We stayed behind at Winton House to eat the nicely prepared buffet and cakes that had been put on for us and the visitors, and it was a marvellous spread. Obviously, the college boys were meant to win the contest, so the after party was supposed to be a good victory bash. It appeared the head master had vastly underestimated the strength of his squad.

After a few days had past, we boxers were made to mow the cricket pitch and roll it repeatedly. There were no breaks, we just spent all our time on the cricket pitch, mostly rolling it. The roller was made of solid iron, and heavy. It took at least four of us at a time to pull it, and we did this for a few days until the head master had cooled down. Why he blamed us for just winning our bouts was beyond me. He must have really thought he would be in with the Winchester College governors. This may have been down to his background as he was obviously well reared and educated.

When all was back to normal I remember a new PTI had started, which I think was to make sure there was no more boxing going on. I quite liked the new PT, he was a very fit person and regularly had us running around the field and also had us using newly delivered weights, which was to help build up our upper arm area. Then the reason for this manoeuvre had become obvious, Mr Thomas was a very keen canoeist, and we had an inside swimming pool so he was in his element. He was often canoeing in it or practising, and eventually he started to teach us how to canoe. It was very awkward at first, just to stay upright, and was demanding while paddling yourself along. I took to it quite easily though in the end and so did our group. He took us under his wing. Reg was in the group with me, he was also a natural sportsman and seemed to take to every sporting activity the same as myself. When we got quite good at canoeing in the pool, we started experimenting with what was called the Eskimo roll. Now this was very hard at first – you had a waterproof cover (don't remember what it was called, I find remembering names from childhood very hard indeed, and this seems a common thing when one gets older) which you placed over your head and it then fitted around the hole of the canoe you were sitting in, forming a waterproof seal so as to stop any water from getting inside the canoe. You then placed the flat part of the paddle flat on the canoe front, then held the back of the paddle in the palm of your other hand, and you rolled the canoe over holding your breath, upside down, then flapped the paddle on the pool water surface and pulled down on the paddle, then pulled yourself up to the surface again. This got quite easy when you got used to it, and the weight training helped to give you that powerful and muscular upper body strength to be able to pull yourself up through the water. We were shocked one day when Mr Thomas told us as we had taken to canoeing so well that he was going to take us on a trip canoeing on the Isle of Wight. This was to do some, what he called, open canoeing on the sea, and goes to show he was well liked by the head master, as we had never been allowed to venture out of the school before, let alone stay away for two days. What a bonus, I thought.

We travelled in a minibus down to Portsmouth and via the ferry to the Isle of Wight. When we arrived on the island, we went to the campsite. This was situated quite close to where we got off the ferry. At the site there were four other groups in the camp, all for this canoeing convention. The ages seemed to go up to the age of 16. Our oldest was 15, but still we all mucked in and it was fun. There was one boy there who we were told was a local, he was very mouthy and loud – a real show off. He made a beeline for me, now there was a definite clash there. Well the inevitable had to happen, and eventually we had a fight. He seemed shocked when it started but the reason for this fight was all down to him. He tried to bully me and that just wasn't going to happen. I planted a few hard punches to his face area. This drew quite a lot of blood, in fact his face was soon pouring blood from his nose and mouth, and it looked quite bad, so the fight was soon broken up. Mr Thomas was OK about it, but did say keep away from that big mouth. He had obviously noticed what the boy was like, and he said he knew what was coming knowing what I was like.

The couple of days went nice and smooth, in fact it was a really good laugh and a very enjoyable break. We only slept one night and the next day went back to the ferry and returned back to Winton House. On our arrival back everyone wanted to know how the trip had gone. I guess they knew I would fall out with someone, and had anticipated me having a fight. I wonder why?

Looking back, Winton House School was a violent place to be, not so much for me as I was strong and would never let anyone take me for a ride, but for the weaker ones in the school. It would have been a vile place to be put, they were beaten regularly even in the shower when nude, not a nice sight to see a hand mark deeply embedded on their backside, and the staff had no qualms. They just hit out at any time and on any part of the body, even kicking out at times. Horrible to see from so-called trusted staff. That is when you realised you weren't getting discharged anytime soon.

Here I was, a teenager at 13, I first came in here in September 1961, but exactly where that first year had gone I couldn't envisage. The main thing was, I felt older and stronger and nearly a man. I ran and trained nearly every day, the only thing that never changed was that I remained thin with wide shoulders. I must have been running and working off all the extra calories I was now consuming. Also by now all the inmates knew how good I could fight and look after myself so I had no worries in that department, no singles would pick on me at all. The only thing that would happen now and again was that two or three would gang up on me, to try and bring me down a peg or two. When I found myself in one of these predicaments, all I would tell them to do was meet me around the coal hole, my favourite fighting place, then if there were two or even three I would deal with them accordingly. I would knock one of the boys over with just one blow of my fist, this was a gift I had acquired. If say three moved in on me I would then get away from the other two by biting and kicking them off, which gave me time to line them up knowing I could now punch them clean and they couldn't take the power my fists could dish out. When it was over, and as always minimal if no damage at all to myself, we would go back to living our normal life in the home. Although at times I found you would get a group of inmates who would load the gun with chit chat, but would never pull the trigger. These were the sly ones who had no bottle at all, little worms I would call them, who were frightened of their own shadow, but they still had the front to stir up other inmates into believing that they could beat me at any time they chose. I would also call these fools. If anyone told me of a shit stirrer I would give them a slap, as hitting them was of no point, they would just cower away, cover up and let you hit them at will. Just like a snake, this is exactly what they were.

Chapter 6

I was now well into my teens during the very bad winter of 1962–1963. The snow was about four to five feet deep, and so cold you would feel the chill cutting you in half. Yes, it was a terrible winter that year. I remember we were just talking in the dormitory just before we were due to get up at 6.30 am, and we had woken up the duty staff. They used to stay overnight in an adjoining bedroom. One of them came in screaming and shouting, "GET OUT! COME ON, GET UP YOU SCUM!" he called us.

There was about six of us just having a chat before we had to get up and back in the robot routine. This is what I called it in the home. He singled us out, made us get dressed in shorts, a vest and big studded boots. We were sent to run around the playground that was covered in snow at least four feet deep. We had to keep running to stop us from getting hypothermia. Round and round, you soon forgot how many laps you completed, but you just had to keep going.

In these conditions you wouldn't make an animal do that, it was nothing short of criminal. Then again who would listen to you? No one.

The rest of the school would now have got up, showered, dressed and had breakfast, yet we were still running round in the freezing snow. At this point we were now developing chafes on our hands and knees, even the Nazis wouldn't put you through this, I was thinking. The teacher responsible for our cold and pain must be a psychopath, the bastard. His name would forever be engraved on my brain. It was Denis Barry Norman Chin Chin, yes some mouthful, but what he put us through was nothing short of diabolical, a real misfit. I remember him often losing it with an inmate, he would hit, kick, punch them with no let-up of a madman. I used to notice when he went into one of his rages, the veins in his neck would stick out bulging as if they were about to burst. He was on the verge of being a lunatic, yes a real nutter. I knew a man like that was not going to let us stop running around the yard in the snow getting chafes and frostbite. Then when he was ready, he told us to go and have a hot shower, get dressed and go for our breakfast. The other inmates had long finished theirs, but ours was left out on the table and frozen stiff. It was streaky bacon, fried bread and freezing baked beans, and frozen toast with butter and marmalade. It was frozen so hard you could have hit the plate and broken it. The food was in fact frozen solid, and we held it in our hands trying to thaw it so we could eat it. If you didn't you would just starve. Some state to leave young people in to survive, they had not a bit of feeling, the pigs.

One of the worst things that used to go on at Winton House was when someone had to have the cane. Unless you saw it you wouldn't believe it and how it was done. The one who was ordered to have the cane was escorted by two prefects, they were older inmates, and were near the time to be discharged, normally larger than the one who was to be thrashed. That is a better more appropriate name to call it. Anyway, they took them into the long dining room (this had a highly polished floor), they were then held over a table with their shorts or short trousers down. They would then by struck with the cane with tremendous force – this was absolutely barbaric. After a few of these lashes, the boy getting hit would either faint or start to scream out so loud that other members of staff would usually appear at the scene thinking someone must be getting killed. They were only to be sent away by Mr Bottom the head who was a very cruel man.

After seeing this I made my mind up, that if I ever had to get the cane they could whistle. I would not let this happen to me, I would fight whoever with whatever, but no way was I going to let anyone cane me without a real struggle. I think this got around all the staff, as many times I should have been ordered to have the cane, but that would never happen. I know for a fact I would have put whoever in hospital just to save going through that punishment. It was a no-go area in my mind.

After someone had been caned you should have seen them after in the shower. Their backside was red raw and the welts from the caning left them looking just like raw meat with blood oozing out of the cane marks, and the dark black bruising clearly seen running away from the welts caused by the beating they had just received. You had to feel sorry for them and the pain they had just endured, you wouldn't do it to a dog, it was nothing short of barbaric. The beating they had just been through was certainly not a thing that should have been allowed to have happened under any circumstances.

Chapter 7

Every Sunday we would dress in long grey trousers, shirt, jumper, tie and highly polished shoes with a blazer, and then we would walk into Winchester to church. After a few weeks, Mr Bottom asked if anyone would like to be in the choir and sing while we were at our service. I put my hand up and Mr Bottom accepted me straight away; I got on well with the sadist head and his wife. In fact, I used to sit with them on their table in the dining room, a real privilege then. His wife was the one who told me to eat with my mouth closed as she didn't want to see what I was eating, and this advice has stayed with me all my life, a manners thing really.

Being in the choir meant we would have lessons every week. This was good because we had fruit juice and sandwiches after and also they gave us some honey sweets, which stopped us getting a sore throat when we used our vocal cords to excess. I also did a bit of acting while in the home, and starred in *A Midsummer Night's Dream* and acted the part of Thisbe. We put on two shows one week and had a full paying audience and they came in from outside. The money raised went to Mr Bottom's charity, but I liked the cheers and clapping we got at the end of the play and found this invigorating and very rewarding. One of the teachers spoke to me at some length after rehearsals one day saying I should consider trying to get into acting as a career, even starting in an amateur society locally. He obviously liked the way I performed on stage. Mind you, I looked at it as if only wimps did acting, and not a real manly thing to do. Why I came to that conclusion I don't know, be it right or wrong, I just could not see myself spending hours and hours memorising the words for the play when I could be out and enjoying myself with mates.

Not all of the times at Winton House were that hard, in fact we had many good and funny times as well. We were allowed hobbies, and my time was used up following Tottenham Hotspur football team. That's when Danny Blanchflower was captain. I used to look forward to Saturdays to get the football results and see how they had got on. They were then and in fact still are a very good team.

I remember when they signed Jimmy Greaves. He was nicknamed 'the poacher', and that was because he would hang around the goal area then strike any loose balls into the net. He was a true wizard of the game, who could create a goal from nothing.

When Spurs signed him it was for a record fee. The sum was actually £99,999. The chairman put up the extra pound to make him the first £100,000 player. It was some sum in the early sixties, mind you his goals would so often win a game and so it proved money well spent, and he repaid his massive signing fee many times.

Next door to the grounds of Winton House was a girls' remand home, and some of the girl inmates would often come to our chapel on a Sunday night. I was often the one chosen to hand out the hymn books to them as they entered the chapel, and if one of our inmates took a fancy to one of the girls they would ask me to pass on a letter to them. I would do this by placing the note inside a hymn book, then let the chosen one know as I handed them the book. If a date was arranged I would let them know the same way, but hand them a note on their exit when taking back their book.

The meeting would be quite easy. The boy, whoever it was, would simply wait until after lights out in the dormitory and when all was quiet, he would sneak out of the home, and then meet the girl in a clump of trees just off Winton House Drive. This is where the girl, or in some cases the girls, would meet their dates, and it was easy as there was just a wall dividing the two buildings, so the girls could get over and outside without too much trouble. Whoever was first there would hide in the trees until the date arrived. The trees would hide whoever from either school. They would return to their beds and no one would be any the wiser.

Some of the inmates from our school said at different times that they were abused by some of the masters, but I can't say much about those allegations, as I never experienced anything like that myself, but pupils often talked about it. I would say to whoever talked about it that they should retaliate by kicking out, or better still hitting out and screaming, but it appeared most said they were too scared. I could imagine that most of them were frail or feeble, others were given treats like sweets or cakes as a reward; mind you, I thought they were sick and only encouraged the assaults to go on.

Another thing that came into force was home leaves in summer and at Christmas. You only qualified for these if you had a term with no trouble, so not all were allowed to go. If you were, wow what a bonus! And great to get away for this short but appreciable break from this enforced incarceration. It was while I was on one of these breaks that I learned Dad was made to pay by way of a charge, the sum of ten shillings a week just for us staying at Winton House. A tidy sum then considering his wages were only about three pounds ten shilling a week, and he had eight children. I remember there was no dole money back then or anything else for that matter to make his wages up. Dad also had to have his drinks money, food and still pay the mortgage and whatever Mum had on the tick. Looking back, how the hell he managed this was beyond me. This was even harder to take in as I was now of an age to understand the value of money. Talk about the feeding of the five thousand with fish and loaves, Dad would have liked to have had them to break up, why he had so many kids was beyond me.

We used to go on walks most Saturday or Sunday afternoons. There was a teacher called Mr Van Dyke, we called him Dick Van Dyke after the actor who was just making a name for himself. Anyway, the one in our school was just plain Van Dyke. He told us he played football for Winchester City team. How true this was we never knew as we only had his word for this. He was a tall man of six feet ten inches tall, yes a very tall man compared to the size of us kids. What made it even more strange was the fact he had a crew cut. This put another two inches on his height, because his hair just stuck straight up, so now he appeared nearer seven feet tall, a great height and very scary in those days.

One weekend he took the walking group out along Andover Road, and then into some woods. This made the walk more interesting seeing wildlife and plants, and broke up the boredom of a walk along any old road.

While walking in the woods I was talking to the boys in front of me, so obviously a bit out of an orderly line from what Mr Van Dyke wanted. He walked with a very long walking stick; this was nearly as tall as us boys due to his height. I was just walking and chatting away, when all of a sudden I got this almighty crack on the back of my legs. Van Dyke had brought the cane down from what seemed like the sky, straight on to the rear of my legs. God did it hurt, coming out of the blue and striking me with so much force it seemed he had broken both my legs, and the pain was indescribable. There I was, doubled up in agony and laying in old rotting and mildew leaves and stale moss, smelling all fungus around my nose. Yet all Van Dyke shouted to the boys was "Walk on!" and never as much as gave me a hand or indeed a look, some pig he was.

I was left just lying there, I could not feel my legs at all, and they were numb with an excruciating pain. I thought they must be broken. Shortly some feelings started coming back into my legs. All I could hear in the foreground was "CATCH UP TUNGATT!" Rising to my feet I managed to drag myself towards the group. I was looking at Dyke with venom, and I felt all the rage my body could muster over and on to Dyke. I was badly limping while forcing myself onwards towards the others. You bastard, I thought, and the nearer to Dyke I got, I decided to get him. I picked up a broken branch, the largest I could hold, and hid it behind my back as I was approaching Dyke.

He was going to get it good and proper, all I could see was him and I was by now oblivious to anything else bar him. When I got closer to him the rage had now taken over, and he was walking and looking forward not in the least bit worried if I was seriously injured. I got right up close then wallop, I jumped with the broken branch and brought it down with as much force as my trembling body would allow, and striking him with all my might on his head.

Got you, you fucker. He fell to the floor blood coming from a wound on his skull; I wasn't even thinking I could have killed him, it was no more than he deserved for hitting me as he did. All I said then to all the other boys was "Walk on". Giving him a bit of his own medicine, I just left him lying there the same way he had done to me. The boys knew I was in a vile mood so they just carried on walking. Dyke had caught us up just before we were about to enter the school grounds. He was a bit bent over and had blood on his head which was clearly cut, and was hobbling along looking shocked. I had calmed down a lot by now, and thought what the hell is he going to do.

Will he report me for the cane when we got into the school? As I knew I would not stand for that. This is when I talked to him, and said, "If you tell the head or mention it to anyone I will get you again and do it harder next time." This was a ploy but would it work? Well I was about to find out. I even said about stabbing him. His eyes opened up in amazement, but I still never knew what to expect until we got back into the house. When entering we turned left and proceeded to the changing rooms for a shower and got ready for tea. Mr Dyke just disappeared into the confined area of the house. Now I was thinking what was going to happen, would he tell the head or call me into the head's office? I had no idea. All I could do was carry on and you shall see.

So I showered, changed and headed to the dining room for tea, if I was to get some, and just wait for what I thought was the inevitable. Anyway, we finished tea and proceeded to the restroom for reading and games. Here I was, waiting but as yet nothing had happened. How long would it take? I was in limbo not knowing. The anguish went on until we were told to pack away and head to the dormitories and get ready for bed. Still nothing had happened, everyone was muttering, what was going to be the outcome no one knew, but most who were scared of me were hoping for the worst.

While lying in bed waiting for lights out the banter was rife, and the older boys said I had some bottle and that I could have easily killed him. I told them "It wasn't bottle" as they thought "but temper and rage". Why should a man of Van Dyke's size hit a pupil with that force and get away with it? I didn't care if he had died, he deserved what he got the bastard. Lights out came and the muttering was still going on in the dark, and what would happen the next day that was anyone's guess. When Dyke got over what happened would he want revenge? I was beginning to think that he was obviously a bully, (a) for doing what he did to me, and (b) for not retaliating or doing anything about it. I was of the opinion he was in fact a bully so worried of the repercussions he might get, also hoping my assumptions were right.

The night had now past and there was no more said of the walking incident, everything was now back to normal or I hoped it was.

Chapter 8

The maths teacher was another who would always seem to be getting on at me whenever he thought he could; a real nuisance at times his name was Mr Weeks. He would also muck in as a general hand in running Winton House, and looking after the pupils, like a master really. Even so I knew he never liked me.

One day during a maths lesson, Weeks was writing on the blackboard. I was chatting away, and he sharply turned around and swore at us all, "Will you fucking shut up when you're in my class?" There was complete silence. We all looked at one another in amazement at his outburst. Yes, he had clearly lost the plot, but worse was to come. He turned back towards the blackboard, gathered his composure and carried on drawing. After a short while we started chatting again, and we never expected the next thing to happen. He just turned around and this time had lost it big time. He threw the blackboard rubber directly at me. It was a solid block of wood, with the padding to clean the board on the front of it.

He let it go with such great force it hit my head and the corner lodged itself briefly into my forehead. It dropped to the floor, and the next minute I knew, blood started pouring out. Mr Weeks looked dumbfounded by what he had done; he must have lost the plot totally for that short while. Anyway, I felt the red mist coming over me, yes my temper had gone. "BASTARD!" I shouted.

I made my way towards a crate of milk that was in front of the class, shouting "You pig!" amongst other words. I was on another planet at this point. I started to throw the bottles of milk at him, repeating "BASTARD!" He was rushing, ducking and diving until he was out of the door, being pursued by bottles of milk which were smashing on the walls and on the floor behind him. After I calmed down and saw the mess, it was unbelievable. Broken glass and milk all over the classroom. I bet Mr Weeks had never moved so fast in his life, after all it was for his life I suppose, in his mind anyway.

Myself along with the rest of the class were now unattended. I thought, what have I done? Blood was still coming from the wound in my skull. I put a cloth from the sink over in the corner onto the wound, and went to the broom cupboard to get a dust pan and brush, along with mop and bucket.

Some classmates mucked in and we brushed up all the glass, mopped up the milk, squeezing it into the bucket. We even used some disinfectant and mopped the floor again, to freshen the place up, repeating the procedure with the walls, until it was looking clean and smelling fresh again. In fact, it was cleaner than it was before. You wouldn't have known what had gone on.

The bell then rang which signalled the end of the lesson, and we went to our next class.

We never saw Mr Weeks again that day, in fact he never showed for a few days. He must have taken a few days off thinking he had done me serious damage. Anyway nothing else was said about it, and I wasn't going to mention it to any member of staff. Other than the boys talking about the incident, it would hopefully die a natural, just the way anyone involved would have wanted.

As the months went by I was getting a bit upset. My brother Reg was now near the end of his time that he had to serve. Reg was in there a year before I got there, and I had lost all track of time.

Yes, I was about to lose him to the outside world, and I would be left in the school without a brother and no soulmate. I would just have to knuckle down for another year until my time in this place was up also.

Although I had just hatched a plan whereby I may get released early, however this was unlikely.

At the heart of the plan, was a school trustee, we called him Super. A lovely man who would visit bringing sweets and pop most weekends, and he would talk to me most of the time. When he came we would walk the grounds while having a good heart to heart.

I was about to boost my brother up to a high again, telling Super how could I manage with no brother in here, with him giving me guidance, I would even cry when I was in front of him saying, "I can't survive with my brother not with me, and I will be totally lost."

Anyway, this went on for a few months, me chipping away at Super's heartstrings, and hoping to make a breakthrough. For I knew he had so much sway on the board of governors, and he would be there for all the board meetings, but I didn't know if he would speak up for me, to get an early release date or not. This was a thing I had to work on, and say, "I may fall apart without Reg even mentally without his strength to keep me sane, it would be so hard on me." This play would have to go on for ages, weeks or even months, who would know, all I could do was keep acting in front of Super and see if anything was to come from it.

This would have to be done when we were on our own in the grounds, after all I didn't want any of the inmates see me acting and crying, because they knew it was not me, as I was hard to the skin. I couldn't handle the boys thinking I was soft, or had gone that way, so it was just for me and Super to see the act.

After a few months I was walking with Super one day, and he said I was appearing to go into a shell, and I didn't have the flare or talkativeness that

I used to have. So I said, "I am feeling the loneliness of having no brother in with me now to talk to." Also, my school work was suffering.

Bingo! Super said he had a meeting coming up with the governors, and that he would recommend that I be put up for early release. This was music to my ears, all the acting and planning had worked. I was going to be given a chance to be assessed for early release, and I couldn't wait. At last I had some good news to look forward to, an assessment and maybe an early release.

I could not get carried away. Super was only going to recommend an early release, and it was no way a done deal by any means. Mind you I knew he had great sway, so I was in with what I would say a good chance.

A couple of weeks went by, then Super came to Winton House at the weekend and we did the usual walk and chat in the grounds. Jackpot! He told me I looked like getting a release date, and that I had to keep myself calm, and stay out of trouble. I recounted the two misdemeanours I had with staff, which had not been reported for one reason or another. Clearly they wanted me out of their hands, and no doubt out of their minds. I think finally they had had enough of me. After all, what could they do? The staff knew I could be dangerous when I lost the plot, and here they had a chance to get me out of the way yet not lose face. Only the members of staff who had felt my temper knew as they had kept it to themselves, and I wasn't going to hold a grudge, even when I was out of the school and on my way home.

These incidences I would gladly put behind me with pleasure. I was called into the head's office where I was told that the board of governors had granted me early release, and I would be going to a school in Portsmouth to finish my education.

I was ecstatic! Freedom sounded great. Yes, this was my troubles sorted, now I had to put up with all the inmates who I had fallen out with, and there were many trying to get me wound up, to make me bite. I must not get sucked in now after all this planning and acting out, I had to stay calm and this would be the hardest thing to do at Winton House School. If I was to fight now, it could jeopardise my release date, it may even halt it entirely. What a dilemma to be in, I thought. Still I would have to oblige, and not be stupid enough to get involved in any trouble. God was that going to be hard. Yes, all the boys I had upset or hit, were now out to get even.

They even started telling lies to members of staff. Still I would have to get over whatever was thrown at me. Should I have to put one in line I would have to do it slyly, and ensure no one was around to witness anything.

Chapter 9

As my release date came closer, I was more on edge. I just wanted to wake up one day and just leave the school as if by magic, but I knew it would be time only that would determine my going. I had to just wait and keep my head down, counting every day as if it was my last.

Finally the day arrived... I went to the clothes store and got my going out clothes and put them on. I wore grey trousers, white shirt, tie, jumper and black leather shoes, also a tweed coat. I was given another set in a large bag.

I had seconds to change, the clothes were old-fashioned, but they were very good quality. I showered and changed, and waited for Dad to pick me up, and be ready at home to get used to a new school after the Easter holidays.

It seemed strange going back home on leaving Winton House. My parents had moved again, and we now lived in Talbot Road, Fratton.

It was nice to be in the family fold again, but as I say seemed strange. No more jump when told, no more do as I say, no more up early and start your day on a low. Just happy now and free. I could at last go anywhere I wanted, also whenever I wanted. Mind you I had to do as my parents wanted to an extent. Otherwise I could be called back to Winton House to finish my time I had got off my sentence. Not a nice thought at all.

Monday soon came around, I had to put on all my new clothes, and get ready to go to the new school that I had been assigned to. It was in fact Southsea Modern, based in Albert Road, Southsea. My brother walked me there, as this area was new to me.

On arrival I was assigned a class by the head master, and then introduced to them. This seemed very strange as well, there I was dressed up in all new clothes, the ones that the approve school had discharged me with. Long grey flannel trousers, white shirt, tie, grey jumper check sports coat, black leather rounded shoes. I must have looked to the class a right wally.

I could hear some pupils chuckling and even laughing quite loud, jeering and some just sniggering. I was thinking what I looked like, funny to them I suppose. After all most of them were dressed in jeans and had a somewhat scruffy appearance. How was I going to settle in, were my initial thoughts. Not very well, dressed like I was, you could assume.

I was given a desk. After I sat down the giggling started again, then I was getting kicked under the desk. I was knocked in my back, even slapped around the head. I couldn't just sit and take all this, then again, if I started on anyone, would I be sent back to Winton House to finish my time? Would I handle that? No I couldn't, I thought to myself.

The break soon came and we were all moved towards the playground.

What was I to do, put up with the jeering and kicking or make a point? This was hard, as I knew I could end up back at the approve school. Well it was just in me, balls to the consequences. I would put a stop to this bullying, and I knew the one who kept hitting me in the back, he was going to be shown I was not an easy touch.

I went to the playground toilets which were on the side of the play area, in which I had a quick look and saw I could have a fight there, and hopefully get away with it. The area was just out of view from the main play area.

I returned to the playground and summoned the boy to go around the back, his name was Mick Phillips. He was silly enough to do it alone, thinking I was a dickhead obviously. Well the outcome was of no doubt. I hit him a couple of times and he went over and then cried wolf. His face was covered in blood, and for once I felt sorry for him. He was to have no idea how well I could fight. Talk about a lamb to the slaughter, this was a prime example of that.

I was accepted in the class, in fact Mick and I became best of mates, so it didn't end up bad at all. The next day I never went to school, but instead bought some more appropriate clothing. There was going to be no more looking like a poof for me. I now fitted in properly with the Southsea crowd. The boys that went to our school were rough and ready types, not smartly dressed, or mod looking. After all I was now in the fold and had a few new mates. Other than the odd fight with older boys, I had quite a good time at school, but I was always up for a laugh, and even went scrumping with the boys. Taking apples home for Mum to make a pie or crumble for us all saved money as well.

I owe a big debt to one of our teachers — his name was Mr Green. One day the boys talked me into trying out smoking, and one of them produced a packet of cigarettes. We went around the back of the toilets to have a puff. I tried but soon started coughing and spluttering, the taste was terrible. I was told I would soon get used to it, but I wasn't so sure.

We were back there again another day and I was huffing and puffing, then out of the blue I was tugged and lifted up on my toes. The tugging of my ear sure hurt and I was about to hit out, then turning around I saw it was Mr Green. He said to me that if I was meant to smoke I would have a chimney on my head. He took the cigarette from me and stubbed it out, then sent me away with a flea in my ear. This had been implanted in my head and for once the brain had accepted this, and even accepted that Mr Green was right — there is pure fate. In fact, fate has played a big part in my life, even to this day.

The following day we were all told to go to the assembly hall, where we were to be shown a film on the wrongs of smoking. This couldn't have come at a better time with Mr Green's words still fresh in my mind.

The film was a shocker. They had rigged a test tube up and placed it above a Bunsen burner with a rubber cable attached to one end, and then heat from the burner caused a vacuum. They placed cigarettes into the test tube and the vacuum was sucking on the cigarette. The fumes were then passed down the rubber pipe and into a beaker. The cigarettes were placed in the tube one after another – they said it was the same as someone smoking the equivalent of 20 cigarettes a day for a year. The glass beaker soon became full of a thick tar-like substance or pitch.

They got a sheet of white paper and as it was a black and white film in those days it was even more graphic. They tipped the glass beaker out onto the paper, and the tar was slowly poured over. This was just like pitch from the road and made you sit up and take notice, it was disgusting. A speaker then stood up and explained the dangers of smoking, with the heart and lung complications.

I was only 14 so I was very impressionable, just the right time to be shocked by this smoking display. I certainly wouldn't be smoking or even trying it again. Well done Mr Green and thank you.

Life was now a real laugh and didn't we have some. Nothing or no one seemed to worry me. I was free and happy like a bird let out of its cage.

Chapter 10

My Dad was still a problem though. He now had a job with a firm of bar fitters and also delivered goods to the pubs, optics glasses etc. He would have drinks given to him at most bars he delivered to, so when he came home he would be three parts to the wind looking back. When he came through the door at night Mum would be straight on to him and they would soon be screaming at each other. Then I would usually hear "IAN!" shouted out, and I knew Mum would use this to get Dad to stop him getting on to her.

So I knew what was coming, as this had happened on many occasions. He would come running towards the front room with his strap in his hand screaming "I'LL SHOW YOU!" I would not let him get at me. I would make a dash for the front door which was down the passage, open the catch and be off down the road. Dad would not have the speed to catch me on the flat pavement, I would leave him in my wake. I would then stay out for a couple of hours and return for my tea knowing Dad was now in bed, and I could relax and watch TV before I went off to bed.

As I said, this happened on numerous occasions, and always at night when Dad had got home from work where he would be a bit boozy, then Mum would set him off then have him to head for me.

I always made the door and got away, but one night I was in the front room watching telly and heard a scream "IAN!" Aye aye, me again. I made a bolt for the door as always, however this time as I made the door I tried to open it but on turning the catch it wouldn't budge. Dad had dropped the catch. I just stood there shocked and there was Dad storming up the passage with his belt in his hand and shouting, "I GOT YOU NOW YOU LITTLE BASTARD!" What was I to do? I was shaking with worry, this was it I had to do something, so I just turned around and hit him straight in the face. The first punch stunned him, the next one dropped him, and he was out cold. Blood was coming from what seemed like everywhere on his face, but I never stayed around. I approached the door again opened the catch and proceeded to run from the house and up the road. I stayed away for a couple of days, staying at a friend's house, sleeping on the couch. He did manage to get me some sandwiches and some drinks, but I knew I had to think about returning back home. What had I done to Dad? How much had I hurt him? I just never knew any of this.

I decided the best time would be during the day when Dad was at work, then I could talk to Mum. She told me he had gone to the hospital but was patched up OK, and had returned to work as money was badly needed, and that Dad had caused it anyway so he would just forget it, and that I was to come home. I did say to Mum "I didn't mean to hit him as he is my father", it was the fear factor and one that was forced upon me. Even though I was wrong, I had to defend myself from a mad man who was about to give me a severe beating. I thought, sorry Dad not this time mate, I am growing up remember, and that you can't just hit me willy nilly now. I would also like to point out it is not clever to assault one's father, but ALAS, it has happened and I couldn't rub it out now.

My parents were soon on the move again, this time they bought a shop, number 91 on Fawcett Road. It was a sweet shop and tobacconist. A few of my friends from school lived nearby, so I would team up with them and we would make our way to school together. They were good company, we would talk all the way to the school gates. Discussing what had happened that night to us all, or what had gone on at school the day before. It was fun! A real funny time we had.

I was 15 years old now, and it was nearing the time for me to leave school. What was I going to do for work, I thought? I had no idea. Still something would crop up no doubt about that.

I thought I knew everything. By this time I had also had many fights in the area. So I had become a bit of a name around this way. As you entered Fawcett Road from the Fratton Road end, on the corner was a café, which had gaming machines. This was a meeting point sometimes before and after school. The owner of the café was Jim Smith, a bit of a large man who was always a pleasure to talk to.

Jim also managed a few boxers, often supplying fighters for shows put on by a guy named Peter Arnett, or Pippy Arnett as he would be known by. Pippy's main boxing venue was the Connaught Drill Hall. He would put shows on there every month. Jim would give me a ticket so as I could go and see the shows.

Some of the fights would be real bruisers with plenty of blood about. They were even allowed to carry on boxing when a fighter had obtained a badly cut eye or cheek. I remember one boxer having such a badly swollen eye which was completely closed shut. When I moved closer to see, when the bell went at the end of the round the boxer's corner pulled out a razor blade and nicked the eye lid.

At the time I found this amazing as the blood squirted out of the nick and like magic the eye went down. This gave the boxer his vision back, so he could now see and carry on with the bout. This may appear wrong but the fight could go on, which was what the crowd wanted to see. Obviously, these days this would not be allowed to go on, but then what would? Now as soon as the eye is closed shut it would be stopped. Today the fight game is a lot softer, and I would say now it is a lot harder to get really hurt.

Three boys came in to the café to play the gaming machines, and an argument started. They were soon shouting at each other. Jim's wife had become agitated and asked them to stop arguing, they didn't so I told them to stop. They turned on me now, threatening to hit me. That was it. I went at them, hitting the two that were near each other and knocking them to the ground. The third one shot out the door and disappeared. The other two got to their feet and proceeded to leave also. By this time, Jim had come through from the back entrance and his wife told him what had gone on. She told him what had happened including that I had stuck up for her, and given the pair a good hiding.

Jim was so thankful he gave me a nice meal, and a big mug of tea and praised me up to whoever would listen. I felt like a guardian angel, but at the time it was a natural thing to do, they had certainly not intimidated me, although that is clear what they wanted to do. Yes, two bullying fools and the third one was just hanging around with them, and must have been surprised at what he saw me do. So they had no choice but to just get out of there.

Soon after this episode, Jim had become quite close to me and he would always give me a mug of tea or coffee when I went into the café. I was hitting anyone who upset him or his wife. He started paying me, giving me ten shillings or even a pound a week. Considering a youngster's wage was about two pounds for a week's work, I was on a good thing for just hitting a pest or that's how I saw it anyway. Jim knew I was very good at looking after myself, and that knocking people over was a gift I had.

Eventually Jim was after me to turn pro as a boxer for him. I told him that I was only 15, to which he said "Don't worry, I can fix that" and made out I was in fact older, so that he could get me a pro boxer licence. I was not sure what this would entail, so just said I would think about it.

A regular of Jim's friends who came into the café most afternoons was called Topper Brown. He had a broken nose and would always want to watch me fight. Jim would let me take anyone who upset him round the back of the café, out of the way of any prying eyes, and I would give them a hiding. Topper loved it, and so did Pippy Arnett when he could get away to watch as he was a very busy man.

One day Topper got me on my own and warned me, "Jim although a good laugh is ruthless in business, and if you did turn pro, he could throw you to the wolves and have no qualms about it." I took this all in and started to have reservations about Jim.

Topper was an ex-jockey and now a racehorse trainer, this was a great passion of mine. I would just love to ride racehorses and try and go into that profession. I used to go horse riding most weekends over at Jackie Madgwicks stables, which were situated at a place called Drayton off Lower Drayton Lane. So I took Topper's offer of the chance to go to his stables.

Jackie's friend and partner was a man called Ginger Wyatt. He was a lovely man I recall, and always having a joke or playing a prank on someone. Ginger would help Jackie shoe the horses and also help around the stables. I think they used to rely on each other, this is why I thought I could ride quite well, so to me the next step would be to ride out for Topper, so he could show me the finer points of the horse game.

I was now getting excited at the thought of riding a racehorse, something I had always wanted to do. Just think, through me being able to look after myself fight wise, I was at last going to get the chance. I arranged to meet Topper alone at the Corner Café situated on Southampton Road near Portchester. There were two cafés near each other, one called Bert's Café opposite the Smiths crisp factory, and the other one on the corner, hence the name the Corner Café.

I would ride my bike there to meet Topper at about 7 am, then he would drive us to the stables, situated near the war memorial monument on Portsdown Hill. His stables were fairly old but kept clean, and he had a few owners who paid him to train horses there. The two owners I remember, were John Blake and Micky Pople. The horses were called Chastise, Algonquin, Juno Moneto, and the Money Matters. I do have a job remembering after all these years.

Topper was a bit of a playboy really, so most of the running of the stables was done by his son Topper Junior. He was a really nice man and was also a jockey, but he was a more serious but natural person, opposite to his dad who was a happy-go-lucky type who didn't appear to care about anything, or at least that was the impression he gave.

I remember opening a stable door and there was Topper Senior on top of a stable girl with his breeches down his legs. I soon closed the door and bolted into the tea hut with the other lads. Topper soon appeared at the tea hut door with a red face and asked who had opened the stable door just now? I never said a word and the subject was soon dropped. The other lads never had a clue what Topper was on about, but I did.

John Blake was a professional tipster, a real conman I would say, and he would charge customers for his so-called tips. I think you couldn't do worse if you used a pin instead, but he had a good clientele and would get the fees he charged. He got his clients to post the money to an empty shop based in Cosham High Street, near the railway station. I looked at it this way, if they wanted to give him money for tips it was up to them.

He must have been quite successful at it, as he had horses in training and a nice house and a big new car. John told me that he had horses so he had access to the owners and trainer ring at race meetings, and that is where he would hear information from other owners, that he could pass on to his clients. Some would win but many bets would not come in. A very clever scheme he had and not many had the idea of doing it.

Micky Pople was what I would call a wheeler dealer, buying anything to sell at a profit, but he was mostly into property. Buying anywhere and selling it on. A nice clever man, yes he was, very bright. Micky would always have a big cigar in his mouth and a nice roller.

On one occasion Micky pulled up at the stables just as we were coming in from giving the horses a gallop. He was late to see his little mare Money Matters on the gallops, and said "How did she go boy?" "She seemed to want to run that morning," I told him. "Good," Micky said, and put two pound into my hand. "Thanks Micky," I told him, this was nearly a week's wages for a youngster.

My luck was in I thought. She rode a lot better that morning even though she was only a selling horse. Well, I can say now the little mare never stopped improving when Micky turned up, just so I got my tip. Ha ha!

Micky's son is called Acker, and he became a very good friend of mine and still is to this day. What I learned from him shocked me, and that was when Micky died he never left any money. So what happened to it all is still a mystery, because he did appear to have plenty of money in those days. Yes, very strange that, very strange indeed.

Chapter 11

It was getting close for me to finish school so I had to find work – needing money was a must. As I wanted to enjoy life to the full, I spoke to my brother Reg. He worked for the NAFFI at HMS *Nelson* based at the top end of Queen Street, Portsea. Reg said he would go and have a word with his guvnor boss.

A few days later, Reg came back saying his guvnor would give me a job on a probationary basis, but I had to go first for an interview. This was my chance I thought. I dressed myself for this, no jeans or flash clothes, just plain and tidy.

The following Monday, I was on my way to the NAFFI for my appointment with his guvnor at HMS *Nelson*. After a somewhat short chat and explaining my need for a job, I was told I could start work at the base next Monday week.

My wages would only be £2 a week. Not that good but it was a start, I would also get my own wages. This was music to my ears, great! Mum said I would have to give her ten shillings a week for keep. Not bad, as she always needed income due to the family size and all her outgoings.

My job would consist of unloading lorry deliveries, stocking up supplies for our central store, and moving the stock to the different department's individual stores. A general dogsbody to be honest. Still it was my first job, and at 15 good to have job independence, which was the way I looked at it.

After a few months had passed, Reg told me he was having a week's holiday which was due to him. Reg said the guvnor had asked him to show me how to do his job, which consisted of mainly restocking the vending machines. The type the rating got their snacks and drinks from.

One of the machines, which took sixpences, supplied milk cartons – strawberry, banana and chocolate-flavoured milk. In fact, whatever flavour you wanted.

Reg showed me how to top up the vending machines with the different flavours of milk cartons. As we approached the machines, Reg looked at the front of them and said, "That's good, I have had a very good night." To this I asked him what he meant. He pointed to the front of the machines and showed me the boot marks. He explained, "When a rating puts his sixpence in and a cartoon never comes out of the delivery drawer at the bottom, they will mostly just kick it trying to dislodge one of the cartons to drop. So the more kick marks, the less milk has been delivered to the customer."

Most were sailors who came back from a night ashore, and after the boozing they would want a milk drink to sleep on. So they had put their money into the vending machine, but no milk cartoons would drop into the tray at the bottom, hence they'd boot the machine in frustration. Simple but effective.

I asked Reg for an explanation. He began to show me so I would know exactly what to do. The shelves which you had to refill, were designed to drop automatically depending on the type of milk you wanted. There was a slot for each one when a sixpence was inserted.

Reg would not put a cartoon on every shelf but leave some empty, hence when a sixpence was inserted, nothing would come out at the bottom drawer. This is when the sailors would kick the front, and the boot marks appeared. This is how Reg knew he had a good night, as there would be no loss of stock, and the money paid for each carton added up. Reg would soon get his wages over again with his fiddles. There were no flies on Reg, I thought.

I was now working on my own as Reg was away on his holidays. As well as my own, I had Reggie's chores, filling up the vending machines. Mind you, as these were Reg's fiddles he had them filled to the brim before he left, knowing they would probably still be workable until he returned back to work.

One day the guvnor told me to go to the milk vending machine by the main gate. Upon my arrival, I was met by two irate matelots, ranting and raving with complaints about not getting any cartoons of milk for their money spent on the vending machines. I could see boot marks on the front, so I knew the reasons.

I was straight away put on my guard, they had clearly been drinking during the day and were very abusive. I said to them, the machine had been playing up and I would give them their money back.

Save Reg getting into trouble, first I needed their signatures in a book to cover the shortfall in takings. With this, one of the sailor's just headbutted me in the face making my nose pour with blood. This stunned me, so without thinking I just punched him instinctively, knocking him to the floor. His mate who I turned on made his sharp exit and headed to the sleeping quarters in haste.

I paused and then thought, I had better let him go. Try and calm the situation by letting the rating rise off the floor and follow his mate back to the housing block. He had now got a flea in his ear. I had to go and clean myself up, so as to be presentable at the NAFFI shop. I couldn't say anything in case it brought trouble to our Reg. After all, he was getting a nice sum out of them machines, so I wouldn't want me rocking his boat. A can of worms could have been opened. Besides I have had many a bloody nose and that would soon get better after cleaning myself up.

Looking back, it was a good job I never said anything to the guards on the gate. As not only were the sailors drunk, but they had struck a civilian worker. That would never be tolerated by the officers, and the two would have been in big trouble, and that wasn't what I wanted anyway. The matelots probably wouldn't remember much about it after sleeping it off. Fools really. Not thinking that all their futures could have gone up in smoke, there and then. Just by getting drunk and losing the plot. I was now getting a regular income, and just by having that,

I could now afford to go out at night and enjoy my evenings. I would often meet up with some of my old school friends, hanging out either in a café playing pinball machines, or music on the record player. We sometimes made our way to the funfair, hanging around in groups and having a good banter and chatting to the girls.

I would find myself often having fights. The place to do this was an area called the mote. A few of us would go there. I would have a fight with whoever had upset me or our group. There was always a crowd looking on. It would give me a good buzz. The fights never usually lasted long either. I would throw a few punches normally and watch my opponent collapse out stone cold. Or drop them and see them cover up and cry, "ENOUGH!" I was always the victor. Mind you it wasn't just about fighting.

You would also go to the mote if you had chatted up a girl from the fairground, yes a good part of hanging out there. I could always guarantee it seemed to get girls.

I remember one night, we were hanging out with two good friends, Graham and Job. This will show you how stupid you can be when you're young. I was with a girl called Val, who had never been with any of the boys. She was with a friend as well. So I took her for a walk and ended up at the mote. We sat and chatted for a while. Soon after I saw my friends Graham and Job hiding nearby.

Val and I started to get aroused. The boys were watching so I had to get them away. I asked Val to give them a grope and kiss, then they would go and leave us alone, for us to be on our own. She agreed to, and they soon left us and made their way back to the fairground, and waited. After a short time Val and I returned where she meet up with her friend again. We all had a laugh then sometime after we all went home for the night.

A few days later we were all at the fair. Val's friend was there but no Val. I asked her where she was, and she said Val had told her she was pregnant.

How foolish. We never knew how long it was before you knew if you were pregnant or not. I told Graham and Job that they had kissed Val and had a feel, so it could be any one of us who had got her up the duff.

That shows you how young and naive we were. We started blaming one another and were worried our parents would find out. So how could we keep this shock quiet, we thought. This was a big worry. We headed on home still blaming each other and wondering what to do. Should we stay away from the fairground for a while, or should we try and meet up with Val sometime and talk about it? Well we decided the suspense would be too great, so we would go back later to the fair, and see what Val had to say.

Although this would be in a day or two, sure enough we did meet with Val, and her friend as well. I took Val to one side and asked her about what her friend had said, and everything she had told us about the pregnancy. She said she had lost the baby. What a relief, we thought, not knowing she was having us on all the time. That's how stupid it shows we were. Green as grass. It is good to look back on these times when we used to meet up. We still have a good laugh about it to this day. I wonder how many young kids can still get hoodwinked into a predicament like that, just through being young and not realising the facts of life. It is a good thing they teach sex education these days.

Chapter 12

In time, we got fed up with hanging around the fairground. While it was a good place to meet girls and have many a good fight and laughing at the past, we could not forget how Val had used us for a better laugh than we had. Bless her.

We were soon going to the Mecca every Friday. We were a small group. We ended up at the night for ones of our age group to get together, and after just a couple of weeks I noticed a young girl through a friend. I found myself very attracted to her. A lovely looking face and you could tell she worked out to keep in shape. A pair of legs to die for.

After some time had passed, and talking with a group of our mates, I was informed she was in fact, for the want of a better word, a 'prick teaser'. A description of a girl who would just lead you on, and not give you a sniff of sex of any description.

When I heard all this I just looked at it as a challenge. Even so I liked her with her nice face and pleasant-looking figure, I found myself chatting to her a few times one Friday night. The more we chatted, the more the chemistry just kept getting better and better.

Her name was Jenny and after a few weeks I asked her to meet me in the week, not just the Friday. She was training as a hairdresser with her mum, who had a hairdressing salon. It was called Eileen's Hairdressers in Cosham High Street.

She appeared to be a bit scared of her parents, they were very protective of her. This did make arranging a date very awkward. In fact, she was afraid to mention to them that she was meeting a boy. Anyway, meet we did, and I found her very pleasant to talk to. This was when she let herself go. We had a few dates, but the one drawback was that she lived in Drayton, down Lower Drayton Lane, about three miles east of Cosham. The last bus that would take you to Portsmouth was at ten o'clock sharp.

The times I had to run up the lane to catch it was far too many times to remember. Night after night I seemed to be running for that bloody bus. You see, if you missed the last one you would have to walk or jog all the way to Cosham to get one to Portsmouth. Which meant I wouldn't get home till about midnight.

By the time I got to bed it would be about one in the morning. Before I knew it, I was up again to get ready for work. There again, I thought Jenny was worth it.

I met her dad (or rather stepdad) George a few times, but I could tell straight away he didn't like me. To him I obviously wasn't good enough for his daughter. His wife and Jenny's mum was Eileen who had been married before, she didn't seem to get involved. We had by now been going out for about six months but we still had never had any form of sexual contact, but I never seemed to worry about that side of it now, as we were getting on very well and I wouldn't put any pressure on her. It would be her sole decision should intercourse take place. We had only ever had a kiss and cuddle. This often took place in an old disused bus stop in an end lane opposite her house. We would sit there for hours just chatting and playing our radio, myself and Jenny – we were now getting on very well. I think this was because she knew I wasn't going to force her into doing anything she didn't want to. We were still courting after seven months now, and the thing that got to her was my fighting as she was a placid person. Even so I appeared to be fighting every night at the Mecca. Clearly Jenny never agreed with my violence, a streak that was just in me. I thought the best way to keep us together was to stop going to the Mecca on the Friday nights, this was because I couldn't seem to refrain from having a fall out with someone whenever we were in there. This was caused mostly by someone looking and talking about Jenny. I would call it being too young to understand the way the world worked. I would often leave someone with a bloody nose, then being asked to leave the premises early – not a good thing for Jenny to put up with. In fact, me and the Mecca didn't seem to go together.

So we decided to meet near her house in Drayton and hang out in a park, or sit in our bus shelter just talking and playing our radio if it was cold or raining. We just seemed to hug and talk till it was time to let Jenny go back home. By now we appeared to be getting on a lot better, especially as we had stopped going to the night club or our old evening haunts. Mind you, we did used to walk to Cosham and hang out in a few cafés, playing the juke box, and having a good laugh with our friends in the area. One was Parma Court and another Singing Kettle. We used these quite frequently. We would walk from Jenny's house where I met her and use the back road to cut through to Cosham, that wouldn't take too long using that way. We would have a good time with mine and Jenny's friends. One also lived in Drayton Lane, her name was Rose. They used to go to school together so had been friends for years.

The time seemed to fly when me and Jenny were together, and in no time at all I seemed to be taking Jenny back home. It was no secret to anyone even now that Jenny's stepdad and her mum never got on with me, thinking their daughter was too good for me or anyone for that matter. In fairness, as they had a hairdressing shop in Cosham they thought – mainly George – that they were above anyone who lived and worked for someone – self-employed was their idea. Mind you, George was in fact a waste of space, after all it was his wife who was the hairdresser, all he was was a dogsbody, wetting and washing hair, and sweeping all the cut hair from the shop floor. Even with this dead-end job he thought his shit didn't stink, that was the term I would use for him. He would never invite me to his house, other than just to meet Jenny and take her out, so I was never an acceptable boyfriend for their little girl.

I was talking to my sister Pat one day when she had come home to see Mum and Dad because she lived in London in Finchley. She was full of questions about Jenny the girlfriend, she also said I should take her to visit her there. She would take us out for a meal and visit Chinatown, as she was married to a Chinese man and that he was a professional gambler, and he did that every night as that was his income. So I asked Jenny if we could go to London and meet my sister, then stay overnight and come back the next day. It would make a change and be something different as we had never been there. Jenny, after agreeing, said to her parents that we were going as a group and not on our own. This was the only way we could go as George wouldn't trust her an inch. Anyway, me and Jenny would get the train and be met by my sister at the station in London. Pat did meet us and took us to her flat, where we got ready for our night out and a look around London at Chinatown near the centre. After feeling full due to the large Chinese meal and knackered through walking round London we couldn't wait to get back to Pat's flat for a nice sleep. On returning to her flat she showed us to a large room with a double bed. I was puzzled at this. Clearly she never thought Jenny was in fact a virgin. I reassured her it would be OK and we proceeded to get into bed, after a cuddle and some petting we made love. This was certainly worth the wait, the only thing was we kept doing it all night long, and in the morning we were more tired than when we first went to bed. Neither of us knew anything about contraception so in fact we were playing Russian roulette. Still we proceeded to get the train home not thinking of any consequences that may happen due to our night of passion, even though we enjoyed ourselves together.

After some time the inevitable happened. Even though it was still a shock to me and Jenny she had found herself pregnant. How could we face her mum and dad, this was now the burning question. All I could do was in my mind blame my sister for putting us together in that double bed. Still it was too late for that, and now Jenny had decided to keep it to herself for now, and as long as she could.

As I said, I was not liked by either of her parents, so what were they going to think of me now? Yes, I was the culprit in their eyes, and to me it was my sister's fault. Anyway, all we could do was think how we could become parents at such a tender age. Jenny managed to keep it covered up for some time, then she told me her mum had gathered what was wrong, then that she sat down crying and let it all come out. Her dad George had gone berserk, I was not allowed to see Jenny at all, so I went around the house to confront mostly George and wanted to know what was going on, I knocked on the door and was confronted by George. He was fuming at me and started having a row.

How I had no brains and that I had mucked their lives up, I got all the blame with no discussion of what we would have to do. He pushed me out of the front door and then told me not to go there again. I rowed back telling him I wanted to see Jenny just to see how she was. He stood in my way and gave me the strong-arm tactics. He said that Jenny wasn't there and to just go away. I had now had enough, after all Jenny was having my baby, yet I wasn't allowed to express my feelings to Jenny. No, I had to see her and pushed passed George. He manhandled me so I just knocked him out onto the floor. His wife Eileen was screaming out by now and saying that Jenny wasn't there, and also that she was calling the police. I decided that I was best to just scarper out of there and head home. When I arrived home the police were there waiting for me. They told me that George had made a complaint that I had assaulted him. I never said anything then and was asked to go to the station with them. There I was charged with assault causing harm to Mr Wilkins. I mentioned to them that I had got his daughter pregnant and that he had been very abusive to me, pushing me and shouting that I would never see his daughter again, a shock considering we were having a child together. The police understood this and still charged me but bailed me straight away. After all he thought he was so-called upper class but was really only a dogsbody for his wife, yes a pig of a man when you look at it.

Now I had to find out were Jenny was so decided to have a word with her friend who was at school with her, Rose from Lower Drayton Lane. I wanted her to approach Jenny's parents and ask if she could write to her just to see how she was. It transpired that they were so embarrassed by their daughter that they put her in a home for unmarried mothers in Bournemouth. This was just to keep it away from the eyes of the neighbours, and thinking it was a disgrace that they had a daughter who was unmarried, young and having a baby. This was disgraceful in their heads. This shows me they had no feelings for Jenny, only how the area they lived in would frown upon it.

I went to the court with regards hitting George and there in the courtroom stood George rubbing his cheek saying that I hit him, knocking him to the floor, and that it was still sore. A grown man grovelling to the judge and me a 16-year-old waiting to be a future father. Anyway, the judge was understanding, saying he had no power to keep me and Jenny apart and that George had to get used to it as it was fact. I was also fined fifty pounds, a lot in those days but not a world changer anyhow. When I knew where Jenny was I got a train and went to Bournemouth to see her. When I got there it was a large imposing property, and one that had many rooms just to house the unmarried and troubled girls. I knocked on the door and was told by the person who opened the door that Jenny's mother had been there and left orders that I was not to see her, and that I had better leave. I was livid as I had travelled all that way and then told

I couldn't see Jenny. I started to scream to the staff members, I would not be told as I was only 16 and would not be told by anyone. Anyway, the door was slammed shut in my face with me still shouting out to see Jenny. With this a window cleaner who was cleaning the place approached me and started pulling me away and down the drive, so I just turned around and knocked him out. Shocked, I just started to run down the lane and away to the railway station. Amazingly, I never heard anymore with regards the hitting of the window cleaner, then again he had no right to pick on me, that was because I looked young and skinny, a bully boy really.

After a while Jenny went home but she had to stay indoors, this being that she was now getting rather large in the belly and the neighbours were not allowed to see, as to them that would be disgraceful. Stupid really as you could not change the situation now. So when her mother and father went out to their shop in the mornings I could ring Jenny in her house. She appeared to be in a terrible state and only wanted it all over. She was now fed up with carrying our baby. After a short while her waters broke and she was taken to the royal hospital. It was there our daughter was born. I went to see her, but again I was not allowed as her mother was her next of kin, and she forbade me from seeing her daughter, or the baby who was now born. The orders were left with the matron on the maternity ward. Under no circumstances was I allowed to see Jenny or the baby, the staff relayed to me, but they did say she had a baby girl.

Chapter 13

Jenny took her home after a few days, I now would find a way to get a chance to see and get involved with our child. A short while later now Jenny was home I could talk to her at will when her parents were at work. After talking for a few days, we decided as her mum and dad were being like they were that she should leave home with our baby girl, who incidentally we called Julie Ann (we arrived at that name after Julie Andrews, this being as when we had nowhere to hang out we would go to the pictures especially when the weather was bad, and it so happened that a film that was on for some time was the *Sound of Music* so we decided to name our child Julie Ann after her). On Jenny leaving with our child I had gone and got a large double bedsit to live together as a family. It was in Gamble Road Southsea. The problem now was I had to get more money working to pay for ourselves and the rent for the apartment. Someone mentioned to me that I may be able to get a job at the Portsmouth gas works, labouring while they were erecting spheres and floating gas tanks. I got the job, it was a Darlington firm called Whessoe. I was to become a labourer and helper to erect these tanks to hold the gas. I ended up working 12 hours a day and seven days a week. It was hard work but I had to do it for the money so as to give me, Jenny and Julie a living wage. I was never scared of hard work and even worked extra hours after my 12-hour shift. The downside was that I was afraid Jenny and Julie would not be seeing a lot of me and that was heart wrenching. Here we were, in a large bedsit. The combined cost of rent, electric gas, the baby food and nappies, left us no money in reserve. We even had to have a pay-per- view television. You had to put sixpences in and that would give you about an hour of viewing. It certainly ate the money. It was left in the room by the previous occupants, so we just kept on feeding it.

Jenny used to say when I came home from work that the television was eating the money. Mind you, being at home all day with just Julie, as there was no such thing back then as baby group, she had to have some entertainment to break up the monotony. She was good though and would have the radio on to save money for other provisions.

Jenny was smart. Every so often the firm would come and empty the television meter. The collector would give her a rebate, and this she would use to get Julie that little bit extra. This may have been a bit primitive looking back, but Jenny had it worked out to a tee.

She ensured money was put away separately for the bills from the general expense, and always made sure she made my sandwiches for work every day. I always had a lovely cooked meal to come home to after work.

Looking back, Jenny was a good wife for one so young, and she seemed older than she actually was. As it was me who was the trouble you see, I always had to be right. I had trouble with Jenny as I was always fighting, and that was the trouble all my life. I put that down to all the very bad beatings my Dad gave me when I was young. He in fact instilled violence in my makeup and this was a thing I clearly had to live with, and there was no getting away from that fact.

Being with Jenny in the evenings after work, made me come to the conclusion I should come clean to her about all my past. At least that way it would be me telling her, so it would not be coming second-hand. The remand home I was put in, and the approve school Winton House that I was assigned to for three years.

The hardest thing I had to tell Jenny about was my conviction for armed robbery. Yes! Armed robbery! Sounds bad that, but the true story never reflected on the charge. The facts were that a friend, Peter, and I from my school days went and bought two metal catapults. Used correctly they made for very powerful weapons. Add to that Peter was a crack shot. He could hit anything on the move, even when he was running he was that good.

We were at the seafront on the beach firing pebbles out into the sea with the catapults. Then a big fat bloke shouted out, "Don't fire them near me or there would be trouble!" This was like a red flag to a bull to us. So we turned to him with the catapults cocked. He shouted, "No not at me!" and seemed really scared. His clothes were near Peter to which he said, "Give us your money then!" and shook his trousers as a jest and provoked the man.

"Give us some out of his pocket!" It was meant to be a joke, but Peter said, "Keep him covered and I'll take some out." The man said he had none. "I have no money!" he kept saying, but the jingle from his pocket told a different story. Peter said, "You lied to me!" and took half a crown out. The man then started to scream and rant up the beach in his bathers. "HELP, HELP!" was his cry. This was at the top of his voice. Now panicking we ran in the opposite direction, and soon got out of his sight towards South Parade Pier.

Peter saw a pigeon on a lamp post. He drew his catapult, hitting it clean and sending it tumbling to the ground dead. Instantly we continued towards the pier walking at a normal pace. We were approached by a police car. It was about 20 minutes after the trouser incident. We were asked to get into the car, and we were taken to the police station. On arrival the policemen told us we met the description of a complaint made by a member of the public, regarding the taking of money from a man, while aiming a catapult at him. We gave our names and addresses at their request.

The sergeant told us in fact the subject of the complaint was a very serious one. We were asked to empty our pockets. We had the two catapults on us and Peter had the half a crown piece also in his belongings.

While we were being questioned at the station desk, a police officer walked in with the dead pigeon in his hands. We were told someone had rung up and informed them that two boys fitting our description had fired a catapult at it and killed it. I never said it was Peter so they assumed it was the pair of us. We were then placed into separate cells and questioned further about taking the money off the man on the beach.

We were given some food and drink, and locked in the cell for a few more hours to brew on what we had done. One of the officers came back and opened the cell. We were taken to the front desk and put in front of the station sergeant. The sergeant explained how the metal catapults could be very dangerous, due to the power they were fired at.

He proceeded to charge us with robbery, demanding money with menace, possession of an offensive weapon, and going equipped to rob as well. Over the top to what the charges we were faced with, and well over the top of the correct charges we should have been given. Still, it was up to the sergeant and he seemed a real stupid one at that. "He had only just been made up," said an officer. He was obviously trying to create an impression.

Eventually we were bailed to appear before a magistrate at a later date, to answer the said charges. The police were stupid in those days; after all you would think on reading the charges that we were a pair of gangsters.

When we did finally get to court, we were assigned a duty solicitor to talk on our behalf which was conditional, as we wouldn't know anything about the law side of things. After we informed the solicitor the facts of the case, he was very surprised. He thought we should have been given a severe warning with regards to our behaviour, and let go with a caution.

Clearly that would have been too easy for the new sergeant or the police to do. Talk about a mountain out of a mole hill. The fat man from the beach was in court as well, waiting to give his account of what had happened thus making it sound worse than it actually was. It was then our solicitor decided to plead guilty on our behalf and put in a lot of mitigating circumstances. Stating it was in fact a prank that had just escalated, and went wrong by accident.

It was not our intention to rob the man, just have a game with him when showed us how scared he was. The solicitor also explained that if it was an intended robbery, we would have taken all the fat man's money, and not just the half a crown. Had he not run off screaming, he would have had his money back, but we never had the chance to do that as he ran up the beach.

The solicitor gave us a good representation and we were very pleased with the job he had done. The magistrate said it would have been a lot worse had we not pleaded guilty. The prosecution ordered to fine us both seven shillings and six pence each, and ordered the catapults to be destroyed. We were told not to be seen before him again, as next time he wouldn't be so lenient. You could imagine how Jenny now felt. After all, she was with a man who burgled clubs, stole rags by breaking into a store, three years in an approve school, an armed robbery charge, and last but not least a GBH charge on her stepdad. Not a good start to any relationship, let alone one with a baby involved.

I had told her all the bad bits and could not have blamed her if she had returned home and ended our relationship. Thankfully she decided to stay with me and work it through. The good thing was, it was me that told her — she's never had to hear it through a friend second-hand. That would have been a terrible way to find out about your man. It would have been distorted.

Chapter 14

The air was now cleared regarding my past, and in the morning I was off to work as usual. Jenny had prepared my sandwiches, I gave her and Julie a big kiss then it was off to graft.

My job at Whessoe was basically labouring, and now and then helping out Jack who ran the canteen and filling up the water urn, as Jack was an old man who was limited on what he could do.

On site there was a smallish jock, he just couldn't resist having digs at me. Calling me all sorts of things, including little squirt and a waster. I took this biting my lip, as I needed the job to feed Jenny and Julie. He did go on to thinking I was scared of him. Nothing could have been further from the truth, and I knew my chance would come. Not if, but when. There would be only one result. Yes, stay calm Ian, I thought and your time will come.

Sure enough, I remember Jack never came into work one week including the weekend, as he was poorly. I had to do the canteen work and make tea, sandwiches, coffee, and cut the men's cake. Jack was old and could never work on site, so he was just assigned to the canteen. When breaktime came around, everything was in place for the rush for the workers on site. The time period was usually about 30 minutes, then it would go quiet, as the workers returned to their jobs.

After they had left the canteen, I would clean the muddy floors and wash all the plates up, the mugs and cups also, then prepare for the next break. I was ready when they next came in. This time the cocky little jock decided to have a few more digs, like a woman's work is never done, and a woman's place is in the kitchen. A really mouthy so and so, he was saying it loud.

So all the men could hear. "Do you think that's funny jock?" I said. "It is to us," he replied.

I knew I had to shut him up, but I had to wait for the right time, hoping it would come soon. This is how your luck goes. At the end of the day I cleaned the canteen. I knew of a large gas bottle we used for the cooker had run out. They were kept at the back, leading to a separate door that opened up into a store. I went to change the heavy gas bottle.

As I was rolling it into position, I turned around and the little jock was walking passed using the back entrance of the canteen. He had his usual leery swagger about him. I said hi to him, and he approached me asking what I wanted. As soon as he got within distance, I gave him a left hook sending him crashing to the ground. I let him get up, then greeted him with a much harder blow, that sent him flat out on to the floor. He rolled into the very muddy area at the back of the canteen, nearer the back door. He could only get up very slowly and was covered in mud. I smothered in it. "Who has all the mouth now?" I said to said to him. "Don't you dare talk to me again as if I was a kid, you little prick." He walked off out of the back gate.

What would happen in the morning of this I had no idea. All I wanted to do was keep my job as the money was needed for Jenny and Julie, not to mention the rent. Had my temper got the better of me again to ruin my life, I thought? Although the tanks and spheres were nearing completion, so I knew my job was coming to an end soon.

The following day I went to work as usual, and fortunately nothing appeared to have been said. Although now the other men started talking to me. I felt like a man now, and being accepted as one. Jock the headache was moved to another job that the firm had just started. I wouldn't be seeing him again, and that could only be a good thing.

I got to know a very tall West Indian man, and a well-sought-after welder called John. He was a good laugh. He asked me if I could tack weld for him while he held the steel down. He used a large metal bar holding two plates together to get a tack weld together ready for what was called a run weld. He was paid by the amount of welding he completed, which was by the metre. I made his job easier, and he would give me a few pounds out of his bonus from whenever he earned extra. This came in very handy, as the weekend work had now stopped. Now down to just five and a half day weeks.

John told me he used to be a boxer. He was based at Repton in London. Apparently, he was quite good, although he had stopped as he never enjoyed the training side of it. I said I had boxed when I was young. John said with my punch I should go back to boxing, as he had heard about the set to me and jock had. Apparently, jock was a bit of a fighter, or so he had told John. In fact, he nearly came to blows with jock himself. John said, "Jock was a pest on site," so he was glad I did that to him. "He had it coming," he said.

Chapter 15

The man who owned the house Jenny and I lived in was called Tom ('Carpets'). A nickname derived from the fact he sold and fitted carpets. Tom was an Irishman and a terrific man to get on with. He would only ever do you a favour and in fact had no malice in him. If anything, he was a soft touch, and a lot of his tenants would walk all over him. This is where I came in. One door would shut and another one would open. I was now home most weekends. Jenny had told me of a tenant living above us who would never shut up, and played his music much too loud, as it would often wake Julie up. He wouldn't listen to Jenny. I never took much notice as when I came home late it wasn't a problem. Now I was home it became a nuisance, so before I stepped in I had a word with Tom. Tom couldn't do anything about it as when he had complained to the tenant, he was greeted with nothing but abuse and told to piss off. I suggested to Tom that next time he approached him, let me go with him. After all, he was upsetting Julie and Jenny for that matter. Tom agreed to my suggestion.

We went up and Tom knocked on the tenants' door. When he answered, Tom told him to turn the music down. Just like before the tenant told Tom to piss off. I put Tom aside, stepped forward and punched him with my best left hand. He went down like a ton of bricks.

Tom and I hung around for a while, he was out cold. Tom asked if he would be alright. I said, "Yes no worries there." It would take a bit of time to clear his head, then after a time which seemed ages, he made a stir and sat up and asked who had hit him. "Me," I said and that if he played his music too loud again, I would be back and next time it wouldn't stop there.

Tom thought it was funny, and said he had never seen anything like it before. Soon after I became the house minder. Anyone who owed Tom rent, I would get it for him or just sling them out. The house had now become more pleasant and relaxed. Plus, all the rents were paid up.

Tom had learned from me, and I was now on a limited income with no weekend work.

Tom said he would help me out as I could now help him out also. He said I could just pay when I had the money or if not, he would give my rent to his wife as if it was me who was paying. A very kind gesture and an excellent arrangement. Tom was happy, as he now had no worries with tenants anymore and the rents were now all paid up, and no arrears.

Jenny was now back talking to her mum and stepdad George. She would get the bus to see them and loved showing them Julie. Her stepdad always dropped Jenny back. That helped us as he soon saw the conditions we were living in. Although it was clean it was still a bit of a dump with all the bedsits under the same roof, not ideal to bring a baby up he said. It transpired they had a house in Elm Road, Mile End that had now became empty. He took Jenny to see it and offered it to us and Julie. Jenny came back home all excited that we could have our own front door now, as she had put it. I could live anywhere but Jenny was used to all comforts and could now have her own front door so I agreed to move into the house. The only downfall was that I liked a drink and the house was only three doors from a pub called The Nine Elms. Still we would sort something out in that department.

We discussed getting married now that we were settled. Jenny did it all, getting the banns from the registry office and arranging a date and getting them all signed from both our parents, then getting a set date for the ceremony. Mum would have Julie while we proceeded to the registry office. That was no worry as Mum was besotted with Julie and there was more to it as Mum had reared eight children herself so wanted Julie whenever she could have her – it became a job to get her back, but that was in a nice way. She could have memories of her last child reared, and must have given her a great feeling and satisfaction.

Our parents had no objections to the marriage. The bands had to be displayed for so long then a date was given to Jenny for the marriage. The reason for this was to give time for anyone to lodge an objection if they had one. The date for the marriage soon came round and as always Mum had Julie while we made our way to the registrar to get married, a shotgun affair really. I remember getting two people off the street asking them to be our witnesses. After they told the registrar that they never really knew us they accepted them and the ceremony carried on. After reading out the banns, and saying words to the effect that now no one could object to the marriage and that it was now legal in the eyes of our Lord and country, we signed the book and kissed each other. Primitive really but we were now husband and wife. Jenny was now Mrs Tungatt. We went back to my mothers and Julie. Mum had done us some sandwiches and got some bottles of beer so we had our little reception or as you would say, everything seemed to be working out for us now.

I had been driving the dumper at work for some time now and had also been driving a friend's car round the streets with no problems, so decided now was the time to put in for my driving test. I was told the perfect dodge to pass my test easily, all you would do was after you had your test date, book a BSM car for two hours before your test then also an hour during your test. The reasoning was that the examiner would see you had a BSM car and assume you were given correct lessons. Mind, the instructor taught you the finer parts like passing the steering wheel through your hands not crossing them, also checking your mirror and using your indicators correctly. After two hours with him you were ready to go on your test with the examiner. A pass was imminent. This was a great tip given to me, well done BSM! I now had passed with flying colours, and before the job had come to an end I would get a car on finance. It had to be quick as I could fill the finance form in as fully employed. I saw a lovely car, flame red and a Vauxhall Velox, it was priced at £150, a tidy sum in those days. A friend knew the garage owner, so he bumped the price up and put it down as if I had paid the deposit. A very clever scheme so I only had an outstanding amount of the original £150, the total needed by the garage. Job done and the credit was passed. I now had a flash car, a house we could move into as soon as it was decorated, so life was rosy now.

I worked on the house with a friend decorating. It seemed to take ages, all the spare hours I had I would work doing the house up. When it was completed we had to get furniture. Some was given to us but most had to be got. All the boys used a man called Bunnie Austin. He could arrange any credit. He asked me to sign a form and he could guarantee the credit for furniture. Sure enough, Bunnie told me when to be in for the furniture delivery. Now that was it – all furniture and house decorated, we could now move in. The only trouble was we had to make the repayments. So Jenny said she would go back to work in her mum's shop in Cosham, doing the hairdressing she had trained for. It was now, as I still had my job, easy to pay all the bills and also the childcare for Julie. Stepdad George would pick Jenny up most mornings as I was working early, drop Julie off at the nursery then proceed to open the shop at nine. It was a good arrangement. Sometimes when Jenny worked late on a Friday and Saturday mostly I would first pick Julie up then go to the shop to pick Jenny up to bring them both home, to save George doing it. One day I picked them up as usual and we were going on to the Eastern Road when a lorry pulled out in front of us. This nearly caused us to crash. I blasted the horn several times causing the lorry driver to slam his brakes on repeatedly in front of us. Every time

I tried to pass him fuming he would pull in front of us again and nearly crush us. This made me worse, I was boiling over, and repeatedly blasted my horn, but again he would do the same, stopping us overtaking him. I was seeing red, he could make us crash and cause my wife and baby to get badly injured, I had to get him but how? I was thinking what a pig he was being. I followed him all the way to the pet fish and aquarium shop in Kingston Road (it is still there to this day), he pulled up there and moved over to the side. I pulled up and jumped out of the car and approached the driver. I flew at him totally out of my skull. The bastard, I said. I punched him twice in quick succession, he went straight down and out. Jenny was screaming and Julie was crying, this brought me around. I got into the car and drove them off, leaving the driver still on the floor licking his wounds. I couldn't care less about him, it was my family that mattered. Me and Jenny were arguing all the way home. I said, "What was I supposed to do, he could have killed us all?" This I kept repeating, and she kept saying, "You said you would stop fighting!" But how could I in these circumstances? My temper would always get the better of me, I could only argue with my fists, not good but alas true.

When Julie stopped crying, Jenny calmed down saying she supposed I was forced into it. When we got in, Jenny carried on making the tea while I nursed Julie, watched television and had tea. Nothing else was mentioned about it. As the morning was Saturday I would take Jenny to the shop, then on to my Mum with Julie as Mum loved looking after her whenever she could. Mum doted on her, she was Mum's favourite grandchild, a thing she shouldn't have done really.

Chapter 16

My job at the gas works was coming to an end now. I had about two weeks work left clearing up the site and getting it all ready to hand over and the contract would be completed. Knowing this was coming, I decided to put my feelers out for another job. A work mate suggested I try scaffolding as I had worked on open steel works, he also told me there was a firm in Rodney Road Milton called Mills Scaffolding, so I rang them and was told they had a job in the yard and that I should come and see the manager. So I told them I would be down the next morning. I went there to see the manager. He was a short man but the thing that stuck in my mind was the small pork pie hat he wore that looked strange. Anyway, there was another short man in the office called Charlie. He told me my job would be sorting out the scaffold tubs in the yard and loading the lorries with their tubs and also unloading them and putting them all away in the racks provided for the different lengths. The yard foreman was Reg, he was a lot older than me and had been in the yard for some time, and a stickler for everything to be precise. I had worked there for a few weeks now when Reg decided he would start picking on me for no apparent reason. If anyone talked with me from a gang in the yard, Reg went mad that they would be there to get the specific tubs needed for their job. He seemed to hate me talking to any outsider in the yard. He may have thought I was running him down, but I wouldn't know what I was looking for, why he was acting the way he was, he would say I should just carry on working and not get in conversation with anyone who came in the yard. He had become like a sergeant major, the prick. After all we were supposed to be pulling together, but no he now made it into them and me. I told Reg that I had had enough, and that I would sort it out with him outside the gate when we finished work. "You will, will you? we will see about that," he said all bullish at first, but as the day wore on he was getting cold feet I could tell so I said I would wait outside the gate for him, that was a guarantee after we finished.

His demeanour had now changed and we never spoke for the rest of the day, then he came over to me and said as there were no more lorries to come in I could leave early. I said no point as I should be waiting outside the yard for him to finish, after all it had to be sorted, he had to know I wasn't a little kid as he would think. I had a bike then and rode it to work, so I wheeled it outside the gates and waited for Reg to finish and come outside. When he came out little Charlie from the office came out too so as to lock the gates up behind him. They came towards me two abreast. Not much was said, I just approached him and knocked him to the ground. I could see he had a deepish cut over his eye, Charlie chirped up that I should pack it in. Mind, I think he knew how funny Reg could be, and that he was glad someone had shut him up, after all he was a pain, why should he pick on me for no reason? When everything appeared to be running along smoothly, he may have done it to others in the past, but whatever the reason Charlie seemed happy at the outcome.

Next morning I went into work as normal and yet nothing was said, but Charlie said it was now time I joined a scaffolding gang, so would now be working out of the yard and then on a building site where scaffolding would be erected and taken down all the time. The gang I was now in consisted of three men – charge hand or head scaffolder, a spanner hand and labourer. They were Don Omara, Johnnie Davise, and me. There was as a rule three men gangs, it was very hard scaffolding but I never used to mind that.

A funny thing I did, now I look back, was to make my skin darker, as the others were working out in the open and all weathers they had a nice tanned skin, a rich colour. Next to them I looked lily white, so what I used to do was rub the rust off the scaffold tubs on to my arms just to give me that tanned appearance. Silly really, but I did it and as luck would have it I never had a bad comment made about it so it must have looked OK. The main thing about it was it made me feel better and took that white-looking skin away.

We had a good gang, Don and Johnnie were fast at erecting and striking, I was soon into it and working very hard also keeping up with them either passing up the tubes to them or cleaning up all the tubes that were dropped down when they were striking a job. We had a very good arrangement and it worked out very well, Don told me I could work fast and that I would be a big asset when they gave us a job on so many hours. This was when the office allowed you so many hours to complete a job, say 48 hours, and we could complete it in about half the time. My money was soon shooting up and climbing to a respectable wage now for my age. The office quoted us for the jobs in hours, and time it should take to complete them in. As I said, Don, Johnnie and me were very fast, so the money was soon building up fast and that was great. This carried on until the office saw what we were earning and getting a lot more than them. It all boiled down to our gang being fast, also I was now on the spanner as well, so me and Johnnie could carry on and finish a job while Don would go and start a new job as he could set a job out on his own and complete up to the first floor then we would all join up and work on the new job. Basically, the office now had to slow us down as our wages were just going up and up, jealousy sets in when you're earning more than the governors, not that they were working bloody hard while they are sitting on their arses in the office. All they could do now was put us on a site, and stop our so many hours to do a job – they found out the quotes given us were far out.

Anyway the site we were assigned to was Sharps Copse in Leigh Park. This was a large project and consisted of many new houses so would last for a few years, now we were back on so many hours a day, this was a lot easier. All we had to do was erect a lift up or strike one down when the bricklayers required it. We would also leave early as we would be well on top of them most times.

I would now be going out with Don most weekends for a piss up, and we would often meet up with a good friend of Don then mine called Stewart Mcginness. He was a roofer by trade, mostly doing asphalting. We would all meet up on a Friday night mainly and early, then drink right the way through the night and often ending up in a good punch up with whoever used to upset one of us. This became a common occurrence the more alcohol we drank, but a good time was always had by all. Don knew I was a good fighter so for a laugh would challenge any one on the site who became a bit lippy. He would say to whoever upset the apple cart I got one for you and I would fight them even though I was young and thin in those days, so the aggressor would come at me full of confidence, but would then leave with a flea in his ear.

One fight Don got me in stuck in my mind. He was working on a block of houses on the site and me and Johnnie were round the back of it. Then a lorry was driven at speed and into a muddy puddle next to Don – he was drenched and he started swearing at the driver, "You silly bastard!" and they had a large exchange of swear words. The lorry driver pulled up quick, and I heard Don shout out "Ian, here a minute!" I came from round the back where we were working, and when I got there the lorry driver had jumped out of his cab and making for Don shouting and hollering. He said to the driver, "I got one for you," and indicated me to the driver. I looked at him – he was a size, a right lump. A fight started between us and I caught him with a peach and as he was going down he grabbed me and pulled me into the mud with him – we were soaked. I butted him hard and managed to get to my feet, I was dripping wet with mud then as the driver rose I sank a left hook into his rib area. There was a large gasp and I heard an exhalation of air from the driver. I knew then I had him and sank a left and right into his head and over he went. He was soaking wet and covered in mud and a broken man. He seemed shocked and had a job just to walk back to his lorry, not believing a youngster my size could inflict so much damage to him. This must have got back to Mill's office as the next week I was told there was no work left and I would be getting stood off. This couldn't have been the real reason as the site we were on had plenty of work left to complete so must just be an accuse to get rid of me – the decision was made. Don even had a word with the office, after all he didn't want me to go, but to no avail and no amount of discussions could alter it. I even had a chat with an ex-scaffolder I knew well who was now in the office. He was Peter who ended up running the firm for many years and was a great success, but even he could not reverse the decision to keep me in the job. I was the subject of my fighting powers again, and now my marriage to Jenny was coming under more strain. Here I was out of work and drinking to excess, we would argue and she would stay at her mums with Julie for longer as I wouldn't be the best husband to be around when in drink.

Chapter 17

I met with some of the boys one day and had a suggestion given to me, to do window cleaning. The firm mentioned was Whites, a window and general cleaning firm – they were quite a large firm, who did all the shops in Commercial Road. We would meet early at about 5.30 am and start cleaning all the shop windows before the shops opened at nine. We also had all the shop fronts scrubbed out and cleaned ready for opening. Also a lot of people seemed to use the shop fronts to go to the toilet during the night, the dirty lazy buggers.

My best mate then was Johnnie Stanley. We had so many laughs together and soon became inseparable. Our humour seemed to just click and we were always in hysterics. Me and Jenny were trying to make a go of it for the sake of Julie. I told her I would stop fighting and work hard to look after the pair of them. Mind, me and Johnnie would become inseparable and be out drinking most weekends. I was still fighting but if there was any blood on my clothes I would leave them with Johnnie's aunty Gwen who would wash them for me and I would put some of John's clothes on before I went home, so Jenny never knew I had been fighting. Most nights I was out, Jenny was usually asleep when I got in so never knew of my evening exploits as I would be gone early in the morning to work. Jenny was back getting picked up by her dad again while I was cleaning shops early, she would drop Julie off and go to open the hairdressing shop, so never saw any bruises or marks I may have acquired in the evening brawls I had.

I could only assume why, but my marriage was getting harder and harder. I was beginning to wonder if I would be better off on my own. In the end, we did decide to a joint decision to have a break from the marriage and Jenny would move back to Drayton and her parents. I would miss Julie most as I had so many feelings for her and as I said Mum was besotted with her. Still, I could take her to see Nan whenever I could take her and that could soften the blow to Mum. I must admit George seemed relieved the split had happened, after all he knew about the rows we had and knew he couldn't do anything about it. He wouldn't have to talk to me again at least for a while, and you could see he was glad of that. After all I had calmed the bully that he was and that must have brought a lot of hurt on him. This was simply because he wasn't in control whenever I was around. He must have put the flags out at his house as he now appeared a free man!

It was nice to be in a position where I had no one to answer to. This may have been due to being too young for the responsibility of a marriage with a child. Me and John were together nearly every day now and we had some great times, just coming home and going out whenever I pleased was a relief. I would take my washing round to my Mums, she was a diamond in that respect, even giving me some cooked meals to make sure I was getting my food OK – a real worrier about me was my Mum, bless her.

All us boys were always very smart, we would all have new suits. How this was done was we would give our names when getting measured up and place a deposit, but would give a friend's address not our correct one. When the suit was completed and ready to pick up a card was sent to the address that was given, saying the suit was done and ready to pick up. Whoever got the card would inform the real one measured up for it that the suit was now ready to pick up and give them the card to confirm that so they could get it. This procedure continued till we all had our new suits. When the asking of the money was sent they were just told that the person involved never lived there. We would all have new suits for peanuts, so to speak, real spivs!

Now as I had the complete house on my own anyone in our company could just crash out at my place if too drunk to make it home, so I appeared to always have a full house. One day me and John and our other friend Johnnie King decided to put a party on for a good friend's birthday, Billy Plummer. He was good and one of us, and we painted the house up a bit psychedelic looking, even painted the ceiling black and covered it with gold butterflies and connected a lamp that revolved round causing a moving picture effect. We did it and it appeared very impressive. The lights were dimmed so as with the music playing it appeared to be a private club and not a house as it was. The job now was to get Bill to turn up without a clue what was waiting for him. This task was given to two good friends. They would meet Bill and go for a drink with him for his birthday. They said me and Johnnie couldn't go as we had an appointment that had cropped up. The two said they had heard of a party on later in the evening that was supposed to be a great one, and the plan was in place. We were all at home waiting for Billy to arrive. I had already informed the next-door neighbours about the noise to expect and that they could come. After a while the door was banged quite hard, the music was loud and the door was opened as the chant rang out "Happy birthday to you Bill, happy birthday to you!" Bill was absolutely flabbergasted, he had not the slightest inclination of what we had arranged. He nearly cried with excitement and shock, his face said it all. The preparation had all been worth it. "Let the party begin!" I said and hoorays rang out. What a night was in store and Bill enjoyed it from start to finish. After the party, most had left and a few others had just crashed out wherever there was space. In the morning, I noticed a new leather coat and transistor radio was missing, they had clearly been taken by a party-goer. As they were all waking up we started putting all the names forward who were at the party, and as it was packed it took some doing.

In the end it wasn't too hard as only about three ended up just acquaintances not friends. Johnnie would go and get hold of them, it shouldn't be too hard. Two names came up to be living quite near us in some flats, so off we went and entered both flats one after the other. We gave them a very good search and never found my leather coat or my transistor radio. That just left one name not accounted for. We had to find out his address, he was just a gate crasher it transpired and no address was known. John and me enquired all over Portsmouth, it was a tiresome task as there weren't many who we never knew or had not heard of. Anyway, the same name kept coming up – James Spencer it was – and that he lived in Stamshaw. We got a number of a house he was supposed to live in and the road. Me and John went there, pissed off by now by all the searching we had done. This appeared to be our last port of call. We approached the house number we were given, there was nothing but anger running through our veins. We banged on the door hard but no answer, so we banged really hard and shouted through the letterbox, but still no answer came back. "Fuck it, John let's push the door in, he's in there hiding I think." With that the door was pushed open, we entered and looked in every room and cupboard, also drawers, wardrobes even under the bed, couldn't see anything we were after. I was sure he must have taken them I said to John, and with that my temper just flipped. Let someone in my house and they steal from me the prick, I proceeded to smash everything in sight, bath, washbasin, toilet, cupboards, drawers, television, radio, cups, saucers three-piece chairs everything. It looked like a bomb had hit it. We left it totally wrecked, I would not stand for anyone taking my belongings after having food and drink the bastard.

Word had travelled fast, I was fuming and everyone knew, and within two days my leather coat was returned along with the transistor radio. I went straight to John and let him know I got my things back. Imagine how surprised I was when John told me he had heard that the house he had wrecked was in fact the wrong number house. What a shock that was, still the man must have heard and returned my goods. I wonder if they had come back should we had not retaliated, the bastard. Still had to feel a bit sorry for the one who lived in the wrong house – he must have been frightened to death.

Chapter 18

Johnnie was now starting to go out with a girl called Christine. She was a nice girl and never poked her nose into me and John whenever we went out. I think that is why they stayed together, John wouldn't want a person telling him what he could do or couldn't as he would have just moved onto another. One weekend we were out drinking in the Cambridge pub Southsea. We used to use the back bar in there and this night Chrissy came in with a friend called Rita. She was a really smashing looker who was of very smart appearance and very clean. I noticed the scent she had on – it was like a spell was put on me. This would be a challenge for me. I tried to talk to her but was just given what I would call a cold shoulder from her. Mind you, every time I looked around at her she seemed to be looking at me only to glance straight away if our eyes met. Anyway, I never tried talking to her again, just looked at her as someone to just look at not one to get involved with. Johnnie knew I fancied Rita but he told me that Christine said she wasn't interested in me at all, mind I was convinced she would go out with me if I could just have a bit of time on my own to talk to her.

On a Friday night when we were in the back bar of the Cambridge a fight started. It was a bit of push and shove at first, then Johnnie started having a word with someone in the bar as well. Chris and Rita moved away thinking a fight was about to kick off, then Johnnie hit a bloke knocking him to the ground. His friend who was with him called Brian Burrows started to get involved as well. He was a hell of a size and they said he worked in a scrapyard that was in Portsea. He would have been over 20 stone, a real big man and a hell of a lump, a giant. Anyway he moved towards Johnnie and this is when I moved forward as well on John's side though. I hit Brian so hard he went straight over. I let him get up but he was groggy, then I struck him on the side of the head this time and as before he went down again, but on hitting the ground he rolled over like a big beached whale. His nose was burst and he had blood all over it, so no way was he ever going to carry on with the fight.

I looked at Rita and she shied away from me, not too pleased with me at all, but there was a spark there. Then when Brian got near me on his rise he was all dazed but Christ he was a large man, as wide as he was tall. Good job I could hit hard as that was what was required with him if he got hold of you he could pull your head off, the size of him. Still no good saying what might have happened – it never did, I was too hard for him and he honestly looked stunned. He was dazed and still wobbly when he left the bar.

After the pub we went to the curry house we used in Osborne Road. Chrissy and Rita were already in there when we got there. After the meal Johnnie and Chris were coming to stay together at my house, but Rita was having none of that and said she was going home, so we dropped her off in a taxi and carried on to my house. John used the back bedroom, and in the morning me and John carried on to work, leaving Christine in the house so she could leave on her own when she got up. We knew the windows were calling and the shop fronts had to be cleaned, it was about 6.30 am and we had a good chat on the way and as always a laugh at what had gone on the night before. After all, when you're young nothing seems to faze you and life seems a big happy rollercoaster; you had to be hard in your mind and that was what me and John were, no one bothered us and never would. We used to go out all the time especially at weekends, we seemed to always bump into Christine and Rita was now with her more and more. I thought it was because she fancied me, yet every time I approached her for a date or ask her to come with me and Chris with Johnnie to the pictures, all I seemed to get was a cold shoulder. No I was thinking she liked me a lot and just putting a front on, or was she?

Then after a few weeks we went to a pub we used called the Railway near Fratton Bridge where a man called Snowy was the landlord. He was a jovial type of man and always game for a laugh, and a nice person with it. He liked a fight as he used to box when younger and everyone seemed to like him. This night the bar was packed and all the boys who were usually in the pub were there, but some that appeared to be bikers were in the pub this night. They had come from out of town so never knew of me. One who had long hair started giving me little jibes and taking the piss out of my clothes as I was in a black leather coat and ice blue flared trousers. I must have looked a bit of a pansy thinking about it. Anyway, the chap kept on at me so I punched him, which sent him flying and out cold. Snowy shouted "What's going on?" so I disappeared into the toilet to give time for the argument to calm down. When I came back into the bar I saw the man I had hit and he never had a mark on him, so I walked over to him and knocked him straight out again and called him a bastard. Unbeknown to me they were in fact twin brothers so they both ended up with a good hiding. Then it came back to me that their biking gang were outside the pub and wanted more of our lot. We never needed another invitation and made our way outside the bar. There were about six of them out there and a hell of a fight started. Me and Johnnie started knocking them over left, right and centre. I had one on my mate Tony's Mk10 Jag, it was a white one, and I was hitting a biker on it when all of a sudden blood came spurting out of my face. I was getting glassed from what appeared every angle and from behind me the gang ran to their bikes around the corner. They were chased but picked up by the mates who had started their bike up ready to shoot off. My face was cut to pieces and I remember asking Johnnie to look for my ear, thinking it had been cut off as my fingers were deep into a big hole at the side of my head, it was gaping open. After John had looked for a little while he said,

"You idiot, mate it's on your head, there's just a very large hole cut under your ear, not your ear off!" Blood was pouring out now and I was starting to feel really weak. I must have lost so much blood I was passing out. John held the gaping hole together to stem the blood flow while we waited for the ambulance that had been called for. I got weaker and weaker until I must have passed out as I remembered nothing else.

I came round on the hospital table being sorted out. I came round with a load of police officers round the bed. One said, "Ian you're a good lad, this is attempted murder. Can you give us the names of any that done this?" I said no, as I knew if the police were involved I couldn't get them myself and that's what I really wanted, that's all that was on my mind at the time, not getting anyone charged. Then I looked and saw who were in the hospital room – there was Johnnie, Chrissy and Rita crying in the corner where my saturated clothes were. Rita was on Chrissy's shoulder crying, she obviously thought I was going to die. Mind you it proved that she was thinking of me all the time and only making out otherwise. After I was stitched up and had blood put back into me I asked to go home. I never liked hospitals and against their advice I left the hospital, got a taxi and went home. Rita came with me, and we all stayed at my house all night. I stayed with Rita all the time after – we were now a couple. She had so much love to give me the time flew by. In the morning, I would start to clean the stitches up, the way I used to do this was to put some butter on a tablespoon, warm it on the gas and put the fluid butter on the stitches and this broke up the congealed blood and left the stitches clean and clear of the congealed blood, leaving them looking like plain neat cord.

A few weeks later I saw my mate Tony George who owned the Mk10 Jag. He said it was not white after but pure red with my blood spillage. He said he thought I wouldn't pull through as I had lost so much blood, and he was relived I had and said I must be very lucky. How could I not agree with him there? The trouble is when it's you and you're young and fearless you think you're indestructible and you don't look at the negatives, only the positives in life. By now the stitches were all out and all there was showing were thin red lines where the cuts had been. I could see a cut had gone very near my left eye only just stopping very close to it, so lucky I never lost it. Also, the cut at the back of my right ear just under was not quite deep enough to hit the jugular vein. If that had happened that would have been the end of me. I would have bled to death, I nearly did anyway as it was.

Chapter 19

Shortly after this episode I got a letter from Jenny's stepdad asking me to sign a paper. Not knowing what this was regarding I decided to go to the hairdressers at Cosham and ask George what I had to sign the form for. He told me it was to take my daughter Julie out of the country when they go on holiday, unless I didn't want her to have a holiday. I said I would never stop her from having a break away with the family, George said then sign the form and next time they go on holiday Julie would be allowed to go with them. I said it would be nice for her and that I would never stop her going so I signed the form and gave it to him, he said it was very wise as now she would go with them. I carried on seeing Julie and taking her down to my Mums, everything was going along smoothly and Mum loved having Julie. It seemed to be working out just fine, then one day I was near her school so went to the playground to see her. All her friends who I knew said that Julie hadn't been to school for a few days but never knew why. I was thinking something must be wrong with her so went to the nursery where she used to stay while they were working in the shop. I was told she had not been there for a few days and also never knew anything being wrong. Now I was worried so I went to the hairdressers and found it shut up, so I panicked and rushed to their house in Drayton as I knew something had to be wrong now. On reaching the house I approached the door and banged it as hard as I could, then again the same, but no one came to it. Then next door opened and the next-door lady said, "Who are you after?" I said, "Julie." She told me, "You won't see them, they have all emigrated," and she thought Australia was the country. I was fuming. Now I knew why George had asked me to sign the form, not to take Julie on holiday but to emigrate.

I was flabbergasted how could they do that? It couldn't just happen as they all needed visas and they take time to obtain them. George must have been planning it for months, the sly bugger, what could I do? After all I had signed Julie away on paper. Anyway there was no answer to this, I was stumped the bastard of a man, nothing but scum, catching me out like that. I had no idea, not a clue, the fox and bully boy had the last laugh.

I was so stumped, now I had to start and get about finding where they had taken my daughter. I was told Australia but that was a very big country, where would I start, that was the question. My head was pounding. What could I do? Who would I ask? How could I do it? All these things were flashing through my mind, this was not going to be any easy job to sort out. George must have known and would now be having a good laugh on me. He was a pig, I knew that, but how big a one was only just coming out. He must have been screaming for at least the last six months. I was told it would take that long to get all the paperwork and visas in place. I never had any idea it was or had been going on that long. I talked to the Salvation Army and donated a sum to get them to look where Julie was taken.

The real con-flab I was now facing was the thought of not seeing Julie again, I still had the hope that the Salvation Army may come up with something, but at this stage I had to just assume I would not be seeing Julie again and this was what I had to learn to live with, there was nothing else I could do. I told Johnnie what had happened and he couldn't believe it. He agreed nothing could be done, we just had to wait for whatever outcome took place later. A drink was the best thing, John suggested, so out we went with a few of the boys. We were having a good drink and a laugh. There was one chap who used to come out with us in the gang, Billy White. He was a nice chap, that was until he had too much to drink, then he would start. No matter what pub we were in he would start. "I'm the best fighter in here who can fight, I'll fight them," he said. This was his party piece and he did this time and time again, but as he was one of the boys we put up with it. Mind my fuse was getting short. I said to Johnnie, "I can't handle him shouting out all the time, he would keep on every time the drink was in. I can't keep quiet about it." I would have to have a go at him if he kept on, I couldn't keep turning a blind eye it was every time he had a good drink. John said don't worry about it, he's only like it in drink. "But John I've never lost a fight, I can't listen to Billy's bullshit all the time, I'll have to have a go at him." John said, "Well Ian it's up to you mate, I can understand you." Yes, the more I keep shut up about it the more he seems to do it, the inevitable has got to happen.

I didn't know when, but I did know if he kept on he would have to have a fight, it wouldn't be easy for him. I had never lost, that's in pre-school, infants, juniors, approve school, then the seniors, so I did know Billy would have to be exceptional. It had now got to the stage of not if it happened but when, and John knew if I said it I would always do it. The only one who never knew it was coming was Billy himself. The pub we used as our local was The Viking in Arundel Street. The landlord there was Dave, he was a lovely man and wouldn't bar anyone unless it was a very bad thing they did. A fight was regarded as a minor thing in his eyes.

Anyway, it was a Sunday dinner time session – in those days the pubs shut at 2.30 pm – we were all in there and swallowing our pints quick as you wanted a good drink before the pubs shut until the evening session, then he went into one. Billy started, "Who wants a fight then?" I chirped in then, "Shut up Billy you never know who's in here." He said, "I don't care who it is, I'm the best anyway!" he was shouting out. I said, "Shut up, you haven't had a go at me yet!" He said, "Who do you think you are?" Then I replied, "Too good for you!" "Are you?" and he came at me in the bar. I struck him and he wobbled, then he grabbed me so no punches could be thrown. We got pulled apart but saw he had a nice shiner. Billy left the bar shouting "I'll have you!" I laughed at him and said, "I'll sort this no worries there."

Billy had gone home, never waited outside for me. This indicated he had a shock me going at him, he wasn't used to that. We all finished our pints and I asked my brother Ken if he would give me a lift round Billy's house to finish this off. I knew he wasn't in my class and had to be shut up once and for all. He used to live off Shearer Road Milton, he had to get a shock even if it was just to stop him challenging everyone in our company because that couldn't go on. My Kenny dropped me off at the end of Billy's road. I knew where it was as we had used that as a meeting point before going out drinking before. This visit I knew he was going to get a hiding and one he wouldn't forget in a hurry. I knocked on the door and his wife came to open it. She turned and called to Billy, saying there was a friend here to see him. She had no idea what had just gone on. Billy came out and said, "Had a drink now got Dutch courage then?" I knew he was going to get a hiding. As he came towards me I knocked him over. I let him get up then knocked him over again, this time I had to wait longer for him to get up, he was feeling the power of me. I hit him again, harder this time and he went down really hard. I let him get up again and stepped back to give him the room for this, but on doing so I slipped off the curb and fell down. Billy saw his chance and sprung on me grabbing my hair and banging my head on the floor. I said, "Let me get up as I did you!" But no, he kept banging and banging my head. I nearly passed out but his hand was across my face so I bit his finger nearly off. He was now screaming out with pain letting go of me. I got up and proceeded to give him a hell of a hiding.

He ended up in a right mess and had a badly distorted face, there was blood and cuts over it, then there were police horns going and a couple of panda cars came down the road. Someone had rang them saying two men were fighting. Anyway, when we were approached they asked us to get in the cars one in each, and were taken to the police station. I was in trouble as I had gone to Billy's house to give him a hiding so feared the worst when entering the station. Then Billy came out with it, he said we had a barbecue in his garden and he thought I was trying it on with his wife but later found out nothing of the sort had gone on and that he was very sorry for any disturbance he had caused and that it was merely a misunderstanding. We were then warned of our future actions and let out to proceed home. I thanked Billy for getting me out of trouble, but knew he would not be drinking in my company again or Johnnie's for that matter, after all he had a good hiding and so knew he wasn't the best fighter. I was a freak in that department and now he knew that.

I was in town just after and a man came up to me asking for a chat on our own. He was Billy Connors and said he was on home leave from Dartmoor nick. It was pre-release leave and he was back after a week to get ready for his release date. He told me there was a really big gangster in the jail who had no end of money. He said he wanted a job done on someone who had upset him. I asked what he wanted done, Billy said he would give me as much money as I would ever need if I did what he required. He then said a black man was seen going with his wife and that he wanted him sorted out good and proper. He said he had a gun and that when we found out the address where he was would I blow his legs off. Thinking of all that money, I said no worries I would love to. I asked if he had the gun to which he replied yes. All we needed was a reliable motor to get us to London and back without breaking down. I knew someone called Sonner Jones, he had a new Thames Van, a rarity in those days as most only had bangers. Sonner was funny at first as it was a new van, then I told him it was for a big time hood, also that I wouldn't damage it and would give him a nice drink out of the wages I was expecting after I did the job required. But I was careful not to let Sonner know exactly what it was as I didn't want him to get cold feet, because he would be an accessory to what was going to go on. I met Sonner, got the van then went on to meet Billy and drove on to London. Billy had the gun, it was cleaned up. Looking at the shooter it appeared to be a short barrelled one and easily fitted into one's coat quite easily. So now, on the road, all systems go. It took over two hours in those days to get to London, you couldn't do the speeds you do now. Anyway, there was no turning back, I was getting excited at the words Billy used – money was no object. This was music to my ears as I liked a bet so always required money. This was my chance to have as much as I wanted. When we got to London Billy said we had to go and see a man who sold flowers at the entrance to an underground station. Billy had to get the address of the supermarket that the gangster's dad worked as a manager there. It was a Fine Fare one so we made our way there. When we arrived Billy asked to speak to the manager and we were led to an office. The door was knocked on and the manager was told we wanted to speak to him. Billy mentioned the man's son who was in prison on the moor, and he asked for the address where we would find the black man as we would be seeing him for his son, to sort out some trouble for him. The address we were given was a long road and his one was off of that, it was going to be a time as the length of the road looked long. I drove slow passed each one looking my side and Billy did the same his side. I got to the end of the road without seeing the name of the one given us by the manager. I said, "Right Billy, I'll turn round, you look my side and I'll look yours." To this Billy said, "They know I came to London, his dad will tell him we came to do the job and my name will be good on the moor." I said, "Billy don't let your bottle go coming all this way, it should have gone in Portsmouth." He said, "No worries, I'll still get you a good drink for coming." What could I do than just go along with him, but deep down I knew his arsehole had gone. On the way back Billy brought us fish and chips. That was all I could see me getting. Billy ended up a right fool, my name will be good on the moor? Why all he did was drive to London, get a few names – a baby could have done that. All it proved to me was Billy had no bottle and was a fool as the job could have been done without leaving Portsmouth, the prick.

I decided now to collect money owed to people, at least I would get paid for my services. Before long I was on a good income as my services were needed by many. I did quite a few jobs for a Johnnie Wear from Hayling Island. He was a very nice man and knew a lot of people in the horseracing game. His brother was a trainer, Roy. One job I did was for an ex-jockey called Peter Haynes. He was having trouble with a chap going with his wife, he wanted him to have a wake-up call and said he would pay me through Johnnie. My life was going well and I was getting good money, but I still kept thinking of Julie. She had left England and it was getting harder to think I may never see her again. That was a gutwrencher, but life must go on.

I was out one night when I was approached by Dooly Byng. He asked if I still had the house in Mile End. He was. I asked him why and he said he had left Ivy and needed a place just for a few days. I told him I only had two bedrooms and I had one and Johnnie King and Lorraine had the other, but if he wanted he could crash out on the settee. He said that would be fine as he would only come in late at night and be up and gone early in the morning. He was no trouble and would come home when the pubs shut and would leave at the crack of dawn as he worked an early start down the docks.

After a few days, a letter came saying the house was getting pulled down for redevelopment. Now I had to use my brain and try and buy my own house so I would be secured. I had to get a job just to prove I had a regular income to obtain a mortgage, so I went back scaffolding, this time for a firm called SGB, a large firm. Once I had been there a few weeks I applied for a mortgage with a firm called Abbey National. They agreed in principle, but I had to get the deposit. The house I wanted was off Fratton Road and it was priced at £2,300. I offered £2,200 and this was accepted but I needed £200 deposit. My gambling never helped, I couldn't win enough so I went to Lloyds Bank on Fratton Bridge. Some of the boys knew the manager so he lent me the deposit. I was now a home owner in my own right. I asked Dooly (his real name was Julian) if he wanted to move into the new house. His money would help the mortgage repayments. Dooly was really pleased to be moving into a house where he would be able to stay and have no worries of getting kicked out.

When I was at work I was with a scaffolder called big Roy Clay. He was living in a council house in Sultan Road. My mortgage repayments were £19, 19 shillings a month, Roy's rent was £2, 10 shillings a week. He said I was still paying twice what he was I would never benefit. I tried to explain to him his rent would soon double, yet my repayments would stay the same, but he couldn't grasp it, he was adamant I was paying much too much. It wasn't long before I was right. Roy's rent soon doubled – you should have heard Roy moan, he never stopped, but I just ground it into him that I warned him.

After I moved into my new house with Rita and Dooly, I took a bit of my old furniture with me, but bought some new stuff as well. Rita was a machinist and always had work as she was good at her job and had a good income for a young girl, and with Dooly's rent the mortgage was easy to pay. We spent out some money decorating the place and did a bit of modernising. I was still going out Friday nights with the boys, but our night out with John was getting a bit rarer as he was now getting more involved with Christine so going out less. Mind, I had a few good close friends, one was Freddie Hodgkins. He had been a friend of mine since I was 15. I first met him down the Camber Docks where my uncle Dave Crouch worked. He would get me a bit of casual work bagging up the broken bags of New Jersey potatoes that had burst out in transit. The money was good as it was run by the union, that's how the wages were kept high. The shop steward was a man called Ronnie Turnbull, he was a brilliant union man and was liked by all the dockers. There were some hard men in the docks and Dave and Ronnie and Freddie were in that class, a real family where they were so close no one used to argue with them. I was in that gang through our Dave, even though I was only nearly 16.

Chapter 20

Now I was older I would often go out with Freddie Hodgkins, sometimes on our own, other times a group of us. One week there was Freddie, Les Fyfield, Johnnie Kite, Peter Kerr, me and a couple of others – Smugger and Bazzle. We were out on the seafront and going in the bars opposite the pier – there were three or four bars we used to go in. Anyway, a fight started between us and a group that were nearly twice as many as us. Soon the fight was in full flow, but as always we were getting the better of the opposition, some started to run away down a side road opposite the pier. We had been hitting out at most of the gang against us so no wonder they tried running away. We were still hitting different ones of them as we chased them. Freddie had just knocked one over as I turned around. I saw him trying to throw him into a garden of one of the houses in the road. I couldn't understand why he didn't just go with the tide and let Fred stuff him into the garden. He was holding onto the garden bars like grim death, so I went back to see and help Fred. That's when I saw the chap Fred had struck, he was still clutching to the garden bars and shouting "No, no!" That's when I looked and saw the bars weren't just round the garden but going round a basement. That was the garden forecourt where Fred was trying to throw the man, not in a garden but down a deep basement and it was a big drop. No wonder he was holding on for his life, he probably was. If Fred had heaved him over he would have been seriously injured or even killed. That's when I explained it to Fred, he was in his madman mode so it took a lot of getting him off, but he did let him go in the end and off he ran to join his group and away from us lot. He didn't know how lucky he was to be alive, the drop was that deep. We ended the night as always having a fight, plenty of booze and a good meal with a laugh and again a night to remember.

The next night I was in The Viking pub, my local, and telling the gang of ours how the night before had gone and about the luck and laugh we had. We said how Freddie was lucky not to get done for murder in the road we chased the gang down and about the deep basement he tried to toss the man down. I was still going on about the night and the good time we had, then a friend we knew said he was in Southsea that night and knew my friends I was with and how fiery they could be, so said what did I expect going out in a crowd like us, it was asking for trouble. I said all you lot are the same, you could start at the drop of a hat. We all had to agree in the end as trouble could flare up at any time so the story ended there. As I turned around, a man I knew as Tellog Singh (he was a Sikh from Delhi or his family were) appeared in a bad mood and demanded a drink off Dave the landlord who asked him to calm down if he wanted to be served. It appeared he had been rowing before he came into the bar. I said don't get on to Dave, he was alright and just doing his job running the bar. Tellog was Indian, some used to say a Pakistani, but I heard they came from Delhi. Anyway, he had a turban on and jumped down my throat telling me to shut up or I would get one. I said don't be silly, you'll get yourself hurt but he took no notice of my warning and came straight at me and tried to punch me in the face. I just punched him and he was lifted off his feet and knocked to the ground, he hit it with a thud. I thought that would be the end of that, but no he got up and came straight at me again. I dropped him a second time and he got up again, so I had to hit him again but with much more force. In his time he got up again, I never thought he would have got up but he did. I was beginning to think how could he, it was impossible. Over he went again, yet struggled to his feet again, I have never hit someone so hard and so many times dropped them yet he managed to get to his feet. I was now thinking what was he on, Tellog was a very hard man not a fighter as I never got hit, but it was beyond me how many times he got up. Beggars belief! After all I had never in hundreds of fights hit someone so hard and the fight was not over, he came again and over he went. This was going on for ages, me hitting him and Tellog hitting the floor. Now my hands were swollen right up, they looked like I had a pair of boxing gloves on they were that large, and now every time I hit him my hands throbbed and they were now badly jarred up. The pain travelled right up my arms. His face was now looking like a football, his eyes were shut and his lips badly swollen; his nose looked broken and was pouring with blood. It wasn't normal, he had to be on something. I was just praying he would stay down to save him such a bad beating or a more severe one. It was like a planned film, no one could take such a beating in real life, yet Tellog was. Now he was having such a job just to rise, I was feeling sorry for him. His face had become unrecognisable, he was bleeding from all over his face and he looked like death. I decided to hit him with a hard one but forget the face it looked terrible, I hit him up the body. That was it, he couldn't take any more and my hands were fucked. The pain in my fists was excruciating. How Tellog was still alive was beyond me he was in a terrible state, I had lost count of the number of times he had gone down yet got up. I looked at his face – it was like neat mincemeat.

He just approached the front door to leave the pub, as I looked out the windows I could see a lot of Sikhs outside. They had turbans on, or most had, they were waving machetes and knives near the front door. My mates said let's go out the back door, I said no, I don't go out the back door, I'm going out the front. My friends who saw the machetes and knives wouldn't come out the front, none of them. I approached the front door to go out, fearing the worst when Dooly said I'll come out with you, I've had a good life. I said, thanks mate and we went towards the front door. As we were about to go out we heard two panda cars sirens. I have never been so pleased to see police before. They were all broken up and a lot with the arms ran away. It soon cleared. I still thought there would be some outside when I left to go home, but no it was in fact all clear. Before I left the pub, though, Dave gave me a bucket of ice to soak my hands in for the rest of the night to take some of the swelling down. I can say I have had hundreds and hundreds of fights as I said before and never lost. Yet Tellog was the hardest man I ever fought, that's not fight wise as he hardly hit me once, but for determination and for keep getting up. Tellog was out on his own, a true grit man, and after the battle we had and the time it went on for the only result was for me and Tellog to end up best of mates. And the more I got to know him he was a true gent, one who would do anything for you, and I used to look after his brother George who loved his drink and needed looking after, but the same as Tellog, a lovely man or more boy in those days. He once made a truly nice curry for my wife and her friends a few years later, yes a true gent in the best of terms who also had a heart of gold and I still miss him to this day.

Chapter 21

I was in a bookies shop near Fratton Road snooker club when a friend got talking to me. He was Billy, or Hamburger Billy. Apparently he had booked a site to sell burgers and hot dogs etc. at a site on the top of Portsdown Hill. There was a travelling fair there all weekend – this happened every year at this time, a bank holiday. Apparently it was expensive for him to book all three days on the site as he would be the only food outlet on site. He told me it normally was a brilliant time to unhitch his wagon and park on the site to sell his burgers, hot dogs and drinks, however this year it had pissed down all three days and he hadn't taken a bean. He asked me if I could help him collect his trailer, hitch it up and take it off the site, then drive his car home. He would give me a good few quid. As I was free and extra money would come in handy I agreed to go with him to get his trailer. This was his only way to earn a living so needed it to get his wages for the week, also he was a compulsive gambler and this was his income to also feed his habit.

The burger van had to be hitched up and dragged off site which was absolutely saturated as it had rained for three days solid. He asked me to be there in case of any trouble as he had no money to pay for the three days and as I say, although he never told me how much it was for him to pay prior to taking his van off, it was expensive. He was in fact in the bookies trying to win the money required, but as always he lost what money he had. He told me he would pay me later if successful and he could always get hold of money so that was a bonus. All I had to do was give him a few days to raise it and that he would be very grateful for my help. So off we went heading to the fair site on top of the hill. Well that was all he told me and said it was a formality if the site was accessible due to the heavy rain and the trailer could be pulled off. It transpired that Billy had been to the site in the morning and told the head traveller who managed the fair that he would bring a fighter with him later and if I beat their best he would not have to pay his site fees. If his fighter lost he would pay double the fees, and leave his trailer there till money came across.

When we got there, Billy got out and proceeded to have a confrontation with the site manager or fair owner. Bear in mind I never had a clue what the arrangements were and certainly never knew a thing about a fight. Anyway, Billy called me over to him so I got out the motor and went to him. He said, "Ian you would fight anyone wouldn't you?" I looked at him and wondered what he had said, so backing him up said, "Yes course I would." Then the boss called a large muscular chap to him. As he neared, the fair owner saw I was not budging then he said get your trailer off the site and don't ask for any available sites in future. He was done with that travelling fair and every site they ever used again. I had no idea of the arrangement Billy had had so there was no reason for me to back off. All I was there for was to help Billy with the trailer and getting it off the muddy field, or so I thought.

After when Billy told me of the blag he had just done I was mad at first but afterwards we saw the funny side of it. He had played a real poker hand and won the bugger, what if I was caught cold and not prepared for a confrontation, anything could have happened, we could have been jumped by a gang of them. All Billy said was that he had faith in me and that he would pay me later after he apologised and promised me a nice few quid, those were his words. Anyway, he saw me later in the week and sure enough gave me a nice few quid as he promised and when he gave me the money it was badly needed as I was in arrears with the mortgage so how handy was that, thanks Billy.

I was always into greyhounds and would usually have a pup round me. A friend who worked with my Dad called Peter also had a couple of dogs, we used to race them at a flapping track called Aldershot. It was great to train them and get them ready for a race at the flaps, the thrill of winning a race gave me a really good buzz knowing you had done the work on them to achieve their optimum ability. I had one pup we called Boy. Chris liked him and would often take him for a walk when her and John stayed. He was an affectionate dog but I'm afraid of limited ability. I couldn't wait to get hold of a very good dog, but how? At my age money was hard to get hold of, even harder to hold on to as being out all the time and gambling took their toll. Anyway, I got in touch with a trainer at White City track called Pam. She would find homes for dogs the owner had given up on or ones that were surplus to the owner's requirement. They would have not only run at the Derby track but also at the next big track, Wembley. She let me have a large white and black, I think he used to run at Wembley and he was a fast dog she told me, but he had to have a toe amputated so the owner called it a day with him. All I had to do was promise a good home and agree that he wouldn't run on any registered track. I was only too pleased to accept him on these terms.

I went to pick him up with Peter and signed a form to accept responsibility for his well-being and took him home. He was a very imposing individual and had really muscular shoulders, a sign I liked to see in a dog. I worked him and walked him to get him ready for Aldershot so he had to be nice and firm to the touch. This also would make him less likely to pick up any injuries. Me and Peter took him to the track so as he could have his grading in trial, on account of the time he achieved would be the grade he would have to compete in. He was a very fast dog and the grader, Frank, told me he would be too fast for most dogs at the track but that I could enter him in an open race. These were races for the better class of dogs and I had two options – a five pound open whereby the winner collected 30 pounds or a ten pound open where the winner received 60 pounds. As money was still on the tight side, I chose the five pound one so would be running for 30 pounds – a fortune then. I paid the money to Frank and I was in the open race Saturday. He got extra work that week, had his teeth cleaned, brushed every day leading up to the race – he looked a million dollars.

On the day of the race I had butterflies. Here I was, a youngster with a dog good enough to go into an open race. I was so chuffed. on the day of the race he was massaged well, given a light breakfast and cup of tea, then in the afternoon he had pasta and fish and some more tea, He was gleaming and shinning like a new pin. Great, he was ready to run. On the way to Aldershot we stopped at a field, walked round so he could empty out fully, then there was nothing in him to restrict his stride from opening out fully. On arrival we got a race card and saw we were in the fifth race. I waited in the car with him for the race time to come around. I got him out, let him have a pee and took him into the stadium. This being one of the top races you would have all the spectators watching you get the dog ready. We called him Tiger and he would nearly pull your arms out when parading. Most of the other runners had older paraders, clearly ones who had been in the game ages. Now I knew I didn't just have to beat the other dogs, but also the more experienced handlers. I had enough ability and had the dog to give a good account of ourselves. He was looking superb. Peter came over to me just before the start and told me he put five pounds on Tiger to win and that he was five to one so we would get the same each if Tiger won. Let's hope, I told Peter. My stomach was now churning as I put his race jacket on, which was the five coat, and put his muzzle on for the race. My heart was pounding as I made my way with Tiger to the traps. He was still pulling like a train, really keen to run, and the crowd was at fever pitch as we got near the starting traps. I put Tiger in the traps and made my way to the other side of the infield where I would collect Tiger as the hare stopped after the race was over. I was standing on my own waiting for the hare to reach the traps so the race could start. I was praying Tiger would get out the traps fast and make the bend in front or as near the front as possible. Bang, the traps opened. Tiger was in amongst a few dogs going to the first bend, there was crowding on the bend and Tiger went around the field and came away winning easily. My throat was hoarse through shouting, "Come on Tiger, my beauty, home you go!" was my call. This was now a very proud moment for me, here I was a young lad taking on the old experienced handlers and had just won an open race, one of the best races at the track, yippee! Frank came over and gave me the winning prize money of 30 pounds and a cup. I was elated. Peter joined me and they took a photo of us and Tiger. Bless him he had run his heart out for me and I was so pleased. Frank said, "Well done Ian."

Next day we all went out to celebrate as I had the equivalent of 300 pints – you could get ten pints for a pound in those days. Johnnie was on brown splits and I used to have a bitter top, then Chris joined us and the drinks flowed. On the way home on the bus and in a very merry state I started to sing to all the passengers. I used to love to sing, not that I was any good but I was to myself. I sang at every opportunity I could. Chris thought that was so funny and Johnnie used to like it too. Some weekends when we were short of money we would go in The Cambridge pub Southsea. I would start to sing and Johnnie would throw some money on the floor to encourage others to do the same, then he would crawl on hands and knees collecting it all up. We could often drink all night on the proceeds.

Chapter 22

One night I recall I was in an argumentative state and during the night had had three different fights. I proceeded to a curry house we used to frequent in Elm Road Southsea. I had some blood on me from my addictions that evening. I thought a curry and break would calm me down before I returned home. In the restaurant I met my good friends John and Bobby. I sat near them and started to explain what a night I had. The waiters were looking at the blood on my attire and seemed apprehensive to serve me. I demanded a speedy service. I was told to wait and they would serve me as soon as they could. This wasn't good enough for me so I started shouting to them to hurry up and serve me. I was now in full cry, why don't they serve me and let me get out? The waiters were now frightened as I was punching the table. Two chefs from the kitchen came out to the noise, waving ladles and a knife about and shouting. I struck one of them who went over, then left before the police arrived. I told John and Bobby I would see them at the fun fair in Southsea then shot off out the door. Outside I jumped into a taxi that was there and proceeded to the fair. The fairground staff were very cliquey and used to think they could rule anyone who entered their domain namely the fair.

I walked through the grounds and could see some of the staff duck away from my path. They clearly knew me and the sight of blood on me put them off hanging around – they were off. I could see others get behind some stalls and cower down. I just grunted loudly at them to put some fear into the little shits, then proceeded to the main area, passed some rides seeing different staff and snarling at them. I was clearly in a funny mood and they knew that it was as if I was challenging them looking back. On looking around I could see a crowd had now gathered and were following me through the area. As I went they were clearly trying to get the courage to attack me, and who could blame them the way I was acting. In the end, I could see a dozen or more had gathered behind me. I said, "Come on then, you pricks!" and proceeded to wade into them. This was great fun at the time. I was just knocking them over, two and three at a time, then I was getting hit and kicked till I went over. This would put me out of my stride. The blows seemed to come from everywhere. I rose and started laughing at them. The fight intensified and it became a fun time for me, after all you couldn't beat me and my ego in those days. I kept going down, getting up and putting a few more of them over. I was now really enjoying the scrap and still laughing at them as they weren't really hurting me. The adrenaline was flowing and I was having a great time, after all I was a true fighter and out to enjoy the moment. They weren't used to someone taking their bulling ways and coming back at them. Scum was the only name you could give them. Imagine how many they must have given hiding to and would just take it then leave with their tails between their legs over the years. Well I was a freak and not one to take it and I enjoyed every minute of it. Mind, I was the only one standing in the end, they had all scarpered. I had hurt so many of the bottlers they were bottled. Mind I was hurting all over when the adrenaline rush had finished and my face was the size of a football. Yes, I was beaten really badly but still came through with flying colours. Mind, I knew from experience I would be hurting badly in the morning. When I next talked to Bobby and John they said they watched it and enjoyed it. I asked why didn't they get involved to which they replied I was doing so well I never needed help, but it was brilliant to watch! Cheers boys! I went and got some chips from outside the fair and caught a taxi home. I hadn't been in long and throbbing all over when the door was banged loudly, you could tell it was the old bill. Yes when I got near the door I could hear them talking and their walkie talkies were clearly heard. Well I certainly wasn't going to open the door, I was hurting enough for one day, certainly not a night to spend in the cells as I was clearly battered and bruised all over. No, what I would do was put my dog in the passage – he was mad on anyone who entered so the bootless police would not risk an argument with him, this I knew from passed experiences. A lot of them I came across used the uniform as a back-up to their bootlessness, not many of them could have a go at a mad dog. I left him in the passage and proceeded to bed.

In the morning reality had now kicked in. The drink was out of me and God did I hurt. I was battered and bruised all over and my face was so swollen I had to pull my eyes open to see how bad I was. There was a glint showing through the two slits that were really eye lids. Christ the size of my face had to be seen to realise the size it had become. On viewing it I decided the scumbags who did this had to have another visit while it was still in their minds. Yes, I would take some painkillers, calm myself down, unwind then get the bus to the fairground to give them a rude awakening.

My face was getting bigger, my eyes were nearly completely shut so I broke some matches up into small pieces and held my eyes open to insert the matches to hold them open enough to let me see out. You would have thought I had been in a fight with a whole regiment the state I was in. I spent the rest of the morning cleaning up my face and body, changed the bloody clothes and had some tea and toast. Basically I was licking my wounds and recapturing my thoughts, then at just after dinner time I inserted the matches in my eye lids, got ready and made my way to the bus stop to go back to the fairground to make my presence felt. Mind, this had to be in the afternoon anyway as it was shut in the mornings.

Now I was ready, fed and watered and had a night's sleep or a part of it anyway. They had to know who they had attacked, even if it was to put them off doing it to anyone else. So at two in the afternoon I was off to catch the bus and looking like a zombie. When I got on the bus I could see through my slits that some passengers were scared of the sight I must have given them. I could now imagine what the workers at the fair would think, after all they were only bullies, yes liberty takers and bastards. I got off the bus outside the fairground and proceeded in. The ones that saw me couldn't believe their eyes. There I was with a badly battered face with matches holding my eyes open so I could see, yet here I was to see them.

One who I saw was a Ricky. I vaguely knew him. He would have known me before the trouble in the grounds. He was from Fareham way, just after Porchester. I shouted at him that I wanted to see him, but he ran like greased lightning through the arcade and he was gone. I proceeded through the middle of the fairground and it was like a ghost town. I think I made my point. Not one came out to challenge me, so I strolled through and to the bus stop just outside the ground and then home to recuperate, but it was a pleasure none the less to show them wankers. After all a dozen of them couldn't stop me then to get a wounded soldier to return to the battlefield. Must have made them shit themselves.

I got on the bus, took the matches out and by then it just looked like I had taken a few punches to the face, but the shock factor had been removed. The way I looked at it, if the shock I had given them made them stop the bullying and picking on anyone else then I had achieved my aim. It may stop the stories coming out of the fairground workers who took liberties with young non-fighters and put them in line. Not many people would have done what I did.

Chapter 23

At the end of the sixties, Johnnie and I decided it may be a good idea to join the army just to get away from all the rigmarole of life in Portsmouth, so we went to Barnaby Road Southsea to where the recruitment offices were and as far as I know are still there to this day. We filled in all the appropriate forms and were then told thanks for that they will be getting back in touch with us in due course. We had been waiting for a few weeks, say three or four, and had still not heard from the office regarding recruitment, so we returned to their offices thinking our forms may have been misplaced or just to seek an answer to the applications we put in. It was then the sergeant in the offices told us they no longer required – and the term he used was – bayonet carrying squaddies, just ones who could go down the computer route. We thought that was strange to hear in those days as it was a new angle for recruits to venture in to. We were told we should get some qualifications in that field then return to them with any we had obtained, so basically as we had no qualifications we were rejected. Strange, there we were, two young healthy chaps yet not able to fight for our country if needed. What on earth has England come to, was our initial thought and here I was not able to go in the navy or army as I was basically not acceptable in either. Still it must have been meant so it would be back to normal for me and Johnnie who just took it in his stride and working as normal then going out at night and generally having a good laugh.

One night Johnnie was out with Chris and my brother Kenny and his girl Sue; me and Rita had been to the pictures. After I said I would pick Johnnie and Chris up, then we would go to some pubs in North End. The car I had in those days was a small Ford Anglia, just a two-door job and one where you put the front seat forward to get in the back. I did the honours and let Chrissy and Rita in the back, me and Johnnie sat in the front. I took a short cut through Copythorn Road to go that way to North End. We were all laughing and joking, when all of a sudden I noticed a give way sign in the road. I remembered saying I should have stopped there, bugger I was in the process of braking when a taxi struck us in the side at full pelt. It knocked us over and we turned over and over and ended upside down and wrapped round a lamppost when we came to a halt. It took a bit of time for me to compose myself, then I was thinking who was alive or dead, let us all be OK please. I could still feel my arms and legs so I must be OK, could I say the same about my passengers? They were still screaming so at least alive. I squeezed out and Johnnie followed me. We had no visible injuries, now to the girls. First I pulled Chrissy out over the seat that was pushed forward in the front, then I proceeded to get Rita out who was still screaming so I thought she must be hurt anyway. When she was out, apart from a few aches and pains she also appeared to be OK and Johnnie said Rita had a nice pair of legs as he was observing her while she was upside down in the back, the dirty sod. Now the thinking had started how could a car get knocked over and over and end up wrapped round a lamp post upside down yet the four occupants get out without any serious injuries. It had to be a minor miracle and that is all you could call it or pure luck, certainly nothing else. Someone from the houses near the scene must have rang for an ambulance as one came quickly. We were checked over, taken to the hospital where they confirmed that there were no serious injuries, but even the nurses couldn't believe the story we told them. I got a flashback to when I got glassed outside a pub and how then I was lucky to be alive. Now this, I suppose it's better to be born lucky than rich, after all how could four people be crushed in a small car yet all get out unhurt considering the state the car was in? It would seem impossible but it happened.

Johnnie was now under pressure to get married. That was the gentlemanly thing to do as Christine was pregnant. I was gutted at first knowing I would lose my soul mate and dedicated drinking partner, still it had to be done as they were in fact a lovely couple. So all that was left now was for me to give them my blessing on Johnnie's stag night.

I remember trying to climb onto a police car saying you have to lock us up, the officer replied why should we take you two to the station, I said because he is getting married in the morning and that I didn't want him to as we were great drinking buddies. The officer asked our names and I told him them. On hearing them he said no, I will take you to the service myself just to get you two off the books, we were that bad he said and laughed,

Johnnie asked me to be best man. I saw it as an honour to be best man for my best mate – a fitting tribute. I spent a few hours writing a speech. I had to have all things in it, the good bits, bad bits, and some right ugly bits. On reading this back, I had composed what I would call a damn good speech or send off if you like.

So now to the marriage service. The time soon came round, John was very nervous and suggested we have a couple of stiff drinks, so we called into a pub on the way and we swallowed two doubles each. Would this now settle John? I was hoping so. We carried on to the registry office all suited and booted and John had those spit and polished boots on you could see your face in. He took ages perfecting the glass look on his boots a perfect shine, bless him.

When we arrived there Chris and her family were already there. She looked prim and proper and immaculately dressed. We were then given flowers to pin on our lapels. We proceeded to a room for the actual marriage service for coming together in marriage. I noticed tears were all over the place – you would think Chris was going for execution; but was looking relived it was now over. We had some cars waiting to take us to the reception that was held in Sultan Road. The pub opened up into a nice area to hold a fair size gathering. Just as well as a nice size gathering had turned up. I looked at Chris's dad, he was still a bit embarrassed as I said in the register office that I had lost the ring. I was so convincing I had her dad pulling at his own ring but one that was too fixed on his finger he couldn't get it off, before I got the wedding ring out of my pocket and he calmed down poor bugger.

At the reception two of the area police officers turned up for a while just to make sure the wedding had gone off OK and that they now have two troublemakers off their books. It came to my speech and I would give it my best shot. Basically they made a lovely couple and I was sorry John was leaving the out-every-night gang, blah blah blah. After the speech I got a stunning applause which was shown as their appreciation. I must have done a good job, that night John and Chris stayed at my house, they ended up well drunk so had a peaceful night. In the morning I did them both a nice breakfast then went to the pub. Chris said she better not drink anymore as she was carrying and that was a thing she stuck to all the way through her pregnancy.

One day a girl called Doffy who used to stay at my house sometimes with her friend Lorraine came to wish the couple all the best for the future. Doffy was a very pleasant girl who often tried her cooking skills out on the household. She respected me and could call me a good friend, as I was one who never tried to get hold of her, not even once and that must have been a rare occurrence as she was a real stunner and one I also had respect for as she was a person who would always do anything to help anyone.

I used to get a good income from doing jobs for the Portsmouth big boys, one had hundreds of houses, one had houses and betting shops, one had thousands of slot machines, one had a night club amongst other things, so I was often asked to sort out rents, non-payers and ones who had to be got out for non-payments, debts, and also any fiddles anyone done against them. With these assignments I started to get too violent so had to ease off or risk getting locked up, so wasn't fun anymore. When I was hunting anyone for a job, I learned a lot on my approach. I used to look for their puffer hand, as this would be there punching hand, at least as I looked at it. I would stand on the puffer hand side when moving in, that way they couldn't take a clear swing at me. As I stood on their punching hand then they had to take two bites at me, by which time they would be knocked over, normally out asleep. These were little tricks you picked up when you did have to get tough with some one.

Once me and Fred had to go to the Isle of Wight for a friend of a big car dealer we did jobs for. The one from Wales was owed a lot of money from a frozen food outlet on the island, so me and Fred went there to put the pressure on. We were all done up in suits and ties and we had a long discussion with him and explained that money had to be paid. We also read him the riot act and explained it fully. He left the offices and asked us to wait till he returned, we thought at first he may go to the old bill but we only used a verbal explanation, there was no violence involved. Anyway he returned after a short while with 4,000 pounds, it wasn't the total amount owed as this was considerably more but he bought some more time. So we told him we would be back in a few weeks. He gave us the hard luck story and said he was virtually skint. Anyway he was told he would have to come up with more next time and we left.

A few weeks later we did return and he told us this time he had no money and that he couldn't get any from anywhere as he had reached his credit limit and was now in fact bankrupt. We told him what had to happen now and were told to wait while he made a phone call. This we did and he came and told us that he probably could get some from his bank in Portsmouth, so would have to go there to try and get more cash. We proceeded to follow him to the ferry back to Portsmouth, off the ferry Portsmouth side and he asked us to follow him. He was heading towards Commercial Road with us just behind him, then he pulled up outside a hardware store called Ben Grubs. He went into the store. We waited a short time outside when he appeared waving an axe about and screaming, "I can't take any more!" then came at us with the axe. He was clearly near bursting point. Fred just stayed calm pulled a gun out and said, "Don't be silly, put that down now."

He looked so shocked and made his way quickly to his car and drove off, I turned to Fred and he said I don't think we are going to get any more off him mate and I could not stop myself from laughing, it was funny though.

Fred was so dry, a great friend and one who would literally die for you, a great, great friend and one I truly miss so much I can't explain the feeling. After this I thought I better get a regular job. I asked my uncle who worked as a stevedore at Albert Johnson Quay. His best friend was Ronnie a stevedore also but was port convener as well. They got me in there as an odd job man or handyman. The money was good as you could work as many hours as you liked; plus weekends this added up to a nice income.

They had to work weekends as boats were in and out, to and from the Channel Islands seven days a week. The work was very backbreaking as it was mostly done by hand in those days. Ronnie was a good negotiator and had a deal for the docker where they would get so much a ton for all cargo on and off the ships and it was shared amongst them all. Ronnie made everyone benefit even crane drivers and banks men. My uncle Dave was so clever but couldn't put his ideas to the management as his skills in that department were limited, that is where Ronnie came in. He could really put a case over, so him and Dave were unstoppable in obtaining the best deal possible and fair play to them. I would often have a ruck while down the quay with a lorry driver or anyone who would come on the quay working, I would take them to an old cemetery that was reclaimed and had a nice grass area where you could have a good set to. It was secluded so no one would interrupt you, you could fight to your heart's content and fight till the end – lovely!

One day Johnnie told me Chrissy was due to give birth and had been taken into hospital for the delivery, he was so nervous and couldn't keep still so I said let's go to the pub and talk it through. Anyway we decided to go to the hospital for the birth. On arriving there Johnnie was now panicking, would it be a boy or girl, would it be OK? All these things came out as we waited in a room just off the delivery area, John was up and down like a jack in the box, I had never seen him so nervous, as he was normally calm. The nurse came in shortly and asked who the father was. When John told her, she asked if he wanted to go in and watch the birth. He declined and said he would get too emotional and that he would wait in the waiting room for any news. Chris had now been moved to the birthing room. We waited a while then the nurse came to see us again after a while and congratulated John on the birth of a beautiful girl and she was perfectly healthy. As Chris and the baby had been cleaned up we could now go in and visit the new addition. Chris was in bed and looking knackered and the baby was in a cot at the side of the bed. John looked at the girl and became all of a jitter. He just appeared to freeze. So I leant forward and picked the baby up and cuddled her. She was a lovely girl with big eyes and a pouting mouth. She looked like a little dolly, bless her. John and Chris had a name ready in case it was a girl and decided on Nicklare. I handed her over to John so he could hold her but he was still in a shocked state, he couldn't believe it was his little girl. The pregnancy, birth and now she was actually in his hands! He was still shaking. I knew when we left the hospital our first port of call had to be the nearest bar for a drink to calm him down.

Chapter 24

I had to return to boxing to keep me out of fighting due to the slightest upset someone gave me. My temper had to be calmed harder. I soon noticed the difference. Ray soon knew I was so good he couldn't hit me and I often would slip his advances and hit him not too hard as he was a lot smaller than me, but enough to let him know I was now a real force to be reckoned with and he couldn't just hit me at will as I could now return the favour but a lot harder. This was the start of Ray getting in with me less and less till he never sparred with me anymore. I trained very hard, doing twenty rounds on the bag top and bottom ball and skipping most nights – I was as fit as a flea and now ready for my first fight for Portsea. I was matched with a man from the Isle of Wight in the Nelson Barracks, Queen Street. A few of my mates came to watch – the buzz was something else. I won easily enough and was now back in the groove, the only thing now was I had to get top class sparring and that was hard to get as my speed was back. I also had that cockiness knowing I was good and that was a big plus to have, they had to then not only beat you but your self-belief and that is a big hurdle for them to get over. Not many could hit me clean or hit me at all, I had found so much speed and could slip punches at will. This was enjoyment to the full. I was getting faster and faster, the more I trained the better I got and I used to train every day. The fitter I got the easier the training became. I then started to visit different gyms just to try and get the best sparring possible. I'm afraid this usually was only the once at whatever gym, as I was too good for whoever agreed to a sparring section. This would be the first and last visit to most places I ventured to as no one wanted to get in the ring with me. I could hit whoever at will and they couldn't even catch me to land a clean blow.

I was feeling good at this point, not many I sparred with could now put me under pressure. I was bobbing and weaving and was never put under any strain at all. A prime example was when Spider Kelly was in the ABAs championships. I sparred with him all the time he needed that bit extra. His trainer and overall navy boxing trainer, a Tony Oxley, asked me if I could do extra nights in the gym to put the edge on Spider from the quarter finals till he was knocked out of the championships or progressed to the next round. I agreed to this request knowing it would only do me good and help Paul through till he was out of the ABAs. We sparred many, many rounds together and low and behold he reached the finals. My sparring was good for him and me as we were both southpaws so would make each other fast at the counter punching – a strong point to any southpaw's armoury.

Anyway, should I have to fight him for real I knew I would knock him out if it came to it, as he would move out the same way every time I backed him up, so all I would have to do was throw a wide hook and he would walk straight into it so making the punch double the power it left me at. Anyway, my sparring with Paul had been concluded, he was a week away now from his final but to be honest I couldn't see him winning as I was now hitting him and dealing with his moves with ease. But what I did know was that he couldn't get any fitter. Tony had him as fit as a flea, it was now down to him as me and Tony could do no more. He was ready and trained to perfection.

Well what did I know? Paul was to win the final easily and I was so pleased for him and for Tony. Also what a boost that gave navy boxing, a great feeling for everyone involved. What I was thinking now was how good I was getting. Surely I could now go right to the top in boxing and the work I put in this was rightly warranted. Portsea was matched up with opponents from a Brighton club. The matches would be made at a night club called Sherries.

I was not on the bill as my match up had pulled out, but I still went along to watch the other box anyway. When we arrived we only had three that could box. The show would have been a flop so I agreed to fight a person a lot heavier than myself. It was like an exhibition bout but would be scored. I won easily only for the result to be announced the other way. I was fuming, what a farce. I was so annoyed and lost it. Tony, a trainer in my corner, calmed me down saying it was a home decision but that was no joy for me, the bastards. I asked Keith the matchmaker for Portsea to get a rematch as soon as he could. I couldn't live with a punk like him getting a decision over me, it was criminal. I had pissed it in my eyes and everyone there thought the same. It deflates you if only those three judges knew what they had just done. It meant nothing to them, but my boxing future was now in limbo. Do I carry on or sling this farce in? Let me calm down and decide on what to do after the dust had settled, but Keith told me there was no way he would fight me again. He knew and wouldn't give me a chance to put this wrong back right. I was now clear headed again and wanted to get back in the ring. I had to convince myself it was the right thing to do and started training again but with more gusto now.

I had a match at Kimball dance hall in Palmerston Road. He was a future English boxing rep and I beat him with ease, winning all three rounds by a wide margin. Keith told me my next opponent was a future English boxing rep and in fact was at one point captain of the team. He boxed for Waterlooville as the last opponent and I beat him also with ease, then it was off to Epsom Baths in London and I was matched with a Kevin. I never knew of him but Keith told me he was very useful and had beaten a lot of top class boxers. Well I knew I was good, so bugger I'll take the bout. It was a good tear up and I broke a metatarsal in my left hand. I won easily enough, but was now handicapped with a damaged left hand, my most sacred weapon in the ring. They had to cut the glove off as it was so swollen it couldn't be pulled off my hand. I wanted to get ready for the ABAs, a championship it was a great thing to win that would be my goal when back to normal. I still trained but never hit with my left hand, so punched one handed on the bag and ran every day to keep myself fit. I had to give the championships my best shot so while training I used to use hot and cold treatment on my hand every day to speed up my recovery, or that was what I hoped. Well after a few weeks my hand seemed to be back to normal as I was also soaking my hand in cold sea water to harden up the skin round my damaged hand.

It all appeared to have worked and I was going to try out the hand on the bag, not hard at first but building up into full power. The initial scarring had gone and I could now punch through the pain barrier. Mind the bag couldn't hit you back, that was the only thing so I had to up my work to include sparring. This came easily enough. I was ready to continue my boxing career and hope my left hand would stand up.

Derek who ran the Fareham boxing got in touch with me and asked me if I would box on his bill as they were in need of the money for the club and knew I always sold the place out. He told me he would put 50 pounds in my boot as payment for me taking the bout and helping his club out. I agreed to this and was down to fight, but I did stipulate what Keith our matchmaker had told me that my ability had proceeded me and he couldn't get me fights. Some of my past opponents had let him know they had received broken ribs and one a nose, so was hard for him to get matches for me. Also, Circlal Frost, a trustee of Portsea Rotary, said I had created a new record for a boxer from Portsea getting a match only for the opponent to pull out before – the total times was 13, some feat when you look at how long the club had been going and all the great boxers they had produced.

I was quite chuffed really. This never put Derek off and he seemed sure he would get me a bout. Anyway, the night of the show had come around and I turned up not really expecting to get a bout. The place was packed as the local news had advertised me on the bill. I was hoping for a bout as the championships were getting nearer. I weighed in about a half stone lighter than I had been fighting at 11.2 pounds, my light middle limit. Still not expecting to be matched up but I had kept my side of the bargain regarding the Fareham show and appearing on it. Time was getting on and I still wasn't thinking of getting matched up. Then I saw Kevin from London. I said "Hi" but still never especially as I was now half a stone lighter, he was the one I beat at Epsom Baths, surely he wasn't the opponent? Oh yes, he was. He wanted to clear the loss I gave him and had weighed in as me 11.2. Was this a stitch up by Derek, because it was.

Anyway, the match was on. This time as I knew all about him I knocked him out, easy fight really, and to his word Derek left £50 in my shoe. It was now full steam ahead to the championships.

The southern finals were held in Crawley. I must have been a warm favourite. Anyway I was fighting a local boy – yes a Crawley boy – the crowd went wild as he entered the ring chanting his name all the time. Philips he was called, he had been sparring with world champ Minter who was also from Crawley. Anyway, the bell went, the crowd were going mad chanting my opponent's name all the time louder and louder, but to no avail. I was all over him and he never laid a glove on me. I was thinking a nice easy fight to put me on track for the final. Anyway, the second round got underway, I backed him on to the ropes and was giving him a real going over. I was well on top then he swung a wild punch and I was on the floor, not hurt but shocked as I had never been down before I rose and the crowd were going mad. I was ready to continue but the referee had stepped in and stopped the fight. I was fuming. There I was, perfectly able to continue when I would say the ref had bowed to the crowd and did what they wanted. Bugger me, I thought, well that was me finished with the amateur game it was so corrupt. I would take time out and decide on my future, but I could not begin to accept how a result like that could be justified.

I was contacted by a boxing manager and asked if I would turn pro. It was Jack and he had a gym at Fratton just around the corner from where I was living. I met him there and liked what I saw. The facilities were first class and the terms he gave me seemed fair, so yes I would sign for him and a new future was in the offing. Then Jack got hold of me and said they wanted me to fight in London at the Grosvenor Hotel. It was to obtain my licence. I thought that was a cheek as they knew my past and I looked at it as a stroke being pulled as in fact you are having a bout and not getting paid for it – were the same fiddles going to be in the pro game? I didn't know what to expect. Anyway, I had a lift from Jack and he stayed with me at the venue. It was a bow tie job, all sitting round dinner tables and having a dinner show really. I was soon on and Jack did my bandages and he was very good at that – it was as if I had steel gloves on, he did a brilliant job. We made our way to the ring and there was cheering and clapping. After we were introduced they explained this was in fact an exhibition bout and it was to get the boxers licensed. The bell went and I can honestly say my opponent was not in my class by any means and when I returned to the corner Jack said hit him harder. I told him I can do that at will so there is no point me showing him up, so Jack said hit him more then, as the BBC were watching and they give the licences out. Anyway, I did come out and boxed his ears off for the remaining rounds. After the crowd clapped we returned to the dressing room. When I was there I was approached by many managers who I knew from television – they were the big names in the game! This is when Jack pulled me away and told them he has a manager. It was later through the *Portsmouth News* that I found out he was over sparring with world champion John Conteh and wanted a British licence, no wonder they wanted to sign me, world champion sparring partner and I treated him with so much ease – unbelievable I would say.

I was still working at Albert Johnson Quay, the job my uncle Dave and his friend Ronnie helped me obtain. I was also now into golf and played nearly every day. I used to be on the tee before work at six in the morning. I would play a few holes then proceed on to work at the quay. That is the trouble with golf, it gets hold of you. A guy who was also working with me in the maintenance department at the quay was Peter. He was a good golfer and would play off eight – this means a professional golfer could only give him eight shots in a round of golf and that tells you just how good he was. I used to play golf with him whenever I could and he was also a good tutor who improved my game by telling me my best grip of the club and also how to line up to prepare to take my shots – my stance that is.

Peter was divorced so would often ask to come out with me and the boys. He was obviously a lonely man or that was the impression he gave. I had often told him of the good times me and some of the boys used to have most weekends, and Fridays that was a good night to go to a dance hall we all used in those days called the Mecca. It was in Arundel Street. My girl Rita never used to mind me going and would often come along or meet me in there on a Saturday as Fridays used to be boys' night out. Peter was always asking if he could come along with us, so one day I said he could come along with me and the boys on a Friday and we would venture to the Mecca after a run around having a good drink in various pubs.

I would also try and introduce him to a girl. This was music to his ears and couldn't stop talking about the night he would come with us and couldn't wait to come out. Anyway the Friday he was coming soon came around and me and Peter met up, did the rounds drinking and then ended up in the Mecca. I knew all the doormen so would just walk to the front of the queue.

No waiting or paying, after all I used to help out the bouncers if they got in trouble with a group or a hard man, fight wise, so they wanted me in there should any trouble erupt. I took Peter in with me and up to the bar area. He loved it there. He was out and amongst a load of women, he was just like a dog on heat, poor thing. All he seemed to do was work and play golf – no socialising, a sheltered life. I would say he was in his element, so chuffed he was out with me he said when I asked him. I talked to a couple of older women who I knew and asked them if they would get him on the floor to give him a dance. This they did, but Peter looked a bit of a wally and moved like a robot and had no rhythm at all. I left him with the girls and went to meet some of my mates at the other side of the bar where I had some drinks and carried on having a good laugh with them. We were really enjoying the crack when I heard Peter shouting out, "Help! Help me Ian! Ian!" I rushed to the dance floor and saw Peter on his knees and holding his eyes. He was shouting out, "I'm blind! I'm blind!" I was leaning over him and he said a girl had thrown a drink in his ace and blinded him. He was screaming more and more. I held his head and he was covering his eyes. I couldn't see because all he was doing was screaming. "I'm blind!" I was still bent over him when a good mate of mine, Don shouted "Watch out Ian!" I looked at my side and saw a man coming at me with a coke bottle raised to strike me. He had short blond hair and I had no time to think, just had to stop them striking me with the bottle so retaliated and fast. I just struck out and they went flying through the air. It was now that I saw it was in fact a girl and not a chap at all, which was the first impression I got. I was shocked when I saw her blood coming from her nose and she was out cold.

A bouncer shouted to me, "Ian, follow me mate!" and took me to the locked back door. He opened it so as I could get away. He was the head bouncer so had the key to this door. I said cheerio to my immediate friends and proceeded to the rear exit and away, I thought anyway. As I was running in the back road to the club I heard a police officer shout, "We know it's you Tungatt! Stop now!" I was bang to rights as so many had witnessed the assault so I had no chance of getting away with it, the police took me to the station and I was later charged with grievous bodily harm. I was gutted, me knocking out a girl. How did that sound not very nice? I can tell you, I was bailed till a court date to be determined. When I got home Rita asked me where I had been. I told her. She told me she felt for me but due to my past thought the judge would have to lock me up. That went down like a lead balloon.

Yet I knew she was right I was snookered. There seemed no way out of this one. Too many could finger me so it had to be a guilty plea with mitigating circumstances, after all she was going to hit me with a coke bottle. It had to be something to do with Peter and what he had said to the girls. She had copped and had thrown some neat spirit into his eyes and had momentarily, what he screamed out, blinded him. She must have been a right cow and then to think she was going to hit me with a bottle so it was really her own fault what had happened. Add to that her appearance at a glance which is all I had at the time – short hair and trousers – you would think she was a man and not as it transpired a woman.

I would have to explain all this to the judge through my solicitor Richard who was a good friend of mine also. What had made it worse was that she had also received a broken nose in the con flab so I was in a very awkward predicament and at the mercy of the judge. All he would look at was I had hit a woman really badly and had given her a broken nose. That appeared terrible but I never had time to think as it had happened so fast. Richard said he would put my case and include all the circumstances surrounding the case to the judge. Richard was brilliant at addressing the bench but this wasn't that easy as the case was in crown court due to the severity of it. This being the case I had to have a barrister. Richard still spent a lot of time trying to assure me it would be fine but I should also be prepared for a short sharp custodial sentence. Mind, he couldn't guarantee it would be a short sentence so I should get ready for the worse scenario. He did also say he would try and get it suspended, but could not add to that it would be up to the judge in the end and that was his way of explaining.

I was due a suspended and that would be an easier way out for me but it was more in hope than fact, all what was left for me was to wait for a court date then see what the judge had in his mind. He had the last say on the matter after all, I was just a pawn for him to push whatever way he thought fit. I could only hope he would be understanding and see the predicament I was put in. I had no time to think and had acted on impulse I never had time to think clearly so to strike out was all I could do. You could even see it as self defence if you looked at it on the whole.

Chapter 25

Rita and I were trying for a child and after we had discussed it I would try extra hard, then if successful hope the judge would be more lenient knowing Rita and I were to become parents. Well it transpired Rita got pregnant quick, so a while before my court date was given to me. Would this make a difference? I certainly hoped so, or would he just take a father from his child and show no feelings. Well in court the judge was by my council presented with the evidence Rita was in fact pregnant and how would the judge look at it now that was the question. The child was due the end of December and this was now coming to July so Rita was three months gone. In court some scumbag had gone out of their way to inform the judge that I was a professional boxer. That was a ton weight put on me it certainly wouldn't help, as I should be in control at all times. So the judge wasn't impressed at all; mind my council never stopped going on about it to the judge and putting it all into perspective, he said it was a lot to blame on the girl. After all she was about to bring a bottle down on me. So all I had was a split second to react, so it was an accident not something that was really meant. It must have worked to an extent as the judge gave me nine months, and nine months on a second charge to run concurrently. That means you only serve the one lot of nine months, not both. In fact this would mean I only served six months of the nine months, given not the full time. So the judge must have had a heart after all. He had to give a custodial sentence under the circumstances and severity of it all and so couldn't really expect a suspended sentence being that it was a women and she had received a broken nose.

I also knew I was going down, as in the box stood two prison wardens one each side of me waiting for the judge's decision to be announced. After this I was escorted to the cells under the court house and on my way down I saw Rita crying. That was not a nice sight and one I could not forget in a hurry.

Rita would be allowed to see me before I was carted off to Winchester prison to do my time. She was very tearful. When I saw her in the cells I explained that I had only six months to do and not eighteen months or nine months that she initially thought, and that I would be out for our child's birth. So he wasn't that heartless, the screw who stood in the dock with me brought me some food. He was very abrupt and tried to let me know he was the boss, never mind how hard I appeared to be. As he had heard of all my antecedence so knew of my past, he was a real pig who had a very sly look about him. He was clearly someone who couldn't be trusted. After the court sittings had finished all the ones given sentences and the ones who were refused bail so were put on remand had to get loaded up in the prison bus and would proceed to Winchester prison. Our journey wouldn't take that long. On arrival we were marched into the reception area where we gave our details: name, DOB etc. state of health, smoker or not, weight, colour and given a quick skin inspection for any complaints in that department or anything that would hinder our stay in prison. We then had to have a shower and change into the prison attire that was distributed to us all.

Our own clothes and other belongings were then placed into a large box and placed into storage until our final release. It was then off to the cell you had been assigned to. I was put on the fours, or landing four, that was fourth storey from the ground. They put me in with a chap who on first appearance was a bit of a nutter really. He told me he was in for non-payment of fines and that he never paid on principle against the unjust treatment the court had given him as he saw it as principle. What a dickhead, that was a lot of bollocks as I saw it. Who would give up their freedom on principle?

It was a Friday we went in, so that meant we would be locked up for most of the weekend save the walks we got once a day round the exercise yard. It was nice to get a bit of fresh air anyway, and if not it would be very boring locked in a cell 24 hours. My time in the cell didn't start too well here. I was sharing a cell with a nutter who smoked. I detested smoking so there is no way would I let him smoke in this confined area, breathing in all that shit, that just wasn't going to happen so I had to threaten to punch him if he lit up and he knew I meant it as I growled at him. It was bad enough smelling it in the open air let alone in a closed area, I would have strangled him that was a cert, so I couldn't let him make the cell stink of that shit. In the prison were quite a few people I knew, Pompey boys. Being the local nick it was inevitable. One was a very good friend called Tony. He was the one whose car I smothered with blood outside the pub that time. He was on a different wing to me, but I could have a good chat to him when we were on exercise. He would give me the run down on the place and the things to do to make my time in there more enjoyable. The chap I was sharing with was due out on the Monday so would have to work out a plan of how I could stay in a cell on my own, no more fools in with me, as I could easily lose my temper with whoever and end up doing more time and that just wouldn't go down well with me or Rita.

During the weekend two screws came to my cell and asked me to follow them to have a chat. They were Mr Hales and Mr Hunter and they were in charge of the block. This was an area segregated from the rest of the prison, like down in the dungeons. This was were bad inmates were put or ones that were dangerous or ones that saved all their visiting orders up as they were over from the Isle of Wight Parkhurst or any prison over there, as it would be easier for visitors to see them if they were on the mainland.

These were usually prisoners doing a long stretch or violent ones. Anyway, it transpired that Hales and Hunter knew of my past and wanted me as their block orderly or cleaner. The job entailed bringing food and drinks down for the ones who were in there at the time. They asked me what I thought about smoking. I said very anti and if someone could frighten me into getting things for them to this I said no chance, I just wanted to do my time and get out. They said on Monday we all had to see the governor. All new inmates had to. This is when they were given their chores while in prison and were also assessed by their capabilities to do whatever.

I had to tell him Hales and Hunter had asked me to be block orderly. That was a very privileged position to get so no way would the governor stand in the way of this selection as he knew I had been assessed by them already. That freed me up from any other assigned job I might have been given. My cell mate had in fact left on the Tuesday – his time apparently was assessed wrong when the amount of fine he owed was worked out in days to serve. This is when I decided that I would have a single cell so I broke the single metal bed ends off the springs and placed it on the landing. An officer saw it and asked me who put it there. I told him I did as the governor told me as I was a known violent inmate, I should be in a single cell. My past form had proceeded me so they all knew about me and my violence. All they said was write single cell on the main inmates' board where all prisoners names were placed and named. This I said I would do. The screws were so thick they fell for my story hook, line and sinker.

Now I could serve my time in peace and quiet, no more nutter or smokers in with me, lovely! The stupid officer who was in the dock when I was sentenced was making things very awkward for me and I was scared I would blow my top and get extra time. He was an acting PO so thought he had more power than he actually had, a fool would be the best way to describe him. Anyway, he would search my cell throwing my things over the cell floor, even now and then emptying my piss pot over the floor saying they had noticed that I had things hidden in my cell that I shouldn't have. This was all fabricated to give him an excuse to disrupt my cell. A real pig he was being, even asked me to drop my trousers and bend over in case I was trying to hide things. I was fuming, but what could I do other than do what he asked? I told my mate Tony and told him someone had put a letter in the box or that is what he told me. The box was where grasses could put a letter in and say something they thought the officers should know about someone, just to mainly stir things up. Tony told me he couldn't do that and that if it were true he had to have a medical officer with him at all times. Now I knew that it was the last time he would do that to me, when Tony knew it was the acting PO he knew him and told me he was a prick. If anyone had a grievance or a complaint they would go before an officer on the Monday morning who would put your name in a book so as you had an appointment with the governor. I was in the line to be put in the book, it was the acting PO who was taking the names for governors. That morning when I got to him he said, "Name?" "Tungatt." "What do you want to see him about?" I told him that I was going to knock someone out as I was fed up with him. He asked me who it was and I told him "It's you!" He looked startled and crossed my name out saying I never heard that. I never had trouble from him again lovely, after all I never wanted to get extra time over a wanker like him.

I thanked Tony, it was nice to see his face. He avoided me as many times as he could, fearful of getting a hiding. He was, it appeared, a liberty bully due to his position and this proved he was bottleless. I soon settled into the environment and was soon dealing in there. As I wasn't a smoker I could use any baccy as a bargaining tool. I would buy anything for sale, mostly money fivers and tenners also rings or watches and small radios, they were easy to get as all they wanted was a smoke and that was what I had and plenty of it. I had to get the money sent home, so I devised a perfect way of getting money out undetected. What I used to do was when Rita wrote to me ask her to put a small denomination stamp all around the envelope lightly stuck down and what I found was that when they got to the sorting office they would just put a postal stamp on the corner stamp leaving all the other ones free of any marks at all. So I could peel them off and when I had enough to send a letter I could use them again. Then I had to get a normal envelope, not a prisoner's one as they would not let that go through, as all mail had to be read and sanctioned. So I had a mate called Ted a lovely fellow who was working in the officers' mess. He would get a screw's envelope out of their mess and I would use one to write a letter to Rita, put the money in with it and give it to Ted who would post it in the post box in the officers' mess – a perfect scenario.

All Rita would do was, when she wrote, put "I heard from Peter". That was the clue she got the money – a perfect fiddle. Another scam was to get extra visiting orders. I would ask Rita to write saying she couldn't handle it me being away from her and that she would kill herself as she couldn't live with it. When I got her letter I would ask to see the welfare officer and tell them that she had that on her mind and I had to talk to her to give her assurance they would get me a special order giving me extra visits – a great thing for Rita and this would make the time go much quicker.

As visits were normally once a month, I did have a good time in the prison. I was excused a lot as I had the privileged position of block orderly and as I was a pro when I went in meant the governor gave me permission to use the gym every day. I could only do skipping ground work and shadow boxing but it was OK to keep me fit. They wouldn't allow me to have a punch bag in there as everyone would ask for things and I understood that.

Most days when I was in the gym I could see a young boy watching from the door way. He was closely watching all my moves. After a while I beckoned him in and started a conversation with him. He was a hell of a size, one hell of a unit – he was over six feet six, anyway tall and built like a brick shit house. I couldn't believe when he told me he was only 17 and that he wanted to be a fighter so that was the path he would follow. So I took him under my wing and tucked him up in his stance and shaped him up I taught him how to throw punches yet still keep his balance. He was so large for a youngster he was allowed to mix with the older prisoners so he didn't have to stay in YP (that is young prisoners). He wanted to fight for money so that must have run in his family. He was a young Irish lad called Danny Roony. He would go on to be champion bare knuckle fighter of the English and Irish travellers. This didn't surprise me as he had showed plenty of enthusiasm and this was a pleasure to see. He had all the attributes to go all the way, he was a giant of a youngster, determination aplenty and so keen to learn. He also had bulging muscles not normally seen in one so young and he would go through the pain barrier when doing ground work or shadow boxing, a natural for the fight game.

Rita used to come and see me regularly and more often with the extra VO we had obtained. On one of her visits we talked about marriage, being as she was pregnant it seemed the right thing to do. I said I would have a word with the welfare officer and they would tell me the way to go about it. On asking I was told that we could get married in Winchester registry office, I could have a few visitors and that the welfare would book it for us. All we had to do was fill in the forms required. Rita would have to sign her part of the form and get permission off the governor. I was told this would be a formality as it was a thing a lot had done over the years. I got hold of Rita and told her the outcome. She was so pleased and soon the date game round.

Rita was there waiting with her sister when I arrived. I was allowed to put my own clothes on, not the prison uniform, so would look OK for any photos taken. They even left my handcuffs off for the service and for the after pictures that were taken, then it was a quick kiss for Rita and back to the prison. She looked stunning and shed some tears as I left. On returning to the prison I had to change back into my uniform and hand my suit back to be put back in store till my sentence was over and I was released. The next day when I went back to work in the block, Hunter and Hales gave me a small cake and wished me all the best in the future and hoped I had a happy marriage. I thought that was a nice gesture and one that I wouldn't forget, after all they had no need to do anything so the thought was there.

I used to have to get food for whoever was in the block at the time. This came from the kitchen in the actual prison and as I was the only outsider allowed in the block it was my job to get their food. They had to be confined to the block at all times, they even had their own small exercise yard to walk around so stayed in the block until it was time for them to be moved on. Some were there from Parkhurst Prison off the Isle of Wight so that would be where they were doing their time. They would save their visiting orders up and use them all up at Winchester. They would invariably get longer visits here anyway as it was the mainland so easier for their relations to get to see them. After all their VOs were used up they would be returned to Parkhurst to finish their time. One man who came into the block from Parkhurst was a real villain, and I met quite a few in my time. The one who stood out was a Micky Williams, as big a man as you would ever see, a giant of a man, massive in appearance and all the screws were frightened of him. So he was given whatever he wanted. He was a black man, so looked more imposing than a white man. I had to get him whatever he asked for as I was his orderly and the only outsider allowed in the block. I found Micky a sound man and we had a great understanding of each other and became quite close.

One day I was sent for by the block wardens. On that day Micky had asked to walk with me round the yard. I was to escort him so he would stay calm they told me, I could tell they wouldn't dare refuse Micky's request for fear of him getting annoyed. When Micky wanted anything they jumped, the only question was how high. I had many good chats with Micky while he was in Winchester he told me about a lot of so-called villains, who were frightened to death of him. He got a kick out of it and I told him some things I did that I could never put into a book. Yes, I would miss him when he went back to Parkhurst. When he used up all his visits he had saved up off he went and I never heard of or saw him again, but a very pleasant man to have known.

When I was out the block in the evenings I used to get the evening drinks for the rule 43s. They are ones who have grassed on someone so are scared, or nonce cases (they are ones who have committed an offence against youngsters) or raped someone so could not mix with other prisoners for fear of retributions. Yes they would be given a good hiding so would never be left alone, they had to always get escorted if moving anywhere in the prison. Scumbags, most of them. There was one who along with his brother had touched a young child who was the son of one's partner. All the nick hated them, they were always escorted front and back by officers otherwise they would have been killed.

They would shout abuse at whoever walked on the landings above them, whenever they saw an inmate, they were real scum. I went one day to the kitchen to get their urn of coffee and tea for the 43's last night drink. While I was in the kitchen I saw the head chef – he hated me, for why I had no idea. I saw him through the serving hatch and he was waving a ladle at me saying he would batter me given the chance. I couldn't get at him as the kitchen staff were in their own unit and not housed with the other prisoners. I knew he was gone if I got half a chance. I had to plan how I could get at him and just hope he wasn't discharged before I could get even with him. Anyway, I took the drinks back to the rule 43s and started pouring their drinks out for them in their mugs that they produced after the warden on that night had opened their cell. The one on one night was Mr Hales. He hated this nonce. I asked him when he opened his cell to just turn his back for a second this he did and I tipped the hot drink on his hand and he screamed then tried to throw hot drink at me. Lucky it missed, but then I hit him knocking him cold. Mr Hales shut the door quick, leaving him on the floor. He told me to be careful as he will scream to the governor. Mind he was glad I had knocked him out. He warned me to get my story sorted out to tell the governor as he was sure he would scream. The other inmates after hearing the outcome shouted out "Well done Ian! He deserved all he got!" If they could I'm sure they would have lynched him and if they could would kill any 43s.

When I had finished serving I returned to my cell and got a towel, wrapped it up and started rubbing my forehead harder and harder till I nearly reached the bone. It looked like a burn mark, very red and bleeding. It looked terrible in the morning. I was called to the governor's office to explain the complaint the nonce had given him. I told him I was pouring out the evening drink when he moved his hand and I accidentally spilt a bit of drink on his hand and with that he threw some hot drink that was in his mug over my face, catching me on the forehead. He looked at the burn mark I had on my forehead and commented it could have been in my eyes and blinded me and that the nonce would lose his privileges. I got a brilliant result, it was the quick thinking that did it and all the other inmates loved it when they heard and it got around very quick. He was hated so much, everyone that saw me said, "Well done, the scum bag deserved every bit of it!" I'm just glad the governor believed my story and not the nonce's.

Chapter 26

I got to know one officer quite well in there and he used to talk to me telling me of all the troubles he was having with his wife. He would ask me for advice on his rather mixed up marriage. One day he said he was thinking of splitting up with her as she never appeared to see his side of any upsets that they had and said she never seemed happy with anything he said or did and that it was getting him down. What would I do, he asked. I told him about the party I had put on for Bill years ago and how I painted the ceiling black and put gold butterflies all over thus making it psychedelic in appearance, then I said he should then put on slow ballad type music, make her a nice meal with flowers and low light candles. He said that sounded a good idea and as she was working till late on that Friday he could as it was his day off. He'd get the paint and do the decorating when she was out as he had nothing to lose he would certainly give it a try, so a big thank you were his words.

The next time I saw the warden he came into my cell early one morning when he was next on duty. He gave me some sweets and a couple of Mars bars as a thank you and told me the ceiling was a big plus. His wife loved it and it gave them a reunion to their marriage. He was like a kid with some new toys. I could see I was now God in his eyes, so I would have to use him to my advantage some way or another and I had an idea where it could come in handy. I had to wait until I could get someone who was a thorn in my side and I knew exactly where the warden would be a godsend while I was still enjoying the perks he gave me. All the tit bits came in handy if only to use for deals buying things. The chance came around quite quickly. I always did the late night drinks and was the deliverer of the drinks to the inmates on the fours, amongst other things. The plan I had would come together when this warden was on late night duty and this happened within a week of me making my plans. He took me down to the kitchen to collect my urns of drink for the inmates' late tipple. Anyway when we were in the kitchen area by the hatch way and this was directly in view of the kitchens where the serving took place, I looked and low and behold the head chef was on and dishing out the drinks. He was the prick who was really getting my back up, being annoying when I couldn't get at him as the kitchen was a gated area with no independent access – the gates had to be unlocked first so that was what I had to work on the warden for. After all I had to get my own back for him threatening me with the protection of the secluded area behind him. I asked the warden if he would do me a big favour and open the gate just for a few seconds as this gate was always locked so the screws' keys were the only way this could be opened and I said he did owe me one. He said it was more than his job was worth but I told him it would only take seconds, I do not think he believed me but he did say you only have a few seconds if not I will have to get you out. I said that would be fine and agreed I would come out straight away should he summon me. All I wanted to do was sort the rude prick out.

He opened the gate warning me I only had a short while, then he would take me out and have to lock the gate again. When he opened it I was in like a jack rabbit. I went straight to the chef and hit him so hard he went out cold. The pleasure that gave me was mind blowing, seeing him stretched out on the floor, the prick. It was like winning the pools and gave me a great boost. I had to call the warden to open the gate, it was so quick he asked if I wasn't going to do anything now, then I told him it was done and that when I hit them they stay hit. What a result.

Another time I was on the fours and had just finished mopping and polishing the landing, this was my job. When I was out of the block they gave me the job of number one on the fours. Hunter and Hals had arranged my appointment as a thank you for the good job I had done while in the block and I could now stay in this job until my release date. I was now well off in the inmates' eyes as I got to keep anything left when one on the landing left their cells. I would buy radios, watches, rings, anything for baccy or just a few dirty magazines. I was a very rich man in the nick terms, even had the sugar and jams not eaten by whoever left them. I had some pots full of either and could buy anything that was up for sale to feed their smoking habit. I could now arrange for the distribution of my wealth when I finally did leave the jail.

Just before I was due to leave I had just mopped and polished the whole landing as I always did. It shone like glass, then a prisoner who came from London and had a load of mouth, a gobby sod, just came up the iron staircase and on to my lovely looking finished floor. I shouted at him to get off the floor as it was still drying, you wanker. I said he challenged me and said, "I'm what?" and with that I just hit him flush on the chin and he went flying down the stairs, the ones he had just rushed up, and this is how one's luck is – he was heading straight to the governor who was coming up the lower flight of stairs as it was his inspection day.

I was so lucky, I just headed to my cell and locked myself in. If there were any comebacks it couldn't be me as I was locked in my cell so no one would think I could hit anyone outside it. Any coincidence the con should have been in the workshop and not on the landing, nothing could be said. I was so lucky really and on course again for my discharge and not going to lose any of my remission that I had gained, so if that had happened it would have been a sickener, after all I was locked in my cell so it couldn't possibly be me. Mind the Londoner never screamed about it anyway.

It was now getting very close to my release dates and when I would finally get discharged, so now I had to really keep my nose clean, bugger getting extended time and having to spend more time in this hellhole. Mind there was one warden who used to get through to me, he was a proper pig, whenever he could be. He had a nickname of Pear Drop. This was very fitting as it was clearly a name given to him by the inmates and based on his body shape. He was called Pear Drop and that was the shape he had – smallish shoulders and a large arse area, so clearly the shape of a pear hence the nickname.

He would always throw insults at me while trying to wind me up saying thing like "You'll be back in no time after you get home!" and saying I was a waster, he should know as he had seen so many like me over the years so could tell, and loads of other things. After mentioning whatever he would always add he had seen so many like me over the years, all bollocks and clearly saying things to get me wound up hoping I would bite and then he could put me on a report. He was nothing but a wanker. All I would say was "Yeh yeh yeh!" and he hated that.

One day I was talking to the friendly warden who I got on with and subtly asked him if he ever had a drink outside with any other screws and did they use a pub near the prison? He said yes they would often use a pub on the corner and opposite the prison gates and that was where most would often meet for a pint before venturing home. He also said that was the life he chose so couldn't relax anywhere really as someone was always upsetting an inmate one way or another. It was their attitude, he said. So outside the prison you had to be careful. This gave me the idea of visiting the pub when I was out which I did on two different occasions but to no avail as each time he wasn't in there. He never knew how close he was to getting sat on his big arse, the knob end.

I did not think looking back how stupid this was. Obviously I would have been straight back inside and Pear Drop's prediction would have been right after all. How could an ex-con travel all the way to Winchester, hit a warden and then not get a lot of bird? It would have been a certainty that I would have had a lot of time to serve given my past, but in those days I wouldn't think straight at all, it was when I got in a temper nothing could stop my actions, no matter how stupid they were.

One thing that did come out when I was serving my time was that there were so many millionaires, big time drug barons and gangsters or so. Many had a very large stash to come out to, yes so many day dreamers, it was mind boggling. Also a lot of utter rubbish. All they were doing were convincing themselves because no one with any brains at all would believe the bollocks and bullshit that was spewed out in the prison. I think they were just trying to convince anyone who would listen, so that they ended up believing it themselves.

Looking back, you had to feel sorry for them as their lives only consisted of fabrication and false dreams and I think that's what made a lot of them become institutionalised, so all one could do was let it go over your head otherwise you could get drawn into a false Walter Mitty world and one that had no truthful credence to it at all.

I was just glad I had survived my time in there, so could now put all those lies and bullshit behind me and return back to reality then live a life to the full. Mind, there were some things I would miss now in civvie street, looking back – the good laughs I had which made my time go faster in prison and not like a dull existence a lot of the inmates had to endure. A lot of them were in a little bubble and nothing you could say or do would burst that, still they appeared to be in a time warp and oblivious to what was going on in the real world. Not recognising what was actually going on outside the nick they seemed in a time capsule and were happy that way. I certainly didn't want to go back to prison, this was enough for me, mixing with a lot of idiots was not for me. The only thing that could interrupt my thinking was my temper. When I lost that I would be on another planet, so couldn't control myself and when I was in that mood it was just me, no one else mattered as my brain would go blank. That was until it passed and I came back to reality. I can understand what they say regards the grey mist coming over you and your mind becomes a thing of the past, all that mattered to me was winning; be it an argument or a fight. I had to win there was no coming second in my world only win win no matter what. Sometimes when I came round and back to reality I would be so shocked at what I had said or done I would often feel sorry for who was on the receiving end of my temper, it was horrible at times. Unless you were on my wave length you couldn't understand, sometimes it would even shock me. Still the day did come and I got released at seven in the morning. Rita was outside waiting. It was so nice to walk free and back into reality.

It was so nice to be back home with Rita after being incarcerated for the last six months. She was now getting very large carrying our baby, and it was strange just cuddling her as she was always a fit girl who had a nice shapely figure and a flat stomach. Now there was a large bump in front of her where she was housing our baby. It was nice to know the baby was there and waiting to come into the world.

Rita told me she had in fact been carrying the child quite well during her pregnancy and had not had many bad days or nights for that matter during the time I was away. She had kept on working, so with her wage and Dooly's rent had managed to survive while paying all the household bills – that was a big relief and we had no debts to face. All I had to do now was venture to the docks to see how I now stood with regards my employment status. After all, I had been away for the past six months and prior to that had been a shop steward for the works department, so I knew the job should be kept open for me after a maximum of six months' break. Mind, that was the limit for any break away from work until you return.

When I went in to see Ron the boss, or Mr Barnett, I was informed that my job had been filled while I was away so there was no vacancy for me any longer. This was against the union rules so now I had to go to the TGWU offices in Arundel Street and see the area convener, Malcolm. He informed me he would visit the docks and have a meeting with all the bigwigs on my behalf, then would let me know the results of the meeting and the outcome in two days. So I went to see Malcolm two days later and he informed me that they did not want me back in their employment as shop stewards weren't liked in the labour force, not just the docks, so I was now unemployed,

I informed Malcolm that the rules of the union stated they had to hold my job open for a maximum of six months and that was the time I was away so they should have let me take my post up as it was prior to me being incarcerated. Then he said he had argued my case but to no avail. I had been sold down the river by the union in fact. I now looked at Malcolm as an enemy of mine. I called him a pig, as in my eyes he never worked for me. I shouted at him and could see by his facial expression that he was frightened. I reared up and chased him from his office, just to get him at it. He must have nearly had a heart attack as he wasn't in the best of condition. Mind, later even my uncle couldn't get my job back so that was that – no job and no income. Good job I had my release money – that would have to last me for the time being.

I decided to go to the dog track for their next meeting and God had I missed the racing while I was away. There was a girl who had worked for the trainer who looked after my race dogs. He was Ron and the girl kennel hand was Sheila. She was also my bit on the side so to speak. Once an owner asked her if she would go to Aldershot greyhound stadium, the flapping track I used to go to as well before my sentence. He wanted her to parade a dog for him so as no one would connect him with the greyhound about to race. He was Ken, a butcher, and the dog was a very fast one who had won the Welsh Derby. Basically by the crowd not knowing the dog or Sheila he would get a better price from the bookmakers, thinking there was no tie to Ken himself. You had to be a very fast dog to win a derby and the chances of getting beaten at a flapping track like Aldershot was next to nil barring accidents. So Ken would back the dog big time and hopefully clean up. All I would do, unbeknown to him, would bring Sheila to the track to parade the dog for the race and back him when Ken had placed his bets – any price would have been big knowing how fast the dog was, so it would be worth the trip there and I wouldn't upset the gamble planned. I was standing with Sheila in the bar having a drink and talking to some traveller boys who were always at the track, when Ken came into the bar and told Sheila that the dog wasn't right in himself that day so he

My dad, mum and a friend

At 14 years of age, just out of approved school. I used to breed and show Rabbits

At my sisters wedding, the cigar was just for show, as I never smoked

Portsea rotary boxing squad

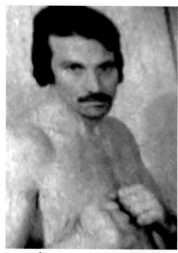

Just after I got my pro licence

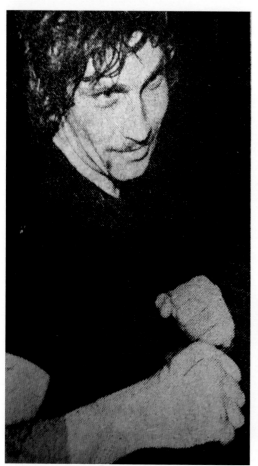

BOXING BOARD OF CONTRO

BOXER'S
LICENCE

My pro boxing licence, I kept this
for my daughter

Me after a heavy training session

Me at a party, with Dave and June
Henderson.. very suave

e Mecca Club many years ago. Me, Johnnie and above us in the middle Polly Hart

The Black Dog crowd, a lot of loveable villains, sadly many have now passed away

Me and Toni, Just married

The first dance after our wedding

Toni and me at Rosie's Christening

England vs Thailand, in Pattaya - I won with a knockout

Me and the boss, Pattaya ,Thailand

Me, Toni and U2 Bob, on holiday in Thailand

Mine and Rita's son Ian

My daughter Claire who found
me after years of searching

Julie my first born who lives in Australia,
I found her after 42 years of searching

Mine and Toni's girl Rosie now an air
hostess, we are so proud of her

Toni's mum and dad

My mum, now 92 years young

Our great bitch Perky, going over the line and winning The Oaks

At the yearly awards, getting the trophy for bitch of the year

Three of us again Toni, Charlie, and me getting The Oaks winners trophy

had not brought him there. He then thanked her for coming and bought us a drink then left. I could now relax and have a drink with the traveller, Jim, who was there nearly every meeting.

We were standing by the window and generally having a laugh while drinking, when I looked out and saw a greyhound winning by half the track. I used to like to see a good dog, which this clearly was, so proceeded to get a clearer look at the winner outside the bar area. I gasped! It was Ken's dog and the bastard had told us the dog wasn't running. I was fuming, being that I had brought Sheila there for him, then to get lied to was beyond a joke. He'd said that the dog wasn't taken there to race. I was boiling up inside and he jumped a fence saying, "I don't run a dog for your benefit!" then scarpered to a waiting car outside which housed the dog. He must have had someone else there to place the wagers and draw the winnings, while he shot off taking the dog with him.

All I was thinking was to get him at Portsmouth on a race night. As I said, he was a butcher and a big lump who thought due to his size that he could fight. I'd soon show him how wrong he was. He was getting a hiding, doing that to me. He wasn't going to get away with that, and word had spread I had to do him. I knew he would be at the track as he never missed a meeting, so I put my tracksuit on and went to the track to level with Ken. I could never do what he had done to me. He deserved all he was going to get, it was of his making. I entered the track and saw Ken. He had a smirk on his face so clearly never knew of my fighting capabilities. I said, "Get round the back of the stadium and we will sort it out." He went willingly, so was clearly green in that department or must have fancied his chances.

On the way to the alleyway at the back of the track I saw a good friend of mine, Charlie Crawford. He knew what was going down and said he wanted to watch the fight. He had seen a lot of my past fights, so I couldn't refuse him. We went by a toilet on the way and Charlie said he had to pop in there for a pee. He said, "Don't start without me, will you?" and I said I wouldn't then proceeded to the designated area. Hurry up Charlie, I thought to myself as Ken was already there with his girlfriend and he tried to get the confrontation started. I was now looking at the track gate entrance waiting for my friend Charlie to appear. All I could do was prance around, fending Ken off and wait for my friend to arrive. He was getting braver and braver, now thinking my bottle had gone. Hurry up Charlie, I was thinking as it was getting harder to hold off from giving Ken a beating. Then Charlie arrived doing up his flies and shouting, "You can start now Ian!" This was my cue. I hit Ken, sending him sprawling to the floor. He looked so shocked. I let him get up then struck him again, sending him to the floor as before. I could see now he had a couple of cuts on his face and blood was seeping out onto his chin and his eye was puffed up and badly bruised. I proceeded to pound him harder every time he rose up. He soon gave up the ghost as he had taken a good beating by now. His girl was screaming out loud "Get the police!" What a cow she turned out to be.

Charlie said to me, "Well done, you gave him a good hiding, Ian!" It was then I told him the whole story and he agreed that Ken deserved all he got then, and we returned to the stadium. After a while a policeman arrived at the track and approached me saying I was to accompany him to the station and that I would be charged with disturbing the peace or something like that. What a joke, there was no one there to disturb. It was a back alleyway, darkish with no passing people at all. What a prick this copper must be, a right wally,

Anyway, on the way to the gate we had to pass the toilet and Charlie ventured into it again. I told the copper I had to go to have a pee and was told to hurry up. Unbeknown to the copper, there was an open wall in the toilet, so I scaled that and disappeared into the night. The policeman who had turned up had no idea I was about to get away so must have been dumbfounded when he realised what had happened. Ken never pursued the case and I never heard anything more about it. Mind, everyone at the track would have given him some right stick if he had, so he stayed away from the track for a while as he must have been embarrassed, the size of him.

Sheila told me what a creep Ken was as he was always trying to take her out and saying suggestive things to her, and that he was an ugly bugger anyway. I missed a few meetings myself as I thought it would be best if I let the situation calm down. When I did go back Sheila had left Ron's and so no longer worked at the kennel. I asked Ron where she was and he said that she decided to have a break from the dogs and had returned home to Reading, her home town. I asked if she had a boyfriend now, as that could be the reason, but he assured me that it was just to have a break away from the greyhounds. I thought that was strange as she had worked for him for ages and had a bedsit at the kennels so had no rent to pay out.

Still life had to go on and I was now looking forward to the birth of mine and Rita's baby, as it was now playing her up. She couldn't wait to have it in her arms and not in her belly. I also had to try and get my boxing licence back that had been taken away when I was sent to prison. Jack, my manager, had informed me he had applied for my licence to the BBBC, explaining I was now out and wanting to pursue my boxing career. He told me I would probably have to go before the board and tell the committee that I had learnt from my mistakes blah, blah, blah, then it would be up to the board if they granted it or not and give me another chance. Jack had a lot of faith in me so took me to the board meeting himself and spoke very highly of me. I was told to wait in the waiting room while my case was discussed. It took about ten minutes for the board to decide and come out and ask me to go back into the room before them.

I was told they had decided to give me a chance and that I wasn't to let them or myself down, especially as it would be bad for the boxing game. Jack was so pleased and told me he had a fight lined up for me as soon as I was back fit. Mind, I needed money now so I put the word out to all my past clients that I would now be able to collect any money owed to them and also sort out any troubles they may now have with anyone.

It was now getting very close to the arrival of our baby. All I could do was a bit of calling during the day so that I would be near for the birth when the time arrived. I was ringing home constantly in case she started and had to be taken to hospital. I would be there for the birth, well in the next room. I never wanted to see the actual birth, just be there for reassurance for Rita.

The day came and Rita appeared to be in so much pain. When her waters did break it was New Year's Eve. I was counting on a new year baby, but alas it wasn't to be. A boy was born on New Year's night so didn't quite make it to the new year. Still Rita was OK, that was the main thing. The bonus was a little boy had arrived. I was over the moon with that and so was Rita.

He was a bonnie looking lad and that is normally hard to say about a newborn. His skin was a nice cream colour, not pale. The nurse said that was down to neither Rita nor myself smoking. She said that was a big plus and would give him a good start in life.

I was as I say, over the moon to have a little boy and as the dogs were on the next night I had to go there and tell everyone I knew that we had a bouncing baby boy. It was the New Year's Day meeting and it was always very busy on that day. I brought everyone I knew a drink, believing that what you spend goes back to your son later in life. I also knew the travellers' way was to call your firstborn son after yourself so he would be Ian. I was so chuffed. I kept getting drinks brought for me as well and getting all the congratulations while taking the drinks given to me. Everyone seemed to charge my glass and I was just drinking as if there was no tomorrow and God didn't I get smashed. I ended up really heavy – out of my skull, is the term to use I think.

Chapter 27

It was alright doing money collecting and sorting out troubles for the boys of note in Portsmouth, but I had to get a regular income now for Rita and my boy Ian. There were three brothers who started me out years before calling, they were Ian, Tinker and Jimmy. At first in those days we would be after scrap metals such as iron, brass, copper, batteries, bikes, water heaters, in fact anything that we could sell. I enjoyed that as it was like gambling, you never knew if you would earn as that was the chance you had to take putting the bills round the doors, stipulating what you were after or buy then leave it to whoever read it to decide if they wanted to sell or give waste away. One day we were away and sleeping in the back of the van, as in those days you couldn't afford bed and breakfast. So we would pull up in an appropriate car park, preferably a nice and quiet one. We had to be up fresh, lay our bills, have a breakfast then go round the doors seeing if there was anything we could obtain by paying for it or getting stuff given to us that was on the list of our bills. We were just dropping off one night having found a handy lorry park, quiet and off the road, then a refrigerated lorry pulled up next to us and had his freezer unit on. The noise kept us awake, it was a racket and we had to be up early for our work. It riled me to such an extent that I had to ask the driver to move somewhere else or switch his unit off so we could sleep. He basically told me to piss off, very rude actually. I went to the van of ours and took out an axe then proceeded to whack the cooling unit with it. The driver shit himself, called me mad and started his lorry and drove off. He used his brains there, as there would have been only one outcome. A short while after, we were calling for scrap etc., an antique came on the scene for us to buy, though we didn't know a lot about them in those days. All I said was if we can get them cheap enough we had to earn, plus we would buy gold and silver – the money you could earn was mind boggling, and a pleasure to put the time in. It was hard work walking miles in our quest, not knowing if we would be well rewarded.

Now the time had progressed here. I was out of work and no prospect of getting a well-paid job. So I decided to go back calling. As it happened Fred had also lost his job on the docks, and had teamed up with a Barry and had been going away with him calling, so he knew how well you could earn. It transpired Barry and Fred had ceased going away together due to a ruck they had, so I got talking to Fred and we decided to team up. I knew I could have a good chat at the door and Fred had learned from Barry who was quite good at it, so it seemed me and Fred would make a good couple. Add to that our close friendship and it had to be a winner for us both. We could earn and have a very good laugh doing it. Fred knew what a good fighter I was so would always be on the lookout for people to challenge me and we would share our winnings. He had a knack of finding someone to have a bet with on the outcome of any fights I had. I never really looked the part as I was quite thin in appearance but had wide shoulders and thick legs so that is where my punching power came from. I used to hit most once or twice then move in and knock them cold. It worked every time. The money wasn't big, the best was £200, but a tidy sum in those days and easy when you added that to our calling money and we were doing well. Fred was a diamond at getting opponents, bless him. He used to have bets with whoever and arrange a match against me knowing the outcome. Mind Fred was an ideal man to have around as he could knock anyone out himself, but he was pure power no finesse, plus he couldn't control himself so would go over the top somewhat. I started to go out with a girl from Cosham called Janet. We seemed to hit it off straight away, she was a good-looking girl. Rita was engaged with our son so never cared what I was up to, and I wasn't going to tell her as I appeared to have the best of both worlds. A very nice wife, very caring and a good mother and on the other hand a good-looking girl on my arm whenever I wanted. This went on for quite a while, then out of the blue Rita started asking me questions about who I was out with and other things like where was I drinking. Looking back that wasn't Rita at all. I later found out she would often go with a friend she worked with to a house she used to clean near their work. It was her friend's brother-in-law, and he used to pay her for it as he lived on his own. A few times when her friend couldn't go to the house she asked Rita to clean it for her and she would get paid for it. It came out the fella she cleaned for used to drink with us in the Royal Albert in Albert Road Southsea. It transpired he was a right snake, his wife had left him and he was sniffing around Rita, and that is how Rita knew everything I got up to. The one I was knocking about with, Janet, and whoever else I used to take out now and again, he was in our clique in the pub so would just relay everything he heard our group and myself talking about. He was a right prick, but fed Rita with everything he thought she wanted to hear. He slowly poisoned her mind against me. What I couldn't understand was how Rita could go with him, he was too ugly for her, she deserved at least a good-looking guy, but she was vulnerable and he knew it, a real piss-hole. Mind I was, I suppose as Rita was a perfect catch, good-looking hard worker and good mother, too good for a wanker like him, but he had sowed the seeds and I knew it was the beginning of the end to my marriage. He was a slimy git and Rita left for his house when I was away working and took young Ian with her. I had got my comeuppance, I could kill the little bastard, and would have but he knew this and the police got involved. I was buggered. They took me in and gave me a warning before letting me out. I would be locked up for a long time they relayed to me, the piss-hole got his way. I was even stopped from seeing my boy as Rita told the welfare I was a very violent man and she was worried for Ian's safety. I was taken to court and told by the judge I had to keep away until it was back before them for a decision on my rights. Rita wouldn't do that, it had to be the prick behind it all. Mind I did get the gun we had hidden and was going to shoot him. My boy saw the gun before I was stopped from seeing him and remembers it to this day as he told me about it, and that wasn't nice for one so young.

I had to let go as it wasn't worth going to prison again and losing my liberty for a long time as I wouldn't be seeing Ian then anyway, and I couldn't join the prison system again. One day a person I was in prison with found me. He was nicknamed Geordie. I was pleased to see him as he was a laugh. He told me he had nowhere to stay at the moment, so I took him under my wing and let him stay in my place for a while. He had no money of note but said he was due to get some back pay from the social on the Thursday – that was his pay day and he got his money from the post office in Bordon. We had a drink in the Black Dog near my house then I took him to the Phoenix pub in Southsea, where a friend of mine, Tom, was the landlord. I introduced them and we had a good drink while talking to Tom then took a curry home for us. I told Geordie he could stay while I was away calling and I would see him when I got back. There was plenty in the cupboards to eat and plenty of tea and coffee to drink. He kept thanking me and I carried on as normal getting up early and away working. Geordie could treat the house as his till I got back.

Me and Fred went away as we always did early on the Monday; we returned as always on the Thursday night. I was a bit concerned as I rang quite a few times but got no reply. Geordie may have been out I thought, so mustn't get too concerned. He may have gone to get his money owed him. Who would know, when me and Fred got home we went to my house only to find Geordie had taken some money I had in a drawer and also some gold I had – not a hell of a lot, but enough to get annoyed about. What a fucker. I put him up, helped him out and he does this to me. I was fuming, I should have known what to expect, after all he was in for fraud and whatever else he wouldn't speak about. Anyway, I was so uptight me and Fred had to have a drink. We would go to the Phoenix and have a run around, a drink may take it out of my system for a while. When we entered the pub Tom came over to me saying was I OK as he had looked after Geordie when he came to see him and he lent him a tenner as well. Apparently Geordie had said I would give it back for him and left it at that. He left a bill in the bar and even gave a few in there a drink. What a liberty! To say I was wild was an understatement. If he was there he would have been put away permanently. I said to Fred I would find him and beat the mother out of him. Fred knew I meant it as I wouldn't say a thing and not do it. Anyone can shout their mouth off, but it takes a man to say it then do it. Fred was the same, he could cut someone up and not bat an eyelid. I paid Tom the money then took a taxi to the Black Dog near my house, and I'm buggered if he hadn't done the same there. He had put the drinks he had on the slate for me to pay when I was next in there. Brian the landlord knew I was genuine and would pay whatever was owed, it just made my blood boil more. I was fuming, the scum bag, I would get him. How cheeky was that? He had to be sorted out properly then at least he wouldn't do it to anyone else.

What was I to do, I suggested to Fred that I thought the best place to be sure of getting hold of Geordie would be the post office in Bordon on a Thursday when he would be cashing his check what would have been sent to him by the social Security, Fred agreed. So I said it would be best if for the next few weeks we worked only till late Wednesday, come back home then I could go and wait for Geordie outside the post office in Bordon.

He said a good idea and asked if he should go with me which was good of him. The trouble with that was that if I did make too much of a mess of him or even kill him, Fred would be implicated as well so it wouldn't be fair. Knowing Fred he would stand by me no matter what would be the outcome. Imagining the worst outcome, Fred could be locked up with me for a long time, what would his family think of me?

No I would venture to Bordon on my own. I sat near the post office entrance in the car park where I could get a clear view of who entered or left the office, praying one would be Geordie. I did this for a few weeks but to no avail, the time dragged just waiting. I used to take sandwiches and a flask plus a few papers to read just to make the waiting less monotonous. Even though it still seemed to drag but I knew the wait would be worthwhile should I get hold of Geordie. What he had done to me after helping him so much was unforgivable

A lesson had to be dished out to him. I waited week after week then one day decided to go and ask for him in a pub just across the road from the post office. I had a pint and got talking to a couple of locals I asked them about a man called Geordie who came from this area,they informed me that yes he did come from an estate across the road and was barred from there so they hadn't seen him for ages.

I drank up thanked them and thought I should go onto the estate and knock on a few doors asking about him and of his whereabouts. I knocked on a few doors but there was no reply, then a man answered and he told me yes he knew Geordie. He was always in and out of prison according to him and that he had a terrible name round there owing a lot of people money, but no one had seen him for ages. suggested that he may be in prison again. I thanked him and at least I wouldn't have to travel all the way to Bordon wasting time waiting for him outside the post office. He clearly wasn't going there for a time,

As the time passed and it ran into months, my temper had cooled somewhat. It was back to normal and Geordie, though still in my thoughts, was not a must-sort-out thing, and I had no inclination of where he might be. I checked with someone who was in Winchester prison and they informed me he wasn't in there, not then anyway so another avenue drew a blank. Well I had to get on with life and just hope I heard more about Geordie later. I certainly would if he was ever in the Portsmouth area. Now me and Fred were back doing a full week calling. We had carried on doing this for a few more weeks, when one Friday we had sold off and entered our local pub, the Black Dog. As normal on every Friday dinner time after selling all we had brought back, we ordered a couple of pints when Brian our friend and the landlord approached me asking if he could have a word. I went over to the counter and he told me he had a strange phone call from a man who said he was a friend of mine, or he thought he was, so that was a funny thing to say were Brian's words. But he said, "Tell Ian it's Geordie and I have the money for him."

He told him I came in every Friday and that would be the best time to come in. He also told him he would inform me of the phone call. I went and told Fred of what Brian had said and also how I thought it was nice of him. He may have seen the light of what he had actually done. When Fred heard that he said, "Ian, don't go soft on him, what he did after all you had done for him." That sank straight into my head. Yes, Fred was right. He had disrupted my complete life and I only helped him. He was only a waste of space, not a person at all – scum.

We were chatting when the door opened. It was Geordie and a couple of friends he had with him. Geordie said I was the only one who had ever helped him and that he was so ashamed of what he had done to me after the goodness I had shown him and that he was deeply sorry, but had the money for me now so had brought it to me. If we went to the toilet he would give me it all and some extra on top. I glanced across at Fred who was taking in all what Geordie was saying. I said it does not matter, Fred was a good friend and he could give it to me there where we were standing.

That was by the pool table. He gave me a wad of money and I placed it in my pocket, then knocked him out. His friends moved in and I knocked them over as well. With that the door was opened. I thought there were others with them so moved to whack them, but it was a man on his own. He said, pointing to his badge on his lapel, that he was a taxi driver who had come to pick them up.

I said pick them up then and he helped them to get up and took them outside the pub and away. That is when Fred said he was only having a game with me and didn't think I would flip as I did. I told Fred, "You know me, it wouldn't take much for me to want to give Geordie a hiding and all you did Fred was light the touchpaper!" We both started laughing and Fred said, "It was good to watch though and you had looked mustard!" Well that was good then, "Let's have a drink now Fred, doubles as I have the money, let's say a repayment owed." We carried on and drank all day as a lock-in was ordered by Brian. We had a really good drink then went for a curry. We proceeded to the curry shop in Fratton Road, just round the corner from the pub. By this time we were both talking silly with the drunken heads we had on. We agreed we should be blood brothers. With that Fred took my hand and bit a piece of skin out of my palm, then I tried to bite a piece out of Fred's palm, but it was no good – it was like a piece of leather! So Fred bit his own hand, taking a piece of skin out, then we joined the skin wounds together and became blood brothers. That sounds silly now but at the time and full of booze, it seemed a good thing to do. It was perfect for us and blood brothers we became there and then. Fred was such a loyal friend it was a pleasure to be called his blood brother, and a relationship that would last all Fred's life.

One day we were away calling in Cardiff. We used to stay in a place called the Custom's House, it was a cheap and cheerful place and a number of lorry drivers stayed there as well, as did a lot of callers from Portsmouth, so you could always have a chat at night. After all it was only a place to lay your head down, so was alright. We had booked in and went into the centre to visit some pubs for a drink that would help us sleep, avoiding the noise we got in the digs. We had visited a few pubs during the evening, then went on to a little club just off the main drag. On the door was an ex-boxer called Joe Erskin, a lovely man to talk to and he said to the doormen to let us in. I asked what he drank and went to the bar and bought him one. I then sat down next to him and we had a good natter about boxing and some fights.

He seemed a bit punch drunk when he talked and kept chuckling in between our conversation. He was really a figurehead to prevent trouble on the door, he clearly got respect from the customers. He told me he never actually enjoyed boxing but got involved in it at a young age. I told him of my past fighting days and that I had turned pro with Jack who he had heard of. I said it was all the beatings my dad had given me that made having a fight second nature to me. We had a good enjoyable chat as the night went on and I kept plying him with drinks. He appeared to handle his booze well and told me boxing was just a normal way of life to him and not a chore at all. Mind, he didn't like to hear my dad used to beat me as he said he had a hard but enjoyable childhood. This I never knew as I could only go by what he told me so never knew if he was telling me the truth or not, but he was convincing.

After me and Fred left the club we went to get a burger around the corner and outside a bigger club than the small one we had just left. The burger van was there and we approached it passing the other club which had a number of large bouncers outside. We carried on to the van and I asked Fred what he wanted. We used to pay for our own when eating or drinking and it never came out of the stock money. This was money kept separate for buying goods to sell on when home. I ordered a burger and called what Fred wanted, a large hot dog, I got the money out to pay and Fred was just behind with his money waiting for the hot dog. The man serving never understood that we paid for our own and started shouting you got to pay for the hot dog as well. I tried to explain Fred was paying but he must have been thick as he began shouting louder – you have to pay now, pay! I told a big steroid bouncer, but he was Welsh so never grasped it either. He thought as he was a giant steroid-enhanced bouncer, that he would frighten me.

I told him to shut up or he would get a hiding. Three of his friends who were also very large, but looked the same, full of steroids and muscle bound, had also come from outside the club. Fred warned them not to start or they would get hurt. They must have thought it was a joke. They became very bullish now thinking we would get frightened of them due to their size. I said, "You have been warned so fuck you now!" and knocked one straight out, then another came near and got knocked out the same, then a third. The three had gone over so easily they couldn't believe it. Then Fred kicked another up in the air and knocked a friend of theirs out. They must have been so shocked. They were so-called top bouncers, steroided up and as big as houses, yet all on the floor. Terry Ross and Smugger Smith who had been drinking in the club came out and saw the mess we had made of the bouncers, then Terry shouted, "Anyone else want some?" He wasn't a fighter but saw he had no dangers there with me and Fred. The bouncers never had a fight in them. With that a smart well-presented man came up to us from the entrance to the club. He had a young girl on each arm and had a large cigar in his mouth. He said to Fred, "You Londoners know how to look after yourselves," and pointing to a bouncer on the floor said, "He is the hardest man in Cardiff." Fred said he was not when my mate is here. Fred said mucking about that I sparred with the world champion and that he was the English karate captain. He winked at me when he said it. With this the smart gentleman with the cigar said he owned the club and they used to look after it for him as he was away a lot on business and that there had been a lot of trouble caused by the bouncers picking on the customers. I said that's because they are nothing but bullies and this little escapade would do them good and bring them down a peg or two.

He also saw that none of them had any bottle as there was no back to them after they got hit. The owner said he had to do something otherwise he would lose the licence to the club due to all the troubles he had there. With that he reached into his pocket and pulled out a large bunch of keys and said, "You boys are just what I'm looking for and I have seen you perform – no one is going to rock the boat with you two around." Then he handed the keys to Fred asking him to run the club for him as we could get it back on its feet and he could go away assured it was run correctly.

Fred said we were too busy and had a lot on, so thanks but no thanks, then wished him well in the future. Then me and Fred went to the burger van, got a burger and hot dog and walked away with them. The one serving never had the nerve to ask us for the money after seeing what happened and then saw the bouncers going back into the club with their tails between their legs so to speak. Then we had a good chuckle to ourselves on the way back to the Custom's House. We still had a good laugh about this incident whenever either of us brought it up.

Fred was a very reliable friend as I stated and would always be there should the case arise, and likewise I was the same for him. We were a real pair together and no one would ever cross us, as if they ever did they would never get away with it, and wherever we went we got respect and you don't just get that, you have to earn it. That is why me and Fred got it and at no time did we ever take a liberty with anyone. We would only retaliate if the case to arose by others. Not us mind, we would always finish it. If ever I lost my cool, Fred seemed to know how to calm me down if he wanted to.

It wasn't quite the same with Fred, though sometimes when his head went no one could hold him and he certainly wouldn't listen. You would swear blind he was deaf, but yes he did seem to know how to get me subdued should it be needed. Sometimes that couldn't be done if I had gone too far over the top, that was when he wouldn't make me see sense.

One day we got back from being away, then on the Friday we were selling off to Colin Macload as we always did, as he was our main buyer. All our stuff for sale was emptied from the van and laid out in the warehouse yard, then we started going through all the furniture and smalls while agreeing with Colin on the prices he offered us. When sold, his staff used to carry it into his warehouse. Then we came to a single pine wardrobe, it was exactly the same as one he had brought off us the week before for thirty-five pounds. This week he said twenty-five. I told him I had brought it for him as they were thirty-fives last week. He said no, they are twenty-five. I told him I brought it on the way home for petrol money only and gave twenty-five for it to earn a tenner. But no, Colin was adamant they were twenty-five. I was now getting really annoyed and explained again he told me thirty-five the week before and that I had given that for it just knowing the price I had got. Colin said I had got it wrong and I knew that wasn't the case. I always remembered prices. It was him who had forgotten not me or Fred and Fred knew I was right.

This is when I flipped and proceeded to smash the wardrobe to pieces, screaming at Colin "You must think we are stupid, you prick!" still smashing it and jumping on it. There must have been a hundred pieces of it all over the yard and while I was copying Colin must have been shitting himself. He bolted to the warehouse door and locked himself in, but there was no stopping me, I was fuming. Then I looked at Fred, bearing in mind it was half his, and all Fred said was, "You carry on, Ian, no worries, I know you're right." I started to shout at Colin to come out, but he said he wouldn't till I calmed down. He said he would pay for the wardrobe but I had to let him finish the buying then pay us so he could serve his customers.

We agreed and Colin came out, added our bill up, paid us and I said see you next week Colin and that was it, no repercussions at all. In fact, he had paid thirty-five pound for a bundle of firewood. Funny really, why did he try it on? As that was what I'm sure he was doing, and what made it worse was that I scraped all my knuckles getting the wardrobe down the stairs of the house it came out of. Then Colin wanted us to give it to him, that's were Fred came in – he kept me from whacking Colin. Not clever and would also have had a night in the cells, no dough, and I wouldn't have had a clue at the time as the grey mist had come over me and I wouldn't have known anything about it till the calmness had returned. Fred stayed quite calm under the circumstances then said should we go for a drink – a good idea, Fred. It was the best way to unwind, as the tension was still there to an extent and that took some time to leave the system. It certainly would happen quicker with a drink inside me. So off to the Black Dog was on the agenda.

The trouble with Rita was still going on and she stopped me seeing Ian and that really hurt as I was close to him. My little man, I called him. Anyway I reared up on Rita and so she got a court order. I wouldn't accept it so was locked up overnight in the local police station. In the morning the judge read out the riot act again and warned me of the consequences should I break the order. The prick she was with came so close to being topped and Fred agreed no one should stop you seeing your child. He was dead against that and told me he would shoot him. I knew if Fred said he would do it he would do it and we always had a gun hidden away so he had access to one at all times. I knew he would use it, no question of that, but I told Fred the judge had given me the lowdown of what to expect should I break the order placed on me. I applied to the courts for permission to see Ian the lawful way and had to have a meeting with the welfare officer. He would assess me as Rita had told them I was a very violent man. The officer who was assigned to my case asked me many questions and appeared to like my answers. He seemed agreeable to me seeing my son.

I left the meeting with him feeling I was sure to get visiting rights, then you wouldn't believe the report when you read it. He said I had been in prison for violence and was known as a violent person and that the recommendation was that permission to see my boy should be denied. I was so shocked at this as he seemed in my favour. I told Fred and he was gutted for me. I said the welfare officer must be a real pig to stop a father seeing his own son. A few days later you wouldn't believe it. We were in Albert Road in Amos' shop when the welfare officer who did my order went by. I said it was him to Fred and he chased him up the road. I shouted out to Fred, "Don't do anything, Fred, he will grass and I will never see him!" It stopped Fred in his tracks as I knew he wouldn't want to see that happen, but he did say he knew him now and he pitied him if he ever saw him on his own with no one around.

Chapter 28

Now Rita had moved out I was becoming closer to Janet. She would be with me from when I came home from away, calling mostly on a Thursday, and stay with me till the Sunday, then I would be away again on a Monday morning early. It worked out OK, but was now becoming a bind as she wanted to be with me all the time and me and Fred liked to go out with no women around. But Janet would bump into us knowing our places we used to hang out at. This just upset the routine me and Fred had, after all you didn't want a girl following you around, that just wasn't on. In the end, Fred and I used to frequent places she wouldn't find us at, places she never knew about. The trouble was that she was beginning to think she owned me so was becoming demanding. She was even staying the nights when I didn't really want her there. This would cause arguments now and then. She couldn't understand that sometimes you never wanted a girl around and only when he wanted so not just to satisfy her needs. It seemed more and more of my time was being taken by Janet being there and that this wasn't always a thing of choice. I used to put up with it mainly so as not to have a full-scale row with her. This was mostly when she had taken a good drink and to say she knew when to shut up was an understatement. She would just go on and on; drink in, mind out, was the way I looked at her, a pain in the backside sometimes, and I often just fucked off so as to be on my own or just me and Fred and leaving her to her own devices. Funny but all her family were really nice, not like her at all, she seemed like a spoilt brat at times and her mum Lil and dad Ronnie knew the score with her and often asked me how I could put up with her. And to be perfectly honest I never knew this myself. I decided she had to be kicked into touch. Mind that was easier said than done, the only consolation being that I never actually married her and I used to think how lucky I was there.

This is how devious she could be. Her brother Micky, a lovely man, got his future wife pregnant. She was Debbie, a daughter of a good friend of mine, Taffy. Janet couldn't stand that she would no longer be the centre of attention in her parents' eyes, so she unbeknown to me left her birth pill alone and hadn't taken one for a while knowing her brother would be a father. And that must have been eating away at her with no pill being taken there was only one result from this and that was Janet would become pregnant. What would I do now? I had to stand by her if just to see the outcome of her pregnancy. I must say I found that very intriguing in as much as would it be a boy or girl, and this was a thing I had to stay and find out, not that it would matter. I certainly wouldn't leave her in the lurch, she never deserved that even though I was not up to having another child around me. Two was enough at my age after all, I didn't want to be tied down again so quickly, and marriage was not an option in my mind. We rowed too much to settle down together, the trouble was though Janet was such a good-looking girl I always gave into her looks when I had a drink, so couldn't bring myself to cut off with her completely. And now a baby was on its way, breaking up didn't seem an option. I had given her so much gold that I had obtained out calling, she was a very good-looking girl, then add to that she was now having my baby, there seemed nothing I could do to get out of this one. I was in a quandary. Then a friend of mine who knew how I felt, Micky, suggested that I should get away for a while and that he was taking his motorhome for a tour round the continent and into Spain and suggested that I should go with him to get my mind straight. I had to have a break away as the birth time was getting near; yes, Micky was giving me a great offer – it was clearly a brilliant idea, at least I would be away from Janet for a while, whereby I could return later with a clear head. Yes, a perfect answer to my troubles, and also this would give me a nice holiday, one badly needed under the circumstances.

We would travel to France on the ferry then travel round France, we even ventured over the Pyrenees, a mountain range, then into Andorra. While going over the mountains Micky stopped near the top and I got out a club from my golf bag and proceeded to drive a ball out into the open air over the side of the range, it's a shame we never had mobile phones then as it would have been great to have captured it on camera or at least taken a few photos of it. After Andorra we made our way to St Tropez on the French Riviera, a great sight to see all the big boats that are there, they must have cost millions even in those days. We then stayed a night here and there and made our way to Monaco where you can see the place and the large square. I would say this would be well worth a visit, the architectural outlook was brilliant there. Then we carried on to Spain where I had arranged to see Fred and Diane, they were with Les and Pam, and Johnnie with Sheila, then the fun began, and the drinks started to really flow as up until then there wasn't a lot of drink involved being that Micky never drank. I was making up for that now and with the company we were now in it was great.

Fred suggested that I rang Janet if just to see all was still well with her pregnancy, and to see if a child had been born yet. I agreed to this and said I would let them know later that evening. I rang Janet's parents' house where she was staying till after the birth. Lil her mum answered the phone. She was ecstatic and seemed so pleased. Janet had just had a baby girl – better out than in she said! That seemed appropriate under these circumstances, Janet must have been a pain in the arse as she couldn't stand pain. After a short while. Janet came on the phone. She was in a right old state crying and telling me what a beautiful girl we now have, I had to come home as I should be there with her and the baby, or didn't I care, while sobbing all the time. What was I to do, after all I was here with Micky so couldn't see him wanting to head back home cutting his holiday short. But I told him, explaining that Janet was in a right state. Micky said no worries, let's head back home then. Janet knew exactly what to say to pull at my heart strings and it had worked, we were on our way back home to see them both. Mind it would take a couple of days as we had to travel through Spain and France just to catch the ferry. I told all the boys we were off as Janet had had a little girl and they said we would meet up back home.

Travelling back seemed to be taking forever as I knew I had to get back as soon as possible just to calm Janet, so as she would be in the right frame of mind to look after our baby girl. Mind, you couldn't wish for better parents than who Janet had, Ronnie and Lil would always help out should Janet need help. This was good because I never had to worry about how our child was, they were diamonds.

The time it took to get back home was nearly two days. The time scale it took to just get through Spain and into France seemed to drag as Micky was such a careful driver, a good thing really on continental roads one had to be extra cagey, and to say Micky was a slow driver was an understatement. When we did get home I rang Janet's house and Lil answered. She was telling me how beautiful our baby girl was and there was excitement in her voice. I had a bath, got changed then made my way to Cosham to see Janet and our little girl and yes it was as Lil said, a beautiful looking little baby. Janet returned home with me the next day and shopped for new baby clothes. She had a cot and pram so we took that home with us to my house with whatever else Janet wanted us to take.

For the next few days it was all OK. I provided Janet with all that was required for us two and the baby food and toiletries and such like. We stayed in for a couple of days, then I said to Janet I would go away on the Monday calling but that I would ring home regularly to see they were both

128

OK. I called her Charmaine after a good friend of mine Denny's little girl. Janet agreed it was a lovely name to call our little girl and that it would be the name she would be registered with. I had been calling home but on the third day I rang and there was no reply. What was wrong? Janet had to be there with the baby or so I thought. I returned home and expected to see them both there, but no. There was a note left saying she was lonely in the house on her own so she had taken the baby and returned to her parents' house. I rang her mother's house then and was told by Janet she couldn't handle being on her own with the child, so she thought it best if she stayed there for a while and a friend informed me she must have been suffering from post- natal depression or that would be an answer to Janet's strange way of acting anyway, so a good excuse to use.

Janet stayed in her mum's house and I went back to living on my own, when I wasn't away calling anyway. It stayed that way for some time. I would still take Janet out now and then and Ronnie and Lil would look after the baby. Nothing seemed too much trouble for them, they were really helpful when they were needed, if we ended up too drunk we used to stay at my house in town then return to Janet's mum's house next day, knowing the child would be very well cared for. Later, while I was away, Janet and her mother went to register the baby. That is when her name was changed to Kelly, this being due to the fact neither Janet or her mother could spell Charmaine, so under the circumstances Kelly was the next option. We were now drifting apart but I made a point of seeing Kelly every weekend and continued to do this for the next few years, as she never deserved to be ignored.

Chapter 29

I was soon back out at weekends and having a drink, usually ending up in the club called Some Place Else. It was owned by Pippy Arnett, a good friend of mine, who I often did work for should he need assistance with regards money owed or trouble from work commitments. Fred was with me most weekends when we were home and he liked the club as well, so we usually ended up in there after the pubs had finished. I never had any trouble attracting female company and one night we were in there at the top bar. This was an area of the club were the older clientele used to drink, a lovely upmarket area of the establishment, everyone knew each other and became regulars quite easily. As there was a draw to the place, you could have a good laugh and usually end up with a girl on your arm, or I used to anyway.

One night I caught the eye of a girl I had seen in there a few times, we got talking together and her friend who she was with had teamed up with a customer in there. The girl appeared to be on her own, as her friend was just looking on and having a chat with her conquest. We started having a drink together, a few dances and generally having a good time. As the night was coming to a close in the club I asked her if she wanted a meal. Her name was Kim and yes she would like to come for a meal with me. She told her friend who had come out with her that we were going for a meal and relayed to her where our restaurant was. She also said that they could then go home together in a taxi, so her friend agreed to meet her in the place. We went on to the restaurant and that is when she told me she lived in a place call Catisfield that was the other side of Fareham so some way from Southsea where we were. By two of them sharing a taxi that wouldn't come too pricey but still a tidy sum then. We had our meal and waited for her friend to come in. After quite a while she said her friend mustn't be coming and that as it was late she had to make her way home. That's when I said she could stay at my house and she seemed relived at hearing that and agreed. I said I would get her home in the morning as that would be no trouble. She stayed the night with me and I took her phone number and told her I would ring her the next weekend when I was home as I worked away. She agreed to that and I dropped Kim home. We started a relationship from that point, a whirlwind romance you could call it, after all she was fun to be with, a nice person who enjoyed a laugh, good looking and above all, like me, enjoyed a drink.

Kim asked me to meet her parents quite soon after we had been together. She was obviously happy with our relationship to want me to meet her parents and I was happy to go along with this. I met her parents who seemed to be happy Kim had a boyfriend and all we had to do now was see how our time together was going to work out and if it was going to progress to another level.

I used a pub in those days called the Florence Arms and a good friend I used to drink with was called Spider – he had spiders tattooed all up his arms and on his chest. This was for his job as he was a wrestler and nicknamed Spider, so all the tattoos were for show when he got in the ring, mostly to boos he told me, but that was good for his job. In those days the pubs used to shut at 2.30 pm or just after. I asked Spider while we were drinking if he wanted to come with me to a barbecue after the pub shut. He was always keen to carry on drinking during the day so told me that sounded good to him and that he would like to come. He was a sight to behold, about six foot eight tall with long jet black curly hair, dyed dark for the audience. To start them going with the boos he loved winding them up. He told me his appearance would be great for the wrestling game and he could carry it off. We got into my car and we proceeded to Kim's parents' house where the barbecue was being held. We had some cans with us but Kim's dad said there was plenty there to drink and gave us a couple of cans. After a short while Kim's dad asked us if we would like some food off the barbecue. "Yes please!" said Spider, and he got a plateful of chicken pieces and a jacket potato. We were drinking and laughing away when Spider asked if I knew them well, whose house it was. I told him it was my girl's parents' place. To that he replied, "OK, I'll leave the bones then." I was in stitches it came out so naturally. Apparently he always ate the bones at any barbecue but he wasn't doing that here, so funny the way it came out, you'd would think he was a caveman. Mind, he had eaten all the sausages and rashers with salad in double quick time.

We were talking about the good times we used to have in The Florence. We used that most days when home as it was only around the corner from where I was staying and that was in my uncle's house while I was getting my house in Fratton completely renovated. It was nice of my uncle to let me stay at his house which was large and made up of a lot of bedsits let mostly to students, so he let me stay in a large double one in the house and that was only a very short walk to The Florence, so handy in that department. Kim used to talk very posh as she had elocution lessons and this took my friends some time to get used to, but that they did and she seemed to mix in quite well. Kim was also a good worker and was well liked at a car showroom where she worked; they even let her have a car at cost, one they had taken in as part exchange, and that came in handy so she could travel to and from work and also visit her parents who were out of town when I was away working. She also pulled her weight when we went out for a meal, often paying for it, and paying her share of drinks when we were out. This was unusual but Kim would insist and I agreed as it made her feel wanted I suppose.

Kim enjoyed her food and would spend ages when preparing a meal at home, spending a lot of time on the finer parts, dressing up a dish and presenting it as if it came from a top restaurant, yet all I did was woof it down, not taking any notice of the preparation. That must have angered Kim but she never showed it. The times I was with Kim were always enjoyable, add to that she was good company and good looking, this I found was a rare commodity in a good-looking woman – most of them thought they were better than they actually were, but not with Kim, she was down to earth and OK in both those departments.

Chapter 30

We were both working and I was earning well but ploughing mine into the house I was doing up. We still used to go out every weekend when we were together and having a great life at the same time. After a while of being together I got a shock – Kim told me she thought she was pregnant, but had to have a test first. She said she never knew how it had happened as she was on the birth pill. She had a test and yes she was pregnant. Well there was no getting away from it, she was pregnant and the only thing to do was as we were happy together was get married. Kim agreed so I would start organising the wedding, but first we had to tell her parents and that wasn't an easy task. The only good thing was that her dad appeared to like me so I found it natural to explain it to him. He was a marine so had heard most things before so it wouldn't come as a shock to him. When I told him I could then get on with arranging the wedding and the reception afterwards. I booked a restaurant which had a club upstairs in Albert Road, got a load of champagne for the reception part as you came into it, also we had a sit-down meal, three courses, for all the ones invited to the day. And my friend Tommy lent me a Rolls Royce just to finish the ceremony off. It worked out perfectly and everyone was happy with the outcome. Kim's dad gave a speech saying he was so pleased at the turn out but added he was glad to get rid of her then stated he was only joking, but it all went well and the drinks flowed. It ended up a very good day, a bit up market really.

Kim's mum had a stall that sold jewellery at weekends but her main job was in care, a worthy job in those days. I used to sell her some gold or silver pieces I got out calling, often waiting for her to sell some pieces before I got paid but I didn't mind as I usually made a bit more by waiting for it. Her dad told me he could never see her getting married as she seemed footloose and fancy free so to speak but I knew what he was on about, that's why it was a whirlwind romance that got her to get married in the end. He also said he was there for us should we ever need him and that was nice to hear. I was in the process of getting a guest house in Southsea right near the Florence Arms. After a few months, Kim had the baby, another girl. We, or I should say Kim and her mum, called her Emily.

She was a lovely calm child who seemed so contented and no trouble at all, even during the night when you need your sleep she wasn't bad and Kim was straight there to change her if she needed it, or give her a bottle if it was needed. Mind I did my share of that and it was nice to get involved should I be needed to give Kim a break. Mind Kim did seem to change somewhat and we were arguing a bit more. Also Kim was drinking more and enjoying her wine even during the day, I don't think that helped as she would get braver after a drink and that did not help our relationship. She didn't know when to shut up when in drink, and this was the best way to get me turned off her. Mind, could it be that she knew I had sold my house and perhaps she was thinking what would she get out of it. Mind I had a bit of luck in this department. She was round my mother's place with the baby, she stayed there for some time telling Mum of all the troubles she imagined she was having and taking tea with her, and my mother was the best listener you could have. She clearly got carried away as the time was flying by and she was so tied up with the chatting that she left her address and phone book by the phone in Mum's house and never realised it till she was in fact back home with me. Kim thought she had left it there as she couldn't think of anywhere else that she took the book out of her bag, only when she used our Mum's phone. I rang Mum and sure enough it was there, so I said when I had to go by Mum's in the morning I would pick it up. I went to Mum's next day to pick her book up and Mum said Kim never stopped running me down and got so carried away she had forgot her book and that she just agreed with all Kim had said just to keep her calm as she seemed on another planet. I thanked Mum for the book and proceeded back to our place to give it to Kim, as she seemed lost without all her contacts and numbers contained in the book.

When I got into my van I looked through the pages quick and on the top of one of the pages was written 'the Matrimonial Act 1967'. Now why had she looked that up? There it was at the top of a page. Alarm bells started to ring, she knew I had sold the property she lived in with me in the beginning of our relationship, I was now convinced she was after some of the sale. I had to decide in my mind if she had Emily just to push home her claim, and if so Emily wasn't an accident at all but a planned act and that Emily was her bargaining tool for a nice pay off. I had to keep this to myself in case I was wrong, but it did seem feasible now if you put it all together. Kim may have had a drink when she was talking to Mum as her tongue was just going on and on. Mum said all the signs of having had a drop of wine but I did hope I was wrong, then there was the piece written above a page about a marriage act – it did seem to be knitting together, or was it my mind? Once bitten twice shy they say, all I knew now was I had to be cagey and not let her know of my suspicions. I never even told Fred, as all this was of Kim's making so no need for Fred to know about it just yet.

I carried on as normal going away with Fred and calling as was the norm. If anything it made me work harder to earn more to put by should I need it if my life did go pear-shaped with Kim. I did hope not for Emily's sake, but deep down I think I was convinced what the outcome would be. Mind, I still had to keep all this to myself and not let on to anyone of the ideas I had and of my future plans. I would just work away, come home, sell off and do everything as if nothing had changed then hope it would all come out in time. I would do all as I always did even to the extent of taking Kim out for meals and buying her wine when she required it and that now seemed every night she stayed in. She may have had a drinks problem but then again that was of my making as I would be binge drinking every weekend and plying Kim with drink also till I went away again on Monday. Mind, I never saw any empty bottles about and surely there would have been some if Kim was drinking when I was away working, so it could be a sign I may be wrong, and I did have a devious mind. Also I may have still loved Rita but I wasn't sure of that as I found it hard to truly love anyone as my feelings I felt were beaten out of me when young by my father, so if a nice feeling was love then yes I did love Rita and of course she did give me a son. And I found that was the women giving you all her feelings but then who am I to get these ideas. I still plodded on with Kim thinking she may change as Emily was such a lovely child and me and Fred were doing more day runs so as I could be home with Kim. When I was about she never seemed to drink so I could keep my eye on her, as drunk and children never seemed to go together.

Chapter 31

Me and Fred still used to go out for a drink and sometimes this would be daytimes. One day Fred said he had to go and see someone in the Painters Arms that was in Lake Road. We were in there and Fred said, "See him over there?" and pointed to old man Stanley who had a fruit stall in Charlotte Street market. He said his boys were liberty takers and that three of them had set about a young boy who wasn't a fighter. They had really beaten him, poor boy, and that they were only bullies. I knew them anyway and agreed with Fred there. Fred said to the old man "Why don't your boys fight anyone who can have a fight?" If he thinks any of them can fight put the money on them and he would see they were only bullies and not fighters. He kept on saying "No, you got no money have you, a bullshitter is all you are." Fred showed him up so much he mentioned a son of his called Ray. Fred said "OK, get you money up together and Ian will fight him Sunday at the stables off New Road. Mind you better get the money together up front." That's when two grand was mentioned.

Sunday was the day and ten was the time he said it was on and left the pub. Good Fred, that was handy, you got him involved he never knew his boys – obviously they weren't real fighters only bullies. I couldn't see him turning up, but if he did as he'd got shamed into it he wouldn't have a cat in hells chance, after all my brother Ken had beaten him and no disrespect to him but he wouldn't lace my boots. "Fred," I said. "This will be easy money, he will get knocked out in seconds." And I laughed, well done Fred, you did well there mate. Putting this into context, a house in those days was £8,000 so a quarter of a house was the fight value. Now a house is about £160,000 so a quarter would now be £40,000 – that puts it into perspective, a lot of money in real terms.

Everyone got talking about it. Now I was thinking how would Ray get the money, after all he never had a pot to piss in. I was now hoping someone would put the money up as it had to be handed over to the minder before the fight could take place, but never mind I had to be ready no matter what the outcome and of that I was sure my money was ready. Then they were all saying he would not turn up but I was relying on the family shaming him into that part. Yes he had to turn up or he couldn't face the family again.

The day and time was fixed and me and Fred could go away and work, me knowing I had a good payday to come back to. This week when we went away I took my tracksuit with me so I could have a couple of runs while away after we had finished work. This would just get me on top form and put the edge on me fitness wise. Mind I was always fit anyway, this was just to sharpen me up so to speak, not that I needed it against Ray – he would be totally out-classed. If money wasn't involved they would have said it was me taking a liberty as there wasn't any way he would be in my league.

Me and Fred only worked till the Wednesday that week and came home. We sold off then I went and had a few rounds on the punch bag to make me razor sharp, then I was one hundred percent ready. A friend of mine who used to box with me at Portsea rotary looked me up as he had heard about the fight and said that he would come and warm me up just before the fight started if he could. I said yes that would be fine and that I would meet him before we ventured to the venue or stables in this case. When we got there it was packed, there seemed thousands there, you couldn't move down the road. The word had clearly got around everywhere. Mind the family wasn't liked at all so many wanted to see Ray get hurt, he was after all a bully boy and they like to see them brought down a peg or two. Fred was there, Big Bob, Johnnie in fact every one of note. I was just focused on one thing – to knock him out. Where was the fight going to happen? I knew Ray would be knocked over so I wanted it on the bombsite as the grass there would help him should his head hit it hard. Brian said it was a good idea on the grass as the road was only cobble stones and they would be unlevel so awkward to move around on, also a danger when he went over. I said on the grass as Ray had turned up late he clearly didn't want it. I could see he was out of his head as his eyes were out on stoppers. He didn't know what he was saying. He kept saying "Here, here", you couldn't get any sense out of him. Never mind he was going, I knew that I made sure a good friend of mine held the money. He was also a market fruit and veg man called Harry, a really lovely man and someone who was well respected and a very honest man. He told me he had the money and that was good for me. Harry was a gentleman.

So now it was on. I squared up on the cobbles, showed him my right hand by waving it out, he looked straight at it and that was my cue – you're going over. I took the weight on my back foot ready to throw my bomb and my leg had slipped off the cobble I stood on and my leg gave way. The pain was so excruciating it was unbearable I thought the bone had come out the side of my leg. I couldn't even stand up so I grabbed hold of Ray and couldn't let go or I would fall over. When I had hold of him I could tell by the feel that I was twice as strong as him, he was like a kitten to me. I took a chunk out of him while I had hold, he started making all different noises and not up to the hustle of a real fight, but what could I do? My leg was gone, to what extent I would only know if I had my tracksuit down. All

I knew was the pain was so bad and when Big Bob threw him across the road I fell over, my leg was well and truly buggered. Bob and Fred knew something was wrong but like me never knew exactly what and Harry said "Shall I give the money back as no punches were thrown?" I said, "Give them it Harry as I will get double that next time," still not knowing how bad I was. All I knew for sure was that I couldn't stand up and I also knew I was right, we should have had the set to on the grass not the cobbles and if he had turned up on time that is where it would have happened. Also who called the police? There were two van loads turned up – some grass must have tipped them off.

I have heard so many sayings from people who weren't there or couldn't see, that he had maimed my leg in a car door, he kicked me in the leg. All bollocks. Now everyone knows the truth, not one punch was thrown. I had a whipped leg on the cobbles and ended up lucky to keep it. Looking back we should have divided the money back up as Harry said, not to let them keep the lot as they got the wrong impression. MP Hancock said it was barbaric and no way should two men fight, the pillock. He must have put it in the *News of the World* as I had a reporter on to me for a story but I declined it, knowing I would knock him over at a later date. The fight was the talk of the city for ages and still is – that will never be forgotten. The turnout was colossal so when I'm dead and gone they will still be talking about it.

After Fred took me to the hospital that was where I found out that the main ligament that runs down the inside of your leg and holds your knee in place had stretched to such an extent that it was now impossible to hold my leg together. They put a support on my leg so I could get about on crutches and told me to return in the morning to see the specialist, but to go very careful on it. I went back in the morning first thing and saw the specialist. He was a Dr Griffins and the top one in England for knee and leg injuries. I had X rays and Dr Griffins said that the main ligament had stretched to such an extent that it could no longer hold my leg together and that he would have to pin the leg or take the lower part off. Mind, he said there was a thing he wanted to try out and asked if I would like to be used as a guinea pig to try his new idea on. Did I have a choice? No, not really. I had nothing to lose but try his plan or lose my leg. I agreed to give it a go. I told Dr Griffins that and he told me it was like my ligament was an elastic band that had stretched so much that it never goes back. His plan was to fold it over stitch it together and hope it takes. All I had to do was take some tablets to stop any rejection that may occur and take antibiotics in case of infection, then wait and see the outcome. After a few weeks, this was done under anaesthetic and when I came round there was a heavy plaster cast placed on my leg and Dr Griffins was there to explain just what he had done and that I was the first one to have this procedure. Up until now it was a success and the whole outcome wouldn't be known for a good while, but he was hoping it was going to be a good result as there would be many after this who would need the same procedure. I was taken home after thanking the doctor for doing my operation and giving me another chance with my leg.

I arrived home on the crutches the hospital gave me, and the plaster was getting heavier on the leg. Dr Griffins did say he had to make the plaster stronger than normal as this was an experiment that he didn't want to fail.

I had to have it on for about six weeks then return to the hospital to have it checked out and the plaster changed if it was needed. That would be the case, I would have thought, as the skin under the cast was itching now and starting to smell, yet only a couple of weeks had past so I was still taking the resistant tablets and antibiotics. I just hoped I could put up with it for another four weeks, and that the leg would stay OK and not get infected.

That was now my worry, and having to use the crutches was a bind. I was so used to being mobile and getting out and about, yet now all I could do was sit at home with Emily while Kim got the shopping in and did the running around. Not nice for me to rely on her all the time – it wasn't my style. My mind was working overtime; why did I not agree with Harry Madgwick and have our fight stake money back? After all there wasn't a punch thrown in anger. So that was the sensible thing to do, all I was thinking about was getting my leg better and arranging for another fight.

Next time it would be for double the money and that would be a win-win situation for me. I never knew the leg would be as bad as it was. Still it may be OK later as I had to knock Ray out to show him and everyone else how the fight should have ended. Still that is why you have bookmakers – there is no such thing as a certainty and I was as near to one as there could be.

After a couple more weeks my leg seemed a lot better. The pain had all but gone and I used to itch inside the plaster with a thin stick. I could also get around just by dragging my leg about and I got rid of the crutches. I seemed back to my normal self. Could the plaster come off now? I was thinking, yes it must. I had to knock Ray out.

I put a stack of pillows on the front seat of my van and then my plastered leg was nearly straight when I sat on them. I would get this damn plaster off and get him and punch his head in; that is all that was on my mind. The job had to be done. I drove the van to Cosham and saw a mate who had a yard just off the high street. There a spray garage and yard. He would help me get the plaster off. He was Peter Essary, a brilliant sprayer and still is. Anyway I asked him to get his big bolt croppers and chump away at the plaster to cut it off. He didn't agree with it, but still did what I wanted anyway. When it was off, my leg looked so thin I had muscle wastage. There was no strength in it, never mind I thought, it would still be strong enough to knock him over, but as I turned to go from the garage I couldn't stand and had no strength in the bad leg so fell over. Peter helped me up and I was taken to the hospital again. What a fool I had been to think I would be OK with the plaster off. I explained to the hospital desk that I took it off as my leg kept itching and it drove me mad. She told me I was very lucky as Dr Griffin was on duty that day and not in another hospital. I knew he was the best knee and leg doctor in England so was always wanted around the country – how lucky was I. I was told to go to the waiting room after being given some crutches and they would get Dr Griffins to see me.

I could walk by not taking any weight on my left leg and only using it as a guide and putting all the distributed weight on the one leg, my right one. I sat in the room and in came the doctor. He asked me what had happened and I told him I had cut the plaster off so as I could get about better. He slapped my face, not that hard, but just to make a point and so I would listen. He said I could still lose my leg as the graft would not have taken yet and there would be a chance the operation would now not be a success. This shocked me – how stupid was I, just thinking of my pride and not the experiment to help others? He also told me if I did anything like that again he would wash his hands of me and I would be on my own. Yes, he read me the riot act, and it was my duty to give the doctor a chance to show that his new knee op idea would work on others. That was all sports personnel – he said so many had this injury and to find a cure would be a brilliant breakthrough, history would be made. Anyone in the same predicament as me would be able to have a normal life.

Denny Huntley picked me up from the hospital after the doctor replaced the plaster on my leg then took me home. I told Kim what had happened and she said how stupid I was and all I could do was agree with her after what I had just been through. I couldn't help but still keep thinking who had told the police, after all they were there far too quick, they were clearly tipped off and it wouldn't be any of my friends – they wouldn't do anything like that. So all I could do was surmise what had happened, and when me and Ray came together in a grapple I was twice as strong as him, he was quite weak really and had no strength at all. How could it end like it did? After all I was so superior in every department, but it was no good beating myself up. I just had to give myself time to heal and forget about it all for now.

I stayed with Kim and we never went out together for ages. I had to make sure I was a hundred percent better before even going out. My sister was good and never asked for any rent for putting us up and as I wasn't earning that was a bonus as I couldn't pay much anyway, my money was going quickly. Time I paid out keeping the three of us.

I was getting bored of Kim now we were together too long without a break. It was best if she moved out and I told her I needed a break for a while to clear my mind – that was my normal method of breaking up. I never let on to Kim we could stay apart for a while then return when I got the new home up together after getting the money through from the house I had sold. Kim rang her sister and asked if she could stay with her for a short time while I sorted my life out. She agreed to this and Johnnie drove us with all their clothes to her sister's house. I kissed her goodbye knowing it was over between us. I did feel sorry for Emily though. Still, I would help Kim out there when I was back on my feet.

After a few more weeks I returned to the hospital and after a check-up I found out all was now well with the graft. It was a complete success and I could have the plaster cast off and stop taking all the tablets that Dr Griffin had prescribed me. It was a lovely feeling – no weight on my leg now, I could build my muscle up again then everything would be back to normal.

It didn't take me long to get out drinking again and I was back earning. Mind, billing was not as easy as it used to be prior to my leg trouble, but I would manage and that I did. Work gave me a buzz as you never knew what you would get hold of or how much you would earn. Just like having a bet, the winnings could be big or there again a loser and nothing to show for your troubles.

I was good on the door so never came back not earning. I had moved to a friend's house now whose house was off Elm Grove next to the Elms pub in Elm Grove Southsea. He was Martin and I used to drink with him in the Albert. Mind, he told me he had a large room, but no bed in it and as I was waiting to move into a guest house just laying my head down was the main thing. So I had a double mattress on the floor to sleep on in a large bedsit with a sink cooker and telly in, but the toilet and bathroom were on another level. That was no problem as I wasn't home that often and when I was I had a good drink in me so would sleep anywhere.

I still used the Phoenix pub and could get a lift home any time I was heavy in drink. One day I was in there and the barmaid had a cousin in there who had just finished with her boyfriend. She was so beautiful and what stuck in my head was her very long well-conditioned hair. It was down to her waist and made her look somewhat stunning. I brought her a drink and sat down chatting to her. Apparently she was going out with her cousin after she had finished the night in Tom's bar. We got on so well I asked her if she wanted to come to some place else with me then go for a meal. She lived in Leigh Park so I promised I would get her home after, seeing that it was a good few miles from Portsmouth. Her name was Lee and she was very bubbly after a few drinks. That said, she wasn't a big drinker so refused one every now and then while I still had mine.

We got into the club and made our way to the front of the queue. I was like God to the bouncers as I used to help them out when they had a difficult customer – I found a confrontation a job of work, not a worry as most of them found it. The leg was stupidly the last thing on my mind – it was back to normal in my eyes. Lee was what I would say very impressed by the way I was treated in the club and we made our way to the upper bar where all the older people used to meet up. She was such a lovely girl, Lee, and brilliant company. I could see me getting involved again and that I did. After all she was beautiful but it was the hair that impressed me so much. Waist-length hair was a real plus for a girl. We had our meal, she stayed with me and I got her home in the morning. Then my brother Dave told me he was getting a group together to have a holiday in Spain and there were a few places left.

I asked Lee if she would come with me for a holiday and that I would pay for her. She agreed to go so I booked two places with my brother and we would have a holiday together. Wherever we went all eyes were on Lee and her hair – you couldn't help looking at it – and she was a bit concerned that I might get jealous. This was far from the truth so I reassured her that it was all OK in that department. The holiday came round and we had a brilliant time. On returning I asked Lee to come out and meet me at the club. She said she was washing her hair and that took ages to dry. I could imagine that as her hair was so long, but at the time I did not listen to her excuses and said to get a taxi and that I would pay for it when she got there. But Lee was adamant she needed time for her hair to dry and wouldn't be able to make it. As I was well heavy with drink I wouldn't listen. I told her if she didn't come we would be over. Stupid really, but that was the end of another relationship.

Chapter 32

Here I was on my own, so hunting for another good-looking lady to have on my arm. I was at a club enjoying my time being single and on the hunt for a single lady to have a good time and laugh with when I saw a friend who I hadn't seen for some time – Lesley Devenish. He was a good time mate who also, like me, loved a bet. We got talking and that's when he told me he had just finished with his girl and like me was now footloose and fancy free. So here we were, two single chaps with no ties. As the conversation was going on and the weather was now getting quite cold we decided it was the ideal time to get away for a holiday in the sun. Where would we go, that was the question. Then after a few suggestions we both plumbed for guaranteed sun in Barbados and we would spend that Christmas there. The idea was to have a nice hot holiday and return looking nice and brown to face the remaining part of the winter. There was a fiddle going around in those days whereby you would go to London and a British Airways main office, book two tickets for a flight to Barbados, when they had put all the details into the computer confirming our flight and the seats we had which were now down to us. Then we would have a row between ourselves so it seemed a genuine argument and storm out of the booking office leaving the person who had booked us on the flight in a quandary. This was because in those days they couldn't let anyone else have them seats as they had been given to us on the computers which they couldn't change. Then we were to go round the corner to a shop that was classed as a bucket shop in those days, explain that we had booked two seats on the flight in question, tell them the seats and let them book us onto the flight, bypassing the British Airways booking. This would save us about £100 each, a tidy sum now, but a hell of a lot then. Now we had confirmation, dates, seats, flight all booked down to me and Les. What a fiddle that was in those days! And a legal way to obtain a cheap flight. We were so pleased with the result we had got that we came home and celebrated with a night out and a good drink. So if this was the way the holiday would go, I couldn't wait!

The holiday soon came round. Now we would in fact be in Barbados for Christmas and wave goodbye to the cold weather.

When we arrived there outside the airport we asked a taxi driver if he knew a place we could book into that wouldn't break the bank and we would give him a drink for his know-how. He told us he did and proceeded to take us to an area called St Laurence Gap, a short drive from the airport. The guest house he took us to was not too big and a quaint place; not too many rooms but nice and clean with the beach just a short stroll from our room where we would spend our days.

After the second day we were woken early in the morning to a chap shouting up at one of the windows in our guest house and after a while he started firing a gun into the air calling to a girl who was in an adjacent room to us, saying she was his girl and no one else's. It was quite stupid really. Apparently the girl had been with him a few times and had now found another chap to go with, but the first one thought he owned her and that she should not leave him for someone else. After a while, a window was opened by the man who owned the house we were in and he shouted out, "You can pack that in!" and waved a shotgun at the man below, telling him to piss off or he would shoot him. This was enough to put the one outside off his stride and he left the girl shouting abuse at him. Me and Les decided we would have to find another place to stay as this was no way to enjoy a holiday. This we would do in the morning.

After breakfast I told the landlady a girl had given me her address there and wanted me to meet her as she was on holiday with her parents. When the landlady was told the address, which was Sandy Lane Hotel, she told me you had to be very rich to stay there and that I was to go and find her as she must be a bit special. Me and Les decided to visit the place and my was it upmarket! We had to get interrogated just to enter the place, which also had its own stretch of beach. There were guards everywhere. I asked how much it was to stay there from a porter and the costs were incredible – you could buy a house for how much a fortnight would cost you!

The girl I was meant to see was out with her parents with no time she would be returning mentioned, so me and Les returned to our area to find a new place to book into. We found a nice smallish hotel just up the road from the guest house we were already in, booked a double and went to fetch our belongings. The owners were understanding in the guest house after the night's disruption. After depositing our cases in the room we put our bathers on and proceeded to the local beach. We got talking to a chap who was there and he also had been booked into our hotel, but had a two-bed apartment as he was overbooked. He was a painter, he told us, and had just split up with his wife so decided to get away on holiday to get over it.

The next day was Christmas Day. Here we were walking on the beach, a painter, window cleaner and bricklayer, that was what was written in our passports so we all had a laugh about it walking on the beach – Christmas Day and mixing with the jet set! It did seem strange, as all we would do was live off our wits. In the night Les suggested we should have a night out in Bridgetown the capital, so we got ready and ordered a taxi to take us. While I was on the beach during the day I got talking to a young girl who wanted me to meet her that evening. She wrote where on a piece of paper. Now Les had suggested a night out I gave the girl's details to the friend we had been with during the day and he said he would see her and hopefully go out with her while me and

Les went to a place we had tickets for in Bridgetown. Apparently it was a dance with food and drink thrown in, these meetings would be on every two weeks, it was for holidaymakers and friends and it worked out a cheap night on paper anyway. The taxi came and charged us two dollars. There were quite a few there, but not many good-looking girls so me and Les would have a run around and return to the dance later. Mind I could tell the so-called free drinks were nothing short of coloured water so a rip off. Me and Les went into a few small drinking haunts and one I had to call Les out to leave – it was a very dark smoke-filled place, not a place you would feel safe in. As I pulled Les away he was talking to a very black girl, all you could see in the room were the whites of her eyes and couldn't determine the features at all. When I was getting Les out of there all he kept repeating was that she smelt lovely but you couldn't see what she looked like so I said forget it and let's go. As we were going out a group of men followed us. They must have been making sure we were leaving, you had to feel uneasy with all them eyes on you.

We returned to the dance place and after a short while decided it wasn't for us as we were now paying for proper alcohol as that wasn't free. We went out and summoned a taxi that was waiting just outside, we got in and asked for St Lawrence Gap. He turned round and started driving telling us that he was an educated coon, his words, and that he went to a private school on the island. Then I asked him how much was it to take us to our hotel and he said ten dollars. Bear in mind it was two to get there, I went mad and told him how much we had paid to get there. Then he said it was late at night and that was the cost now. I told him I wouldn't pay that much and started an argument with him, and with that he turned off the road and onto a beaten track. It was quite dark and all you could see was some beaten down old shacks on the way up the muddy track. He pulled up at the top of the track and it looked like a field of sugar cane. Then he said get out and walk down there, he added "You'll be dead before we reached the bottom." I was shocked and thought quick to get out of it. So I grabbed the driver's hair, pulled his head back and held a metal comb I had in my pocket to his throat and told him I would cut him if he didn't drive us back. He must have shit himself as Les said that I was mad and that I would do it mate. He turned the car round and drove quick back onto the main road and headed towards our hotel. As we arrived I got out and slammed the door saying, "Now you will get fuck all!" Les said, "Give him something." I said, "He gets nothing the way he treated us," and we entered the hotel we were staying at. I couldn't believe the way we were treated and said to Les let's go and tell the one who was supposed to have met the girl I gave him and tell him, then see how he got on with the date. We knocked on his apartment and he opened the door slowly. You could see he had been asleep, so we were the last ones he wanted in. I wasn't having none of it and we went in to have a drink that was in his fridge. After a couple he was on our wave length and enjoying the crack. It transpired that the girl I gave him to meet was not interested in him so he returned back to his rooms and had a quiet drink on his own. We drank well into the night and slept there before returning to our room. When we got there earlyish next morning the door was ajar and the room was trashed, a lot of stuff was slashed up and some clothes cut to pieces. How lucky were we that we stayed in the other apartment. It must have been the taxi driver who put them onto us. I'm certain we would have been killed if we were in the room at the time. We went just along the road to a small kiosk that had just opened and asked for two coffees. The bartender was cutting up oranges, apples and pineapple ready for his cocktails. He looked at me and said "You're the man with the tattoos [they weren't on everyone in those days], you have crossed the Flyers [or a name like that], that's a gang you don't muck about with." On saying this he pulled the large knife he was using across his throat as if to say you will end up one way. I looked at Les and him at me, we clearly got the message. All there was now, we had to get out of here and quickly.

We went back to the hotel, paid our bill and asked them to call us a taxi to the British Airways office to get our tickets changed. A Volvo estate turned up and I asked him to take us to the airways offices. On arrival I talked to the girl who was behind the desk and told her someone in my family had died and I had to get home to England. She was very argumentative and said she could only take Barbados dollars not the British pounds which was all we had on us. She wouldn't budge but I kept on and on. Les was very nervous by now. Yet we had to get to the airport and away while we were still in one piece. I asked the office girl to let me talk to the main British office. To this she reluctantly agreed. The taxi was still waiting for us which is what I had asked for – I told him I would pay him to wait. I spoke to the head of British Airways in Barbados and convinced them I had to get home due to the bereavement, not that our lives were in their hands, and they agreed to take British pounds as that was all we had on us, no dollars. She wrote us a ticket out and said we were booked on the next flight to England. It was music to my ears. On hearing this we would now get away with our lives in one piece. We went and got into the taxi and he drove us to the airport. On the way he told us he was Bob Marley's brother or cousin, I'm not sure, but something to do with him anyway. We got to the airport, thanked him for waiting, gave him a nice drink on top of the fare asked and waited for our flight time to come round.

While we were waiting in the airport I thought I would have a game with Les who was clearly concerned about whether we would get away scot free and in one piece. I would say, "Look at him looking at us, Les, he could be one of them after us." And "Look at them over there, Les, they could be after us." Les was shaking, then I said "Don't go to the toilet on your own as you may not come out mate." Yes I was getting him well wound up. It seemed forever, but then after a few hours our flight boarding was announced – we were on our way out of there and good riddance to Barbados. On the flight a young very attractive girl was sitting next to me and she became very talkative – a lovely girl. She told me she went to Barbados regularly as she liked the black men who used to service her well. One thing led to another and we were soon kissing and touching each other. Les said ease up but we were too involved to listen. We had a great flight and we exchanged our phone numbers. I gave her my mother's number as I never knew if I would be home or away calling, not that I thought she would ring. How wrong was I! My mother said she had rang a lot of times and asked me to ring her.

Chapter 33

She was from Ludlow and lived in her parents' hotel where she also worked. I agreed to visit her later and that I would ring her before I would be coming. Les had a nice newish car and I asked him if I could borrow it for the visit as it was quite a long way so a reliable car was a must for the trip. He said I could use his but to be careful and not to hammer it. I rang and told her I would be up there on the Friday night. She said she couldn't wait. Now the visit was on and I was looking forward to meeting up with her again. When I got there her father showed me to my room and told me when breakfast was and the cost of the room, this was the least of my worries as I had brought money with me for our nights out while I was there. I was just having a shower and getting ready to go out when she came into the room. She got undressed and got into the shower with me, she couldn't leave me alone it was a real thrill! God she knew what she wanted.

After we got changed and had some drinks we then went onto a night club. She was very romantic and kept kissing and touching me. I felt special, it was nice. When we got back to the hotel she joined me in my room and we went to bed. After a good time we had we were knackered and went to sleep. During the night she woke me up by touching me and we were at it again. This happened all through the night, she was nothing short of an animal, yes she was a nymph as simple as that. She was never satisfied. I was more tired when I got up than I was when I went to bed. It was lust so I made up my mind it would only be one night I would stay. So after breakfast I made an excuse and left for home, never to see her again. All I would add is that Barbados had opened my eyes, if that is how the rich and famous lived their lives you can keep it!

Chapter 34

I still used the Florence Arms where they sold a good rough cider or scrumpy as it was called. Every afternoon I could go in there and see a good drinking buddy of mine, Roger Harper. He drank with me for years. One afternoon while we were drinking in there an oldish man came in and after a few drinks got into conversation with Roger and myself. He was moaning at some length about a bad tooth he had, to such an extent he was nearly in tears. He was saying no one would pull his tooth out due to an infection he had in the gum. He kept on about it so many times and would not stop saying how painful it was. It started to get through to me how could someone be in so much pain yet nobody would help him. Well Roger was the local handy man who did all the odd jobs in the area, he could turn his hand to anything to do with the building trade. Mind he only worked in the mornings as every afternoon he would be in the Florence on the scrumpy, so would not be working. He was purely a morning man. Mind he had a few houses left to him by his dad on his death and drew rents, so in fact never had to work anyway. I used to say it was to get him up and out the house that made him take the odd jobs on, also it was bedsit land we were in so landlords used to like him in this area, as he never used to let them down.

Anyway, back to the man with the bad tooth. He kept on so much I turned to Roger who always had his Land Rover outside the pub with his tools in and asked if he had a pair of pliers in his motor. He said yes so I asked him to bring me a pair, not too large, into the pub. I said to the man with the bad tooth if he really wanted it out, he said yes as he was now in agony. I told him I would pull it out as I had done it to a lot of my dogs and many people who had upset me. Roger returned with the pliers and I proceeded to pull the man's tooth out. I said have a double brandy to him then open his mouth wide. I could see the bad tooth and smell the odour it was giving off. I used the pliers to grip the tooth and yanked it out with a sharp pull. It came out before he really knew what was happening. I told him to go into the toilet and get some paper to press into the hole left by the withdrawn tooth. Roger just gasped and said he didn't believe what he had just seen, then I gave him the pliers back to return to his tool kit saying it's all in a day's work Roger and gave out a laugh.

The man came back from the toilet with the paper stuffed into his mouth to stem the bleeding. I gave him his tooth and he brought me and Roger a pint, he was so pleased to now be pain free and then told me of a friend of his who also had a bad tooth that needed pulling out. I told him I was in here with Roger most days when home and tell his friend I would try and help him if he was in the same or worse pain than him. He drank up then left, he couldn't stop thanking me now the pain had gone.

I was in there another afternoon when sure enough in the man came with his friend and I proceeded to do the same for him with the help of Roger's pliers. Mind one day a chap we knew from the pub, he was a bit of a junkie who had long really curly hair, blondish, came in. He had heard about my tooth exploits and told me he never liked dentists as they would only sort his tooth out if he was drink and drug free, but as he couldn't handle dentists due to the fear he had of them he couldn't go into one clean, hence the way his tooth had become decayed. I said I would try and help him out and had a look at it. On inspection I could see the tooth was completely rotten and could see the middle of the annoying tooth was completely rotted away. I told him that but he was still happy for me to have a go at getting it out. Roger fetched the pliers again and after a double brandy he was prepared for me to try and get it out. He opened his mouth wide as was required and I proceeded to try and grip the tooth ready for the extraction. Every time I appeared to grip it enough to get a pull, it just crumbled as the middle of the tooth never existed it was just rotted away. I told him there was nothing to grip so as to get a good pull at it. He said can I please try for him as he was in so much pain. I proceeded to have a go as asked and gripped the gum and the tooth together then gave it a big yank. He screamed out even though he was pissed and also full of drugs, even I felt for him but it did come out with part of his gum also and he was happy, brought me and Roger a pint, swallowed another double and left the pub giving me the thanks he thought I deserved and having his hanky stuffed into his mouth to absorb the blood flow. Another satisfied customer, I said to Roger and he couldn't stop laughing then called me mad.

Chapter 35

Another time when I came back from being away the landlord Ray said that a couple had been in asking for the extractor man and he said I would be in the weekend when back from being away. Roger was in hysterics. I was in The Navy Arms, another pub Fred and I used, when a group of girls came in. One was a friend of our daughter. They were all giggly so had obviously been on the drink even though they never looked old enough. One took my eye, but as me and Fred were going to Southsea I just said cheerio to our mate Ray Deck and turned to the girls and said see you later to one who was Ray's daughter Kerry.

A friend Bobby came with us and we did the pubs in Southsea, then went to someplace else, a night club we used all the time. I never paid to get in as I was a silent bouncer for the doormen when they were up against it with anyone who they couldn't handle. While in there I saw the girl who had taken my eye in there, I mentioned her to Fred and Bobby she had a pretty little face but never looked 18 so that was a bit off putting, but Fred gave her the thumbs up and agreed with me that she was a good looker. I asked for a dance and she agreed to that. While dancing I bumped into a table and could see a very thick-lensed pair of glasses on there. I took them and for a laugh put them on and proceeded to dance away, then there was a tap on my shoulder it was a young man who asked for his glasses as he couldn't see without them his eyes were that bad. I apologised to him and gave them back. I told him it was only as a joke and he was alright about it. I turned to Fred and said Fred she's either stupid or likes me a lot as I told him about the game I had with the glasses and we started laughing about it. He said go for it, me and Bobby are alright anyway. I asked the girl her name, she said Toni. That's when I thought she was now having a game with me but she convinced me it was her real name, not a joke at all. I asked her if she would like to come for a meal with me and before I got the question completely out she said yes! I was a bit shocked as she never knew me, but later I was to find out she had seen me a few times and took a shine to me before really knowing me.

I took her to the curry house we used called Eugene's in Palmerston Road, just around the corner from the club. I asked her what curry she would like, then she told me she had never had a curry and didn't think she would like it. I showed her the menu but she clearly couldn't read it. I pointed to the one that said *Tungatt's Special*, Eugene had it put on the menu as a lot of the boys asked for it by name. It was an omelette with chips, garden peas and Bisto gravy. I also used to have a bottle of Blue Nun wine put into a water jug so I could drink when the restaurant wasn't allowed to serve alcohol after time. In other words, it was funny being with Toni, she was as green as grass but so sweet with it and she couldn't get over there being a meal on the menu named after me, she thought that was cool. After our meal I asked her where she lived and she told me Paulsgrove and that was quite a way from Southsea, so I asked her if she wanted to stay at my place and I would get her home in the morning. She said yes to this and we got a taxi to my friend's house where I was staying, being as I was still in the process of getting my guest house, and this was a fill in between the moving.

When we got to the house I told her I had a nice car round the corner with a brilliant stereo unit in it and would she like to hear it. Toni said that would be nice as I did say it was better than a disco sound. I opened the door as I had the keys on me but wouldn't ever drink and drive so had left the car round the corner. It was a Merc, a 280 SE, and even had my private plate which was Dan but I had the plate made into a narrow D so it looked like Ian. Toni's eyes popped out! It was a lovely light yellow colour and very imposing. We got in and I turned the stereo on and asked her to pick a tape to play. She asked me to put on a Motown tape which I did and she appeared to get blown away.

The shock to her was still to come when we went into the house afterwards. She saw I was in fact sleeping on a mattress which was on the floor. She must have thought I was just bullshitting her and that I was just trying to impress her. I told her my friend had agreed to put me up until I moved into my new house and that he was good to do me this favour, as I was a bit stuck till the move was complete. She stayed the night and in the morning I drove my car to drop her off. She gave me her phone number and I told her I'll give her a ring later. I did ring and said I would be up someplace else that weekend and would see her there if she was out, that way she wouldn't be interfering with my nights out with my friends and could see me if she wanted.

The next weekend I was out with Bobby and we had a good drink around some bars ending up at the club. We had a good laugh in the process of the run around. I was at the bar in the club getting us a drink when there was a commotion going on and on inspection I saw Bobby on the floor. He had been struck by a tall chap, Russell Hood. I copped the needle as Bobby was out with me so I went over and knocked Russell out, I was so annoyed, thinking Bobby was out with me, by hitting him he was in my mind hitting me, so I picked his head off the floor and bit his nose off, the bastard. Up until then we were having a great time and while at the bar before all this had happened I was talking to Toni who was with her friends Christie and Karen, so a nice night had gone tits up. I was simply fuming how things had gone. When I returned to the bar I was just about to get the drinks when Stuart Spraggs had a go at me. He must have been with Russell. I knocked him down but let him get up, he shook my hand then nutted me out of the blue, the fucker. So I knocked him down again and set about him, then a chap from behind me hit me on the back of the head with a heavy pint glass mug. This shattered on my head and all that was left was the chap holding just the handle of the mug in his hand. I left Stuart on the floor, turned to hit the one who had hit me with the mug, saying you prick, who on seeing the glass had shattered yet never appeared to have hurt me just ran off down the stairs and away so I couldn't get him.

None of the bouncers would say anything because it was me. I just slipped away and off to Eugene's the curry house. Toni when in there, was still picking the skin out of my teeth from Russell's nose, and I told her I would go and sort the one who hit me with the glass mug the next day. Toni knew the pub they used, it was the Three Marines in Eastney. She stayed the night again and I ventured to the pub the next day, none of them were in there but I let the customers who were in there know I was fuming and had come to sort them or at least that person who had struck me from behind with the mug. After all he wouldn't be getting away with that, he couldn't have had any bottle to run away the piss-hole.

That week seemed to drag as I had to return to the Three Marines to sort the wanker out who hit me with the pint glass. I thought the best time would be at the weekend to make sure I got hold of him. Toni came with me and the pub was quiet. Whether it was because of my last visit where I laid the law down saying what would happen to the prick when I got hold of him or it just happened to be a quiet weekend I wouldn't know. They knew I was going in there as I had told all of them who were in there the last weekend that I'm coming back the next weekend so they may have kept away for fear of the outcome.

One that was in there was Tony Male. He knew most customers who used the pub but said he hadn't heard who had struck me from behind. He also said that Russell had his nose stitched back on and it had gone well during the op, other than that he had no news. I asked him to get in touch should he find out who the culprit was. He said he would and me and Toni left the bar.

I was moving into the guest house as the deal had now been finalised and the paper work had all been signed and delivered. Work had to go on the back burner while the move was completed. It would be nice to sleep in a bed and not on a mattress placed on the floor. Mind it was good of Martin to put me up, his timing came just at the right time and was badly needed then. It seemed strange at first moving from a one-room bedsit into a five-bedroom house. I was now what you could call upmarket, a guest house proprietor. It had a ring to it, and the bonus was being in Southsea and near my local the Florence.

In those days the pubs used to close at 2.30 pm, clear out by 3 pm, so I used to take a few bottles of scrumpy home till the pubs opened again at six.

That's where a friend I used to mind called Alf Major ran a naval club called Tiffs. We used to drink in there when the pubs closed in the afternoons until the evening sessions would resume in the bars. If there was any trouble in there or Alf had a bad customer I used to sort it out, often having to throw out any troublemakers. Mind they had to be bad as I would know most of the clientele, so usually could just stop them in their tracks, seldom having to go that extra mile and use any force unless they were there as a guest and had too much drink in which case they were ejected as a matter of course and told not to return again.

I used to drink with a carpenter called Jeffro. He was in there a lot of afternoons having worked in the mornings, a bit like Roger. One day we were talking and the bit about Russell came up, then he mentioned that he had been round my house to sort out the trouble we had. I went into defence mode, after all no one came round my house. I would meet anyone anytime and anywhere, why come round my house and upset any of my tenants? I was now fuming. Jeffro was a bit of a shit- stirrer mind, but he had hit a sore point with me mentioning that I would now have to go and find Russell. I couldn't have that getting around, I was no normal person who would just accept a threat like that, I had to get hold of Russell and quick. I found out that most days Russell met a few of his mates in the Railway Rifle Club in Goldsmith Avenue. Jeffro heard me say I would go and see him in there, whether he would relay that to him I wasn't sure but I knew I had to make a visit to the club one afternoon. I took a knife with me, a strong SAS one that could not be bent and it was so sharp it would cut a piece of paper with the slightest of effort. I placed it in the back of my trousers between my buttocks so as it couldn't be detected. This was just in case he had a few of his mates there which was the norm so I heard and they wouldn't stand back and wait for their turn to get knocked out, they would jump in to help their friend out. So the knife was a safety net, mind when my head has gone there would be no holding back as long as I won was all that mattered. So it was silly carrying a knife, it was a thing that could have given me a lot of bird and I could knock the lot out anyway. Still I take it with me I did, no explanation would be needed there.

On entering the club I asked at the bar if Russell was in there. The barmaid said no but his friends were there and they could tell me if he would be in later. I approached them and asked if Russell was due in that afternoon. They said they didn't think so as he was normally in there by then. I said tell him I came in to see him and tell him no one comes around my house, all he had to do was say and I would meet him anywhere. Then I pulled out the knife, why I do not know, and rammed it into the table they were sitting round. I did this with so much force I couldn't pull it out. I never wanted his friends to see me struggle to get the knife out so went babbling on about Jeffro saying about his visit to my place, all the time wiggling the knife backwards and forwards till it was free to pull out. At least I hadn't made myself look a twat as it would have appeared had I not been able to remove the blade from the table, mind my temper was so strong I brought the knife down with such force it went in a long way in to the table top. When I had it out I left the club knowing his friends were shitting themselves and would tell Russell. Now I would see if he wanted to meet me somewhere if he still had a grievance and get it out of his system. I was prepared to settle his mind anytime, after all I knew there would be only one result and Russell knew that.

Sometime after I saw him in a club in Palmerston Road and asked him if he wanted to have a go at me, after all he had been round my house I was told so did want to have a return or that's what I had assumed. He told me then it wasn't him that came around my house and that he would get hold of Jeffro for stirring things up but assured me he had no grievance to sort out. I drank up and said that was fine with me but gave him my phone number in case he had a change of heart.

Chapter 36

Another time just after this I was in Tiffs club and there was a man in there being loud and a bit forceful with the staff. Alf was so pleased I had come in he said could I keep an eye on the noisy one as he was getting louder and louder. He was now getting money out and you could see he had a few thousand on him, he kept on about playing spoof – that's a game where you put a number of coins in your hands and select a few to leave in your hand and your opponent would do the same, then whoever had the call had to guess the total number of coins yours and his added together came to. He would not stop going on about having a bet. He challenged me and I told him I never played the game, but the more I said no the more he went on about playing me. On and on, that was it I had copped. "Right, one game win or lose for a grand or is that too much for you, mouthy?" I said. But he wasn't deterred and said, "Yes, a game for a grand, right". He put his money on the bar and I had my money by me so the bet was on. We had our hands behind our backs and shuffled the amount of coins we would leave in our hand then we put our knuckles together and he said to me call. I said five, that was my approve school number. It came up, I snatched his money and he was protesting he wanted another game to try and get his money back, an enormous amount in them days, it's a lot now so putting it in perspective he must have been gutted to lose that amount.

He still kept on and Alf said, "Get him out, Ian, he's become a pain." I had his money and was so pleased to get him out of there he wouldn't have it back no matter what. I was never going to give him another go at his grand, it was gone and in my pocket and I proceeded to throw him out of the club. Me and Alf had a good drink on him, anyway lovely man he was ha ha!

Then me and Toni ventured out of the club and home which was not too far to walk. When we got home we hadn't been in five minutes when the door knocked to our apartment, which was separate from the rest of the house and the tenants. I opened the door and Jock was standing there with another jock who he said was a friend from a bedsit around the corner from mine. The jock had a microwave and a video recorder in his hands. These were a rare commodity then not like now and just what I could do with. I asked him if they were stolen and he said no he had finished with his girl and they had split the goods in their place between them and he had that to sell. I asked him again as a tenant was passing us so I had a witness. He heard me ask again if it was stolen, but he convinced me they were OK to buy as they had not been stolen. There he was with two things I could do with and I had a pocketful of money I had won so I had a deal and brought the two items off him, closed the door and went into the bedroom for a lay down before going out for the evening.

We had just settled down for a sleep when there was a commotion going on and someone was banging on the back door which was on the ground floor of my flat. He was shouting to open the door up and was banging hard. There was a glass panel in the door so I could see the shape of a man, rather large he was, really hitting the door. I thought it would break the glass, this was strange as there was no natural back way into our garden, you had to climb over a number of garden walls. That's when I feared the worst. I took a knife out of the drawer and stood ready to stick the man. As Toni took the double bolts off I was ready to stab the intruder, but that was when he shouted "Open up, it's the police!" I was shocked and got rid of the knife while Toni pulled the bolts back. In the meantime a police officer in plain clothes burst into our apartment from the front. What was going on, I had no idea. He said he was a detective called DC Wise. I would say a prick, after all what was this all about. Then he let me know. Apparently I had just bought some knocked off gear, namely the video player and the microwave. I pushed him out of the way and proceeded up the stairs to get jock to explain I had bought the two items legally. But Wise wouldn't have any of it and started to wrestle with me. The trouble with this was he wasn't in my bracket for strength or power and I chucked him off with ease, then others came in the front door and arrested me weight of numbers, but I had done nothing wrong so why come to my door so quick?

Obviously it was an informer job or even a set-up. Mind I found out later Wise was said to be having an affair with my sister Pat. Could that be how I got set up? I wouldn't know, all I knew was that I had done nothing wrong so got into the squad car and was taken to the police station. I was later to find out it was called the Bridewell. In the scuffle one of them had lost their radio and Toni had kicked it under our bed so she could hear all that was said on the way to the station. On arrival Wise took me to the desk and as there was a prisoner getting booked in we had to wait. Then I saw the sergeant go at the one being booked in and give him a right mouthful and grabbed him round the neck. The poor chap was terrified, all the sergeant was doing was bullying the bloke so I had to speak up. "Oi, who do you think you are? You're frightening him!" He turned to Wise and said "Who is he, your prisoner?" I said I'm a member of the public and as you work for the government you shouldn't put the fear of Christ up the poor chap. Then Wise said I was his prisoner and that he arrested me for receiving. What a load of cobblers that was, but

157

at least now I knew it was a stitch up. The sergeant who I later found out was Sergeant Batten, he said to Wise "Put him in that cell [which was a holding cell at the side of the booking-in desk] and I will deal with him later." They closed the door and I laid down on the bench in the cell. After a short while the door was opened and Batten came in with another officer and said, "So you think you can fight, then?" and closed the cell door. I told him that I knew I could fight and to fuck off or he would get hurt and to take his man friend with him. He was punching his hand with the other one holding it as a fist. This was a challenge to me, he wouldn't heed my warning so I knocked him out and his friend who had come forward. As I struck, Batten was knocked out as well. What was happening, there were two police knocked out on the floor of the cell so I rang the bell for someone to open the door. It was opened and a couple of officers pulled them out of the cell and locked me in.

I was in there for a while when the cell door was opened again and there were a lot of tall beefy units of officers there, clearly going to have a go at beating me up. I said three Hail Marys and rushed them, knocking whoever I caught. Over six or seven had gone down but they got up and cuffed me, that's when I bit at Sergeant Batten's ear, taking the bottom off. He was screaming like a baby, then with the cuffs on they proceeded to give me a beating and a half. Good job I was fit and a non-smoker as I have no doubt I would have died. The bastards must have beaten me within an inch of my life and when I was on the floor a big useless gabber jumped on my ribs. I heard them crack, I honestly thought I was going to die if not there, then later. I could hardly move let alone walk but they gave me a haul up. I never thought about my leg that had been patched up, it's a wonder it never gave way under the onslaught. How lucky was I.

They pulled me and supported my weight to get me into a cell in the main cell block. I could see there were quite a number of officers there. Now I had calmed down it was registering in my brain a thing that doesn't completely happen when you're in a scrap, you seem to be in another planet, the complete happenings only come back a few days later when the mind has had time to rest and recuperate. When I was now in the cell I was feeling hurt all over, God the pain was terrible. I was pissing blood and spewing up blood, they had done a first-class job on me. Mind I had knocked a few of them over if that was any consolation. I tried to relax on the cell bench but the pain was too much, there was no way I could sleep. I knew my ribs were broken, every time I coughed I had to hold my sides, the pain, I never stopped cursing the pigs.

As it got dark the pain became worse. A young PC opened the cell and asked me if I needed anything. I said no, knowing I couldn't swallow, but

I did say, "Look mate if you don't want a dead body on your hands get a doctor as I am pissing blood and bringing it up in my mouth." I knew from my boxing if you swallowed some blood you could have a collapsed lung as it makes your lungs deflate, so I couldn't go to sleep. Anyway, even if I could close my eyes that would be dangerous. Mind the young police officer looked very worried at that point and said he would get a doctor, bless him. He was shaking in case anything did happen to me. He closed the cell and I sat down on the bench and he kept coming back checking on me. He said on one visit, "Why is the doctor taking so long? How are you, any better?" "No, the same," I said, but now feeling the full force of the beating the pain was coming out. Although I couldn't see I knew the bruising was coming out by the feelings I was now getting.

After a while the cell was opened again. I knew it was late as the bottle holes in the cell were now very dark. The police doctor I knew, he was Dr Constance. I saw him steal some small items off a friend of mine, tattoo Joe, and he knew I saw him so I wasn't getting any favours from him. He asked me if I could stand but he could see by my face I had taken a beating so I held my sides to try and restrict the pain knowing my ribs were broken and I rose up, but couldn't move forward so basically all I did was rise holding my sides. Constance said, "You're alright" and left, the fucker. He should have had me admitted to hospital, the condition I was in if he was doing his job right. I sat down again and kept looking at them bottle holes, just waiting for them to get lighter knowing it would be morning. After a few hours, the light arrived and the cell door was opened. I was told the superintendent wanted to see me and after a struggle I rose and gingerly made my way to a room just up the corridor. The door was open and I stepped in. The officer in there asked me to sit down but I told him it hurt so much I would sooner stand. I also said thinking of just getting out that he should forget it, the officer has a family and can't afford to lose his job. "Forget it, forget it," he repeated. "You have bitten my sergeant's ear off and you want me to forget it?" "But look at what your cronies have done to me?" "I don't care about that, you will be charged," and left me to go to the desk and get the charge sheet made out. God what a stitch up was my first response. I was charged and released.

I had a lift waiting and was picked up by Toni. She couldn't believe what they had done to me. I got home and stayed in a chair sitting up, eating and sleeping in it. I couldn't bring myself to lie down, I couldn't even go to the toilet. I used to shuffle round in the chair to put my bum over the side of the chair just to go in a bowl Toni held – she was good to me knowing I couldn't move properly. She even washed me in the bucket chair that was my home for a couple of days. I was confined to the chair till the pain had reduced and I could move with no restrictions.

I was confined to the house for a few days and Toni was a good carer, she wasn't the best of cooks but with her mum's help she kept my food edible. My ribs and arms were still hurting, God did those police give me a hiding, sadists when they had me restrained in handcuffs just seemed to keep on kicking hitting and jumping on me. They showed their true colours, bullying bastards. I got my mate and friend, solicitor Richard Scofield to represent me. He could not believe how the scumbags had beaten me. What Richard couldn't understand was why after I had knocked so many officers over outside the cell I had only been charged with the one case of unlawfully and maliciously wounding a sergeant John Norman Batten with intent to do him some grievous bodily harm contrary to section 18 Offences Against the Persons Act 1861. All the other charges that they could have put on me with regards hitting numerous other officers seemed strange, but later it became obvious the reason for that. Richard said we had to get a barrister and assigned a barrister Duggan. He was a local brief and one I had not come across before. I was a bit apprehensive with regards Duggan, as surely I would have heard all about him if he was that good beings I was regarded as the daddy about town so to speak. This is where it's better to be born lucky than rich and God was I a lucky man. I was in a club called the Establishment when a piss artist I knew for years, he was a dog man the same as myself, his name was Grenville Mays, came over to me in the club and told me he had been drinking with Barrister Duggan and he had told him he had a lot to put forward during my upcoming court case and that I shouldn't worry myself too much. Now that was a joke to hear, I had knocked numerous police officers out and had bit a sergeant's ear off and he's saying I had nothing to worry about! Add to that he was discussing my case with a piss artist, the alarm bells started to ring. I had to sack Duggan and find myself a good barrister. I went and explained it to Richard and he agreed with me he shouldn't have mentioned my case to anyone especially when he was drinking and told me it was a breach of confidentiality. I told him I would get a good barrister and to give me some time to sort one out. Toni had a little clique of friends who were all at school together. One was called Grant Murphy. He had not long finished a stretch in prison for hitting a landlord and in the fracas he was pushed or pulled through the pub window, so lucky he only had a few cuts and it had not been a lot worse. Anyway I got talking to Grant and I asked him about his case and who had represented him as it was a charge that could quite easily have been attempted murder and he said they told him to expect anything up to eight years, but all he got was nine months. That's when he told me about the brief he used and backed him one hundred percent. My ears were now pricked up. I had to get his barrister's name. I asked Grant and he told me he was the best I could get. The barrister's name was Paul Hymes. That was good enough for me. I wrote his name down and Grant told me he was stationed in Temple London, that is where all the top briefs were housed. I told Richard that he was the barrister I wanted and he got in touch with him and arranged an appointment. I was to travel up to Temple with an ex-cop called Jock Hunter who was a right-hand man for Richard who would do all the running around for Richard and the solicitors' office Warner Goodman and Street. The bit I didn't like was having to make the trip up to London with an ex-copper in tow. Still I could put up with that as he knew exactly were Temple was and what trains we had to catch to get there.

On arriving we had to find the Chambers Paul worked out of and asked a few people who looked like either QCs or barristers, and we were soon directed to his offices which were nearer to the middle of the layout of Chambers. We knocked on the door which was opened by an office clerk who took all the briefs into whomever was assigned a case. He knocked on the door and handed my brief to Paul. He was rather short, bald-headed and quite attractive for a male. He imposed himself on me straight away as he shook my hand with purpose, a firm grip – that is a thing I like about someone, not what I would call a wet fish handshake. On reading my case he started to laugh. I couldn't understand why he was like that, then he explained. "You have all these police officers giving evidence against you" and then proceeded to tell me why he had to laugh. He said, "You got to remember, Ian, police officers in uniforms are thick." His true words. "As if any have any brains they are grabbed by the CID and do not stay in uniform for long; these what I can see of it are all thick officers and if I can't slip a few of them up I will give the game up, you will see."

These are the names of all the witnesses the police had dug up to give evidence against me John Batten (Sergeant), Robert Parker (Sergeant), John Jacob (Constable), Mark Wise (Detective Constable), Gordon Ross (Sergeant), Anthony Reed (Constable), Suzanne Lynas (Constable), John Woodland (Detective Constable), Margaret Bishton (Police Matron), Robert Lamburne (Sergeant), John Smith (Police Sergeant), Brian Hallem (Detective Constable), John Windust (Detective Constable), Adrian Riley (Medical Practitioner), Martin Shuker (Detective Sergeant). Apparently that is what made Paul have a laugh. He said if it was cut and dry they would never call that many witnesses, all it did was make a jury bored in the end and also gave him so much ammunition to get involved with making one lie against the other and so on. That's when he said to me, "See what I mean Ian? They are thick, mate, they should have just used a selected few not 15 dummies. Add to that the two prisoners who were at the desk being booked in when this all kicked off and you have an over-zealous crowd trying to get a conviction and you are the scapegoat they need to protect the bullying Sergeant Batten who really thought he could fight but ended up with a flea in his ear."

Paul seemed to want to congratulate me, still laughing, then he told me just why he was so pleased to get this brief. He said he was at Oxford in a shared house which he had just moved into and was on the floor of the front room revising his homework when a few police officers burst into the room and went straight to a vase that was on the mantelpiece and retrieved a bit of drugs that used to be smoked. Paul knew nothing of this as a) he never touched drugs and b) he knew nothing of what was kept in the vase being a new intern. The policeman handled him and dragged him off protesting to the police station, where he was charged with possession of some drugs. He told the magistrate the true story on how long he had lived in the house – two days to be precise – and that he was in fact dead against drugs. They found him guilty, wouldn't listen to him at all, and that is when he said to himself if that's what they call justice I'm going into law to protect the ones stitched up as he had been. Apparently he had to go before the bar council twice to explain his misdemeanours before they would grant him his law degree, and then he would go on to become a barrister. So to say he hated the police would be an understatement. He told me a bully underestimated his opponent and due to that you gave him a hiding. "Yes Ian, I feel proud of you. Let's get this case on. I am hundred percent on your side knowing how the police work, fabricating evidence and distorting the truth. I will use this case to get them back as that is what is deserved in this instance." He shook my hand again and told me not to worry. Mind, he did say when I asked him that I would be looking at anything from eight to ten years if it did go the other way, but that he did think it would be in my favour when the true explanation was given to the jury they had come to give you a good hiding which was dished out to you anyway.

After leaving, Paul, me and Jock caught the train back to Portsmouth. I would now go before a magistrate to be put over to the crown court for a hearing at a later date. The police who came to the palimony case at the magistrate were looking at me smirking as if to say the old bill would get their own back, the pigs. Mind, I think that is too good a word for them to be called. They are the lowest of low. I was thinking again, if I was a smoker or not a fit person I would have been dead, killed by scum like them. It took over ten police to get me down so as they could lay into me. Just thinking about it again made my ribs hurt more, I could feel the cracking all over again.

The time of the hearing soon came around and my bottle was squeaking. I never wanted to be locked up again, that's all that seemed to come to mind at that time. I was so pleased to meet Paul in the foyer of the court, he seemed to generate calm and my word, was that needed. Paul asked me to go with him into an interview room where he would update me of his assessment of the case. That's when he told me how crooked Portsmouth was law wise. Apparently, the prosecuting side kept on to Paul to try and get me to plead guilty to which Paul replied, "I don't come all the way from London to throw the towel in" and apparently he told them they had a big fight on their hands, after all it just pointed to a stitch-up on their part and there is no way Ian would want to give in. He is not a quitter, he told them. When he relayed that to me, I said "Well done, Paul, at least I have a fighting chance with you in my corner."

The case started and as his word, Paul made the police sound complete fools. At the interval I had a good chat to Johnnie who had taken a week off from working with my brother, to be in the court – he wasn't going to miss this case. I think deep down he thought I would get sent down, mind it was so nice to have him there with his support, anything would be a boost in my position. As it transpired Toni was there with her mum and dad, my brother Ken was there with his wife Maddie, my mate Tony George was there with a friend and quite a few more. They all came hoping I could go against the grain and get a not guilty. One after one the police came into the dock and one after one Paul would make them sound silly. It was like a film. There was Paul shooting all the prosecution witnesses to pieces, he drew them in and then left them high and dry wondering how Paul had made them out to be complete liars. The judge even pulled Paul up saying who do you think you are, Rumpole of the Bailey? That was when I knew Paul had done a good job and had got up the judge's nose. He was called Macrerick.

The case went on for the whole week and my friends had me to Winchester prison to stay overnight. I would be back in the morning for the verdict, that's how bad the judge was. I had been on bail all the time and all that week when the case went on and he had to detain me in custody while the jury decided the outcome. When I got to Winchester a friend of mine called Metal Micky was in reception. He said that he wondered why Macrerick had gone to Portsmouth, as he was near retirement and only did the Winchester cases, and that he was nicknamed the hanging judge as he always gave harsh sentences. Micky knew now why they sent him to Portsmouth, it was for my case. If I was guilty he was going to make an example of me. I said, "Thanks Mick, you prick, that helps me I don't think so!" Mind it was said in good humour as Micky was a good boy and would do anything for you so I knew he meant well. He gave me some perks and I prepared to settle down in the cell for the night.

I couldn't sleep as all I kept thinking about was the trial and what would the jury think of the defence Paul had put up. He had made the police look like liars, as was the case and had proved that they had called them to the police station to give me a good hiding. He proved this as he had shown the jury the custody record whereby when a police officer comes to the Bridewell, which was the name for the station cells section, they had to sign in, so Paul ordered the record book which clearly showed the time and date they came there and would you believe it was when I was incarcerated in the cell area. There was no way out of it for them. Paul had shown beyond any doubt that they were called into the nick to give me a good kicking. There was no way out for them, they were in fact out and out liars and their signatures in the book were there to prove just what went on that night and Paul had picked it up. Mind on Micky's say-so, I was still worried as before the jury was sent out the judge had near enough told them to find me guilty on that point. Paul did say if it did go against me we had a perfect appeal case on his when addressing of the jury he could not lead them into what he thought they should do.

We waited in the court area waiting for the result. After a short time we were called into the court. Paul entered with me and said "Good luck Ian, let's hope we showed the jury the truth of what had happened." I got into the box in the court and waited for the jury to appear. They took up their positions and after a while the judge asked the one nominated as the head juror if they had reached a verdict, to which he replied "Yes, your honour." I nearly fainted when the words came out of his mouth "Not guilty." The court erupted. "Hooray!" boomed out. The judge copped "Order, order!" he rang out.

As much as I disagree with it, the law is the law. Then he said to me, "You have been found not guilty, you can go." I was ecstatic, that was the best feeling I could ever have had, my was I relieved! It was all over, I was now a free man. I grabbed Paul and gave him a big hug. He was to come with us and celebrate our victory. We would have a run around on me, Toni and myself took him out. The result being he ended up plastered and I rang a friend who drove us to London where we carried on our merry piss up, celebrating the court result. That is when Paul reiterated what he had said in Portsmouth and that was where it was the most bent place police and law wise he have ever worked. That's when he told me and Toni that he was an actor as well as a barrister and that explained how he could act out his case to the jury, he was nothing short of brilliant with my case.

Well done Paul, I still owe him one till this day.

Paul said the prosecution had said to him how can a man bite a sergeant's ear off or part of it and get not guilty and he told him it was up to the jury and they decided. In fact, the police had over done it and had too many witnesses, that was where they fell over. He told the prosecution side that he would be advising me to go for compensation. After a while Paul told me they had offered £60, 000, and he had told them that would be chicken feed to what he would be asking for, after all they had nearly killed his client so a substantial amount should be paid out. The injuries I had received were nothing short of scandalous, a real liberty had been taken. I couldn't fail but agree with Paul. The pain they had inflicted on me was nothing short of diabolical, my life was on a knife edge and all down to the army of pigs who had cuffed me then proceeded to beat me senseless. Good job, as I said I was a non-smoker and a fitness fanatic so that must have been how I came through it. Richard heard the result in no time and was so pleased for me, he was a real friend so must have been worried knowing the corruption in the local police force. That is why it could have gone the other way. Even the judge was brought in especially for me so as to try and sway the jury should it be close. What they never knew was that a good friend of mine, Brinley's sister sat on the jury, and when he knew she was listening to my case he said to her that I was his friend so don't let the old bill blind you with bullshit will you. And apparently she was adamant she would not let them cloud her mind and that the truth would come out. Good girl!

Chapter 37

The wedding was arranged there and then at the dog track. A trainer of ours would be best man, Ron Jeffries. He was thrilled to be doing it, saying it was something he had always wanted to do. Another friend who used to have the antiques from me, a Tony Amos, would be our photographer. There, it was all arranged and so I was getting married again, to Toni, but first I had to ask her dad Les.

He was in his local club at Paulsgrove. We had a good drink and Toni's brother was there as well, Mark. The landlord or steward of the club was John Cripps, a lovely man. I kept the drinks flying and John gave us a lock-in, glad he would not be getting Toni in the club again on her own – she was a handful he told me. Les got drunk out of his skull but seemed happy on hearing the news, but it was nice we had his blessing. Now all we had to do was set the date and venue then all was in place. Toni's mum would, with the help of some friends, do the catering. The venue would be the Labour Club in Arundel Street – it was big enough to hold a sufficient crowd. That's it now, all arranged, the wedding was on.

We returned to our place in Southsea, rather worse for wear, but happy it was all arranged. The next night we were in the Florence to tell all our friends the news when a couple who were in there started to argue. They were clearly heavy in drink, and were just in front of us playing pool or trying to. The male started to have a go at me and tried to hit me with the cue. I stepped aside and knocked him out. As I turned around his girl started on Toni and the same result – Toni knocked her out. Why he started is beyond me. We left the bar and were met in no time by the police who took us both to the station. They charged me with hitting the girl and her chap, a stick up again. I rang Richard Scofield and he got us bailed. Strange they only charged me, still I wasn't going to say anything as there were enough witnesses so let them tell the truth of what had happened, those were my thoughts at the time. Mind, they must have been happy, they had me again after the last lot but this time I had a lot of witnesses myself and ones who would just tell the truth so it would be uphill for a conviction. Bearing in mind he came at me with a pool cue and all the bar saw it and heard the argument that was going on between the two of them, I was quite confident the truth would prevail in this instance.

Everything now was geared towards the wedding to Toni who was to be wife number four, not clever but it happened. I used to get bored rather quickly but could this be my last hitch up? Who would know. After a few weeks Toni and myself were up the dog track when who should come in but the big useless copper who had jumped on me full pelt. He was the bastard who broke my ribs the worst, he saw me and offered me a drink. I said, "You prick, fuck off out of here before I knock you out and you mate you wanker." He looked stunned but did go out of the stadium. Just as well because I knew I couldn't have held back should he and his mate have stayed for the racing. Good job, he was lucky that night, I would have given him a right seeing to and after he saw the way I had performed in the station he knew he would have got a hiding and that was exactly what he deserved.

I rang Paul up and told him we are going to sue the police and asked if Richard had been in touch. He informed me he had and that Richard's go-between was the same Jock Hunter, the ex-copper who had come to London with me in the first instance and was the one doing the paperwork. He advised me on being careful as knowing the way the police in Portsmouth were so corrupt they could well stitch me up with something again and that they wouldn't be happy till they had me behind bars and that was not what Paul wanted to see. The wedding soon came round and I went out with a crowd and my best man was under orders to make sure I got to the church on time. We had a run around Southsea drinking in most bars and clubs in the area and there were plenty of them in those days. We got out of our skulls and I ended up sleeping in the early hours on the Common. When I woke up I had no idea where I was. I even had a job adjusting my vision and my head was throbbing. As I came round there was Ron the best man running across the Common with my suit. "Quick, Ian, you got to get ready mate!" he was shouting. What was the time? I had no idea, but it must have been about five in the morning when I collapsed on the Common, so what time it was now, I had no recollection of any time whatsoever, that department in my mind was blank. Someone, but who it was seemed a blur, took me home to shower and get ready. Ron handed me the suit and helped me get dressed into it. I had to have a drink, so swallowed a few ciders in the Florence being prompted by Ron not to get too smashed. I had news for him, it was too late for that Mr Jeffries. I was just topping up, we had to get to the church and that was quite away in North End as that was one of the few churches that would marry a divorcee and the vicar used to go to the dog track so it seemed only right he should marry Toni and myself. He was Father Morgan, a gentleman who was also worldly wise, and liked a drink as well as a bet.

Murphy turned up being in Toni's friends clique and put something on my tongue. What it was I have no idea but later was told it was whizz and that it would straighten me up. And how right he was. I was now as right as rain and my tongue was tingling, it did the trick. It was then on to the church, my lift was there and took me and Ron to the church. We got there a little late but get there we did and Toni was sitting in the carriage waiting to proceed in to the church.

The ceremony was a blur but I remember saying "I do" and going out the back to sign the register. Toni's mum and dad came out back as well, they signed as witnesses. From there we made our way to the reception and prepared to greet our guests. The champagne was there being given out, it was supplied by a racing partner I had, Malcolm Bultitude. He used to have gangs of workers doing roads for his firm and the funny thing is his birthday was exactly the same day and year as mine – what a strange thing that was. Malcolm came with his little daughter so I thanked him wholeheartedly for the toast he supplied. We also had Frantic Fran, a local well known DJ, and he was backed up with an Irish folk band, violins and all. I turned round and one of Toni's friend's mates said hold your tongue out and put a dollop of whizz on my tongue again. I felt a million dollars and sat down for the wedding feast as high as a kite.

Ron gave a good speech and the night went well. All the guests got into the swing of things and the night went brilliantly. Everyone enjoyed themselves. After the night was over we made our way home to crash out, absolutely knackered.

Derek, my friend from the docks, had just lost his mother and said he was going to her house in Ireland to sort out a few things and see the house was still OK, I said that I would go with him if he liked and he said he would be glad of the company. I had been there before and knew his mum well. She had greyhounds all with the great prefix and some were very fast, mind it was a shock that she had passed even though I knew she had been very ill. The house was a three-bedroom bungalow with a separate annex which was similar to a self-contained flat, there was about four acres of land with it and the view from the top of the drive was spectacular – it over looked Dunmanus Bay West Cork Eire. Unbeknown to me at the time, I would end up with it and living in Ireland. The air was so clean and fresh, Derek and I returned to England after he had sorted out a few things there. A man called Herbie who used to court his mother used to look after the bungalow when he was over here, he was like the squire of the village, a laid back man who would really open up when he had taken a drink. A lovely natured man was Herbie.

We were talking about the bungalow all the way back to England and I said when I sorted myself out I would have a deal with Derek. How couldn't you love the bungalow, it had everything going for it and I was thinking of moving to Ireland just to get away from the old bill. Paul had told me they wouldn't leave me alone, and there were police cars going up our road at least twice a day, but it wasn't their money they were using on the fuel not to mention the wage bill. What they were doing really was what Paul had told me – that was harassing me, and that put the lid on it.

Toni was walking near Albert Road traffic lights, plus Portsmouth were playing at home, when a minibus full of the old bill going to the match stopped at the lights. Toni heard them shout out "That's Tungatt's wife!" "Which one?" she heard one say, so she walked on fast and came home then told me what was said. What a load of fuckers. Why say that? It upset Toni so much so, that she said let's get out of here and move to Ireland, just what Paul had suggested. I had to sort out the charges I was now facing two – GBHs against a man and one against a woman. Mind, that was Toni but I never marked the card of the filth, let them think it was me as then it would be kicked out after all everyone in the bar had seen the trouble that I was now getting charged with, so knew it wasn't me, bring it on I thought. A bit of trouble that I had no control over. Richard was now claimed by the prosecution service, so couldn't help me but he did get hold of a good solicitor who worked for Stokes. He was called Ken White. I went to him and told him the whole story. I also said that I was sorting out my affairs and moving to Ireland but would be returning for the court case. All he had to do was go to the first hearing, explain why I wasn't at the palimony hearing but tell the magistrate who would have to transfer it to the crown court anyway, that I would be back for the case as simple as that.

I rang Richard and told him what I had arranged with Ken White and he said he would make sure the prosecution department knew all about it, but it was Ken who had to make the point to the judge. I then invited him to my going-away party. It would be held at Tiffs club, Alf's place. I let a mate of mine for years have the guest house – George Russell. It was a ready-made business for him and his wife and he was over the moon with the chance to become a landlord. The going-away party was a great success and a lot of my close friends came along, even a lot of friends from the greyhound world were there.

I told them I would be breeding and training greyhounds in Eire and couldn't wait for the boat over there with my belongings to my dream bungalow. We would be taking two of our brood bitches with us Rosie and Blonde. They would be the start of our breeding operation in Ireland. All my friends were at the party – Fred and his wife Diane, Les and his wife Pam, Johnnie and Sheila and so many. You couldn't mention them all so it was a bit tearful really but I told them they could come for a holiday anytime they fancied it. We would have an open house for them all, mind it was still a choker after all we had been close mates for nearly all our lives, so one would be bound to get upset.

I had already made a trip over there with most of the furniture and had a few nights out in the village getting to know most of the inhabitants. They were a bit inward but enjoyed a crack when the porter was flowing and then I would go into my entertaining mode telling jokes and singing. The foundation was laid prior to us moving there full time.

We moved over completely and Fred came with a car that Toni would be using to learn to drive. With Fred there it was only right that we would go out every night and the drinks flowed. Fred was such good company he never really wanted me to move away and became tearful himself. He cuddled me one night when he was drunk and said if I wanted him for any reason and no matter what trouble I was in just ring and he would be straight over for me.

I told him I knew that Fred and the feelings were mutual. Our eyes welled up, it was emotional but a lot of it was the drink, then again Fred was such a great and loyal friend I would be missing him like crazy. The time came for Fred to return home and I took him to Cork airport for his flight back to England. We settled in quick I would say and seemed liked in the village. One day just after we had made the transition totally to Eire, we were drinking in the village. It was a small place yet there were five pubs there. We were in one called Casey's Bar and I was at the bar drinking and having a great laugh with a couple of locals. That's when Toni came up to me and asked for a punt (that was like a pound in sterling). I gave her it and carried on drinking with the company I was in then Toni came to me again and asked for another punt. I gave her it and carried on drinking. When she came again I asked her what she wanted it for and she told me she was playing darts for a punt at a time. I told her she couldn't play darts then looked at the one who was taking liberties with her. I copped with him and told him she couldn't throw darts at all, but that I would play him for five punts. The jeering started and the liberty taker had to give me a game. I took his five punts and told him not to take liberties again. A scuffle started and I was grabbed round the neck by an arm that was like a vice. It was one of two brother Donavans. They were just trying to calm the situation down but he held me so tight I couldn't move. I was let go when they knew I was not angered any more, but I was fuming. They were, or it seemed at the time, laughing at me.

I told Toni we were going as I was a bit worse for wear but they wouldn't be using me as a joker, there would be a return for me. I drove Toni home half-full with drink but I couldn't let them think I was a push-over, after all we had chosen to spend our life there and I wasn't going to be laughed at. We got home, had some food and laid down in bed to sleep and clear my head. I put the alarm on for two-hours sleep, when it went off I got up, left Toni in bed and put my tracksuit on and put my contact lenses in so no glasses. Then took the chainsaw, put it in the van and made my way to the village and Casey's Bar. When I went in with the saw they left the bar like rabbits, the Garda were called but when they knew what for they made their way through the village at one hundred miles an hour with their siren blasting. There was no way they were going to stop, but they did answer the call on paper anyway.

I came out of the empty bar and proceeded to a stop about half a mile outside the village. It was the place of the liberty taker who would be getting a call from me. I pulled up, got out and banged the door hard. There was no reply so I banged even harder. The door was opened by an old lady who informed me her son wasn't home. I knew he must be as his car was outside. I told her I would get him later and to make sure he was in and that would be the next day now.

I got into the van and made my way back towards the village. On the way I had to pass the Garda barracks or house. I thought as I was living there and the police knew me I should explain it to the Garda, his name was John. The office was locked so I walked round the back as it was his living accommodation as well and opened the back door. On stepping in I was greeted with a shriek. There on the floor with just a tiny pair of briefs on was John's wife doing her exercises. I apologised and asked her to tell John to come to my house in the morning and I would tell him what had gone on in the bar. She was still trying to cover herself up and informed me she would, I left and went home still fuming.

Chapter 38

I was soon a person all the timid ones in the area could look up to and if they had any trouble they could come to me to sort it out if at all possible. One chap was a Mick O'Sullivan. He was having trouble with a person moneywise so was prepared to pay to get it sorted out. He came to me and told me money was no object but he just wanted it sorted out. I told him it may cost as I would get a friend over from England to sort it with me. He said no worries he would pay. I got on the phone to Fred, he was coming over to take a car back for me as they wanted too much tax on it to leave it in Eire. He said as he was coming he would come tooled up to sort the trouble out for Mick and I would make sure he got a nice pay day so would kill two birds with one stone.

With Fred we went to see Mick and asked what he wanted to get done. Fred took his gun out and asked if he wanted to get it sorted quickly. I could see this scared Mick, he was shaking but tried to calm us down. I told him Fred had come over for him and that it wouldn't be cheap to forget what he wanted done. Mick said no worries, but the chap he had trouble with had heard what may come and had sorted out his differences with Mick. I told him he still had to pay as the expenses were not cheap. He never argued and gave me and Fred a wad of money for our troubles. Fred was happy and so was I. Fred stayed a few days, had a nice drink around the area which he liked, then returned home taking the car back with him. He rang me when back home and told me the customs had stopped him at the port and gone completely over the car. They had even taken the tyres off their rims thinking Fred had something hidden in them. Fred said he was so glad they never searched him as they would have found the gun on him and then he would have been in big trouble. Glad they never as it was my fault he was there and I would not have got Fred in trouble deliberately for anything.

Another one who used to ring me to meet me in the pub was a Sonny Hospice. He liked seeing me in the bar for the crack, a lovely man who was very knowledgeable about the farm and farmer's life. He was nearly 80 and worked all his life on the farm. It was when the mad cow thing was going on. I said to Sonny it was a big thing in England at the moment and had he read it in the papers. To this he replied, "I don't read papers as paper never refuses ink." What a thing to say! Yes, Sonny was a very wise man. Then he told me when he was a boy it was called the staggers and that when a cow showed signs of it they were quickly taken to the market for slaughter, so in his mind wasn't a thing to get too worried about.

Another who used to ring me for a drink was a man who had a load of tipper lorries and transport ones as well, Jimmy O'Brian. They were all painted a dark green colour. I said, "Jim, why don't you get your number painted on the side so if anyone wants a lorry for whatever they can ring the number and it will give you more trade?" He said, "Ian, I know I got a lot of money, why tell everyone else of it?" Another clever man was Jim, he wasn't educated but was worldly wise just like Sonny.

My name had got all around West Cork and I appeared to be looked up to and if there was any trouble I was there to help out if needed. One day I was in a village just over the hill from our place, a quaint place where we would often go on a Sunday night as there was an Irish group on most Sundays so it made a change to get out. Anyway, I was in the village there during a week when Toni had returned home to see her family, so me and Johnny went there for a drink. The bar we went to was in the centre and one of only three in the village, a local who used to drink with us was in there also. We were having a good crack and in the corner were two brothers, they were the O'Brian's and there were three of them in their family but only two present. They were a bit of a bullying family and used to scare a lot of the locals. One said to Johnny, "Who do you think you are, venturing out of his area? You should get back before you get lost!" I told him he was with me and I would get him home no worries there. He turned on me saying he was talking to John not me. He was aggressive in his tone so I told him to mind his own business as we were just out having a drink and laugh. The local drinking with us tried to warn me that they were trouble. I said no worries there, they would soon get put in their place. Then one of them came towards me aggressively. I never gave him time to argue, I just hit him and he went flying through the air landing in the fire hearth. He never knew what hit him, he was out cold. Then I turned to his brother and beckoned him over for much of the same. He helped his brother up and took him out of the bar. I had become another hero in that village. All they were were liberty takers, so never expected to get their comeuppance. It did go down well with the locals and also the landlord who was glad to see it. They were obviously troublemakers so it must have been coming to them, they were just unlucky I was in there that day.

Another time I was drinking in our village all day so became very heavy. I had the van with me that was parked at the side of the bar. I was so drunk when the bar closed I could no way drive home, so I got in the van and fell asleep in the front. I was awoken by a knock on the window. It was John the local Garda who had woken me up. He said, "Come on Ian, let's get you home." I told him I was too drunk to drive and that I would travel home when I'd had a sleep. He said to me, "Come on Ian, we will get you home" and told me to follow his light on the squad car. Then he said, "If they get bright stop." Hearing that creased me up and I straightened up right away it was that funny.

John the Garda came to the house the next day. I had invented a story regarding having a chainsaw when I visited the bar in the village. I was just waiting for John to ask numerous questions like, was I getting it repaired, trying to sell it, lending it to someone in the bar?

But no, John never even brought it up. All he was concerned about was me having friction with two brothers who lived just outside the village. He said they can be a handful and could jump me when I least expected it and so on. All I told John was that wouldn't worry me, I would love that as it was just like being back home in England and that it was an everyday occurrence there for me. I would love the challenge, that's when he said he wouldn't like it in his area as he just liked a quiet life. I told him it was up to the brothers if they wanted to have trouble, I was just the man to give it to them and said let's hope they see sense where we can all get on together.

John left knowing the ball was now in the brothers' court and I assumed he would go and relay this to them, basically saying I was prepared to leave it on my part, but that the outcome was now down to them. After a few days, I got a phone call from one of the brothers asking me to meet him for a drink in the village as it would be better to get on together and the drink would be a get-together just to let all around know there was no animosity between us.

One chap who got on with us was a man called Johnny Cockland. He had never left the village so all his life was spent just in his house or walking down to the village for a drink and a chat with whoever was out at the time. He was looked at as a backward lonely fool really, it wasn't that but down to his upbringing and education. Apparently, his dad was a hard taskmaster and even took him to school every day on the back of a donkey, so he was never given the chance to express himself so was on the shy side. That said he was a good friend to us and did odd jobs like some fencing and cutting the grass when needed. Mind, we had a lot of laughter with him, not intentionally but by the things he did not knowingly say or do.

One day Toni said, "John we will put you some dinner up if you like." He was over the moon at this as he had never been invited for a meal in his life. Toni said we were having spaghetti Bolognese. He replied that he had never had that, but would like to try it. He came to the house and Toni put his dinner up on a large plate. Johnny just looked at it and you could see by his expression that he never had a clue how to eat it. Toni showed him how to use the fork to twist the spaghetti round the spoon and eat it with some of the sauce. Well you would never believe how he performed. He was spinning the spaghetti round the spoon and got it everywhere, on the table, on his clothes and even on the ceiling. It was all we could do to stay straight and not burst out laughing. He was so dry, so never knew how to conduct himself in company while eating, so we left him to carry on while we went into another room and give him time on his own to finish the meal.

Another time he was banging on the door in the early hours in just his shirt, no shoes or trousers, just a shirt and it was raining hard. I opened the door and he just stood there stuttering while trying to get his words out. I told him to calm down and explain just what had happened. Apparently, he had a fire in his house and asked me to call the fire brigade as he lived in a remote area with no phone or electric. It was about a mile and a half from us and over a mountain. I gave the details to the fire brigade and told them we would meet them at Johnny's house as I would drive him there. We gave him a top coat and trousers then drove him to his house. When we got there the fire engine was not in site as they had to get the firemen in first, then come to the fire, being part-time firemen. When we got to John's the door was locked so he had locked the fire in. He obviously had not thought how the firemen could get in to attack the fire, and smoke was coming out of the doorway, even with the door locked. I opened the door with the key John gave me that was under a brick at the doorway. I could tell the fire had not really taken hold and there was mostly just smoke and not flames. I went into the house and headed up the stairs where a mattress was smouldering and you could tell that was where all the smoke was coming from, even in the dark. I thought the best thing to do was get hold of the mattress and throw it out of the house and into the garden area. This I did and also took out some blankets that were also smouldering and chucked them out as well. The smoke was now starting to clear, that is when we heard the fire engine. It was a very loud ringing of a bell so it could not be ignored, you knew what was going on. Yes, at last the fire brigade was there with us. It was so comical, the head fireman had a very large hard hat that was twice the size you would expect, which also seemed to go halfway down his back. Also, it appeared so Victorian, certainly not a modern uniform to accompany his hat. It was all I could do to stop bursting out laughing, what a joke. Then the Garda John turned up from the village and he just about put the lid on it. He shone his torch onto a pair of John's what-appeared-like Doc Martens boots. These must have been on the mattress that I had thrown out, they were melted and curled up. He said to John, "You could have been standing in them!" Well that cracked me up, I just couldn't keep it in as it came across so funny to me. Even Toni was in hysterics. Then I had to listen to the head fire officer. He gave me a rundown of how dangerous it was to enter a building that had a fire inside and that I should have waited till they had got there and not done it myself. I felt like saying by the time you got here it would have burnt to the ground, and by the time you had arrived I had it all done so stopped it getting out of hand, but he had to still lay the law down. Seemed a bit of a fool really, but the funniest was still to come.

Once they knew the fire was contained and could return to base they set off with their bell still ringing out. The noise was unbelievable, and it was the early hours so would wake everyone in its path. I suppose they had to let all know they worked now and then, as the row could not be missed it was that loud. The next week I had to go and get the charge sheet at the police station. I was bailed to appear at a later date.

Chapter 39

We were now racing our dogs that we had bred. They were good racers and all the locals wanted to know whenever we fancied one. They loved a bet. One day I was on the phone to a friend I was very friendly with, he was a Bill Shannon. I told him about a dog I was getting ready and that he should win on the Saturday at Cork. He asked to come with me and I told him to be at my place before we left and he could come with me. When we were at the track it seemed a lot of people kept their eye on me. Toni paraded the dog and I moved towards the bookmakers to place a bet, but looking at the bookies' boards no one put a price up so I couldn't get a bet on at all, and all the work I had put in on the dog could not be rewarded with a bet. I was so annoyed at that. How did the track know I got one ready? That's when I thought I must have been right with what I had assumed was going on, that being that our phone was tapped by the old bill, same as England, the pigs. Mind I used to have a game with them after that by letting them think I had a dog ready when in fact I had the dog stopped.

When at the Cork track it was nice to see the Garda move in to back one of our dogs just to get their fingers burnt, I loved it.

After a few years, Toni seemed to be in England more than Ireland. First her mum was bad then her dad and her uncle passed away out of the blue. Her head was in England through her family more than Ireland. Then her dad Les had a heart attack that was also unexpected. She was in pieces as she was so close to her parents. I left a friend to look after the dogs and came to England to be with her. On arrival I rang Richard my solicitor and friend to make sure if I handed myself in they wouldn't refuse me bail as there was a warrant out for me, due to Ken White not going to court for me and explaining that I needed an adjournment seeing as I was now in Ireland. Richard met me and went into the station with me. He explained my case and made sure I got bail. Richard Scofield was so respected even though he was now working for the prosecution. Everyone had known him when he was on the other side so his word was gospel.

He got me bail and Toni and myself stayed at her parents' house while waiting for the case to come up in the crown court. I tried to get hold of Paul Hymes again, but he was already on a case, one of murder that would tie him up for a good few weeks. Mind he did assign me one from his Chambers, a Mrs Williams. I wasn't too keen at first to have a woman to defend me, but she put me at ease and assured me she could not be swayed by the corrupt workings of the Portsmouth area criminal practices and that Paul had marked her card of how the prosecution would try and get her to help them to get a conviction. Good thing Mrs Williams was having none of it.

I had my friends from The Florence there as witnesses, Roger Harper, Ray Browning and a few others from the bar, and Toni who said it was her who hit the girl and not me as the prosecution was trying to make out. The strange thing to me was that when Mrs Williams had to cross examine the witnesses she appeared to be half-hearted in it. I naturally thought she was helping the prosecution out by going easy on the witnesses and not pushing home the points I gave her. To be honest I could not see me getting the not guilty I was expecting with her conducting the case to the jury. How wrong could one be. When she summed the trial up and brought the witnesses' statements into play she picked up on every one of the silliest points and had the jury eating out of her hands. She was nothing short of brilliant. The jury left the room but in no time at all, or so it seemed, they returned with a not guilty verdict. Well done Mrs Williams, you were out of this world, I told her and gave her a big cuddle and a kiss. She wasn't fazed by the procedure at all, lovely woman. It was then she told me she took classes with law students to teach them summing up cases, no wonder she was so good, nothing short of a wizard in that department. She then proceeded to say exactly what her colleague Paul had said, that I should be very careful in future as the system in Portsmouth wanted me which is what I already knew, but I did take it in.

Chapter 40

Back home again and I had to now think of buttoning up all our ties in Eire, but first now free from the shackles of an outstanding court case, I had to come to terms with my freedom. This victory, the feelings were great. Here I was now being able to move around without fear of a warrant being served on me. I was talking to Acker Popel, a very good friend who told me about Trevor and Buncer Cummings who were working in Germany bricklaying, and he said he would like to go out there and see them. That's when I came up with the idea of taking some small pieces of furniture and some bits of bric-a-brac like figurines, China plates and alike. I knew the Germans used to come to England regularly buying these things and taking them back there to sell on, so knew what would sell the best to the Germans. I would fill the van up with small sellables and make the trip to where the Cummings worked over there.

It was the other side of Stuttgart, so we obtained the goods and prepared to make the trip to Germany with a van full of the goods to sell. We had to meet Trevor who would show us where the shops that sold antiques were. We went there and after visiting a few, mostly shopowners who couldn't speak English, we went into a shop were a lady spoke fairly good English and was interested in buying some things to put in her shop. She said the things she was buying over there were very expensive and hard to sell on at a profit due to the price. When I showed her what me and Acker had she liked what she saw and was prepared to take all of the goods off us and that was a great result for us. The only problem was that she had to have a couple of days to raise the money from the bank, so we had to stay there till she got the money.

There was an American naval base near her place and they accepted the English with open arms and told us we were free to use the canteen on the base for our food. You would never believe the amount of food a service man could devour! The plates were very large and they were just for the steaks which were 14 ozs and upwards, so covered the plate completely. Then they used to have the spuds and vegetables in separate dishes where they could keep putting them on the plate and eating them until they were full. Where they put it all was a mystery to me, their consumption rate was unbelievable! Mind, Acker gave it a good go and showed them the English could eat well, but there was no way I could back him up in the eating game. In those days, the Afro Caribbeans never sat with the white guys, but were segregated on different sides of the canteen which had a large eating area. When you look back it would never be like that nowadays as it would be classed as racist, but perfectly acceptable then.

After a couple of days, we got our money from the shop and returned home. It was quite enjoyable meeting Trevor and Buncer as they talked good German, so could explain things if there was a language barrier. We told them we would be back as soon as and have a good drink next time then proceeded to the boat and back to England. I went out and got the next load as soon as I could and in another few days we were ready for the next trip. This time we were told we had to have a T form. This was so as we could go across borders and the customs knew what we had on board. All we had to do was go to the customs office which was on the borders and get them to look and stamp the T form as a clearance to proceed to our destination. When we got to the shop Bernice the owner was there to take in the goods and take the T form to produce to the customs, when she was ready. I never knew that we should have done this, as we came across the borders, not her, so it was really our responsibility. Still she said she could sort it out. This time I brought with us about 15 silver pocket watches. I could get them for five pounds each in those days, but Bernice said she couldn't sell them. What were we to do? Trevor told me there was a large market near Stuttgart and we should go there and see what was selling in the market. We went and I ended up setting up a small stall on a wall then started shouting out silver pocket watches for sale for the equivalent of £20 but in marks.

Trevor kept a lookout one way and Acker the other way for police, as we were in fact fly pitching and that was against the law there, but I kept on shouting out and they were soon all gone. I was so pleased as I didn't want to take them back to England and Trevor couldn't believe what he had just witnessed and said I got some front and we all had a good laugh about it.

After going for a drink and a sleep Acker and me returned home but we had to leave quite a lot of stuff there as Bernice had borrowed her limit from the bank and had to have a bit of time to raise the money still owed. The next time we arrived with some more smalls, we had to arrange to put what Bernice hadn't sold in a local auction and that would take a few days to set up as the auction date was a few days away. We were in a bar talking and asking where the cheapest place to stay was. It was then a young lady approached us and said that she had left her chap and had an apartment which would be empty the next day and that we could stay there for no charge as she was off and would have the place repossessed at a later date, but as it wouldn't cost her anything we were welcome to it. She took us there and we crashed out on the settee and floor and took the place over when she left the next day. This brought our expense bill right down, as guest houses weren't that cheap. All we could do was eat in the American base and drink in a local bar till the auction day.

It was now the Sunday and the auction would be on the Monday. The strange thing in those days was that all pubs closed on Sundays, but we were told we could have a drink in a brothel as they stayed open all the time. As we had no option we made our way to one. It was a great laugh and the views in there were a nice way to pass the time. Some of the girls were very friendly and even bought me and Acker a drink and that must have been a first in that place. We returned to the apartment and in the early morning there was a load banging on the door. I looked out of the spy hole and could see a police officer with a big black hard hat on which was flat at the back as he turned round. I wouldn't open the door for fear of getting locked up, what I thought would be for gatecrashing the apartment. After a short while the door was banged again and I looked out of the spy hole again and this time a plain-clothed policeman was there and he shouted for us to open the door or they would knock it in. On hearing this I opened the door cagily and the policeman was standing there. He was quite irate and kept on about pulling the chain in the toilet before a certain time in the morning as it would wake the people in the flats below us. Strange, but that told me it was a police state.

In the morning, me and Acker went to the auction to see what had sold. Every time they brought out a bit of our wares to sell no bidding had happened. I thought it was strange and asked the one who worked there what was going on as there wasn't one bid. This was when he told me their way of doing an auction was that the public saw it when it was held up for sale and then would make their offers after the sale had finished. A strange way to run an auction, I thought, but all we had to do now was meet the ones who had put offers in, then we would have to say yes we accept that or decline the offer. We soon got through it all and had sold quite a lot of the stuff. The money would be there for us the next day and we had to take away the unsold lots and leave them in Berenice's shop who would try and sell them for us. Then me and Acker would return home and give her a ring to see how the other articles had gone, either sold or left on display in her shop till someone wanted it. When home I rang Bernice after a week or so and she said she had sold some and that I could go over there to get some money. I decided it would be best to venture to her shop and take back any small bits that hadn't sold. Acker couldn't come with me so I went and drove there on my own. I got the small stuff and put them in my van, or as much as I could get in. I rang Toni on my way back from a phonebox and told her I would be getting the ferry from Belgium and would be home as soon as possible and I would ring when I was booked on the ferry. That would give her some idea when I would be home.

When I got to the Belgium border a custom guard approached me and told me the registration of my van had come up on the list as being in trouble for non-payment of VAT, a thing that was newish then. He told me if I went over the border he would have to take me into the offices and that would take all night to book me in for questioning, so if I turn around it would save him all the trouble and he could go home on time and not be late. I got what he was on about, thanked him and turned around to go over another border to board a ferry. It was Antwerp I chose to catch a ferry, at least I wouldn't be locked up all night and it was nothing for me to drive that extra mileage. I rang Toni and told her of my plans and told her the customs officer had in fact let me go to save him the trouble of booking me in. I told her I would ring her again when I was booked on the next available ferry but would be another day getting home. When I was booked on I rang again and to my surprise she told me the ferry I was due on the first time was the Zeebrugge ferry and she told me that it had flipped over and sank and that most of the passengers and crew had died. God, luck was with me. The customs had saved my life and I was so pleased. It was then I told Toni when she could expect me back as now I was booked on I knew about when she could expect me home.

The trip back to England was done with some relief, imagine me getting on the Zeebrugge ferry? I would certainly have been a goner. Luck had raised its welcomed head again for me. God bless that, I knew when I got home I would light a candle in church and say a prayer of thanks. Amen.

Chapter 41

Now as I say I could move freely around, I said to Toni we should go to visit the star of Bethlehem, so booked up to stay in Tel Aviv. That wasn't too far from the Star. At the airport we were searched extensively for fear of something in our case. There was an alert in place all those years ago. A lot of the passengers were moaning about the time we had to wait for clearance. I started to go at them saying it would be better to spend a few extra hours getting luggage clearance than having an explosion on the flight. After a while everyone round us agreed and decided to stay quiet and just wait to board. When we got to our hotel, you couldn't help but notice how clean the area was, you couldn't see any waste on the streets anywhere. They were doing trips to the Star and the Mount of Olives but they were a bit pricey. I told Toni we would go after we had settled in and knew how we stood regards when and where to go. We got talking to a young Irish couple who had been to the Star the day before and just got the bus. They said it saved the rip off of a tour price the hotel was selling. They then told us they were going again the next day and said we could go along if we wanted as they would then show us the way and buses to get. So we agreed and said we would meet them after breakfast in the lobby.

So the trip to the Star was now on and we would go there with the Irish couple, a great idea they had put to us. Next day we met up and caught the bus to the Wailing Wall and from there we could walk around sightseeing and then on to the Star which had a large cathedral built on top of it now so you had to enter the church and go down some stairs to the Star. But before we went to the stairs while in the cathedral, two choirs were in there visiting from countries afar and they started to sing. The sound was unbelievable and the hairs on my neck started to stand up and I felt something either entered me or left me at that time, a truly uplifting experience and a feeling that stayed with me till this day. It was magnificent. Then we went to the stairs and proceeded to the Star. It was a terrific sight and there was a star around where the birth had supposed to have taken place. The Star was made of gold and silver, we were told it was pure gold and silver and there were also precious stones placed around the Star as well. You were told no pictures could be taken, but I ignored this and took a few for my own album. Then we made our way to the Mount of Olives and you could see a large burn mark on the rock face and it gave me the impression that it looked like a mark caused by a rocket taking off. The burn was that intense so a perfectly feasible explanation in my mind anyway.

The Irish couple were great company and seemed pleased they could help us and we were very grateful for their help. It had ended up a terrific day and we had managed to do all we had come there for and seen just what you go there to see. When we got back to the hotel there was a large gathering of police and reporters, that's when we learned that a bus had been blown up right near our hotel. A shock in those days and something you wouldn't expect to see, just as well we were due to return home in a couple of days and after the shock of the explosion that couldn't come quick enough. But we had done all we wished to do and seen all we had come there to see, so a good trip in that respect.

Chapter 42

When we got back to England we had to book a trip on the ferry to Ireland and take a van with us to bring our furniture to England when we were ready, as Toni's uncle had just passed away out of the blue, and her dad Les had a sudden heart attack, so her mind and feelings were now in England and not Ireland.

I had arranged to meet a good friend of ours, a truly doggy man at Listowel races. He was Pat Murphy, a very funny man who was always good company. I had done a few jobs for some of his friends and had always been paid well. When we met up with him he was in a bar area and had a few girls round him. He was a ladies' man big time, so that was to be expected. He had glasses all along the bar and was charging them when needed with champagne and orange juice, or Bucks Fizz. Money was no object to Pat, he had shares in a dog who won the international called Rugged Mick, a really fast greyhound. We had a great time at the races with Pat and he said we were to go to Tralee after the races as he had a dog to back at the track there. That sounded good to us so we were now programmed to go greyhound racing at Tralee dog track.

It was quite a drive, but to hell with it. Pat was now on a winning streak and a bit heavy with booze so a great laugh was in store anyway. When we got to Tralee it was still early and the track wasn't open. Pat said he was now hungry so we went looking for a restaurant. There was one he knew of that had a good name so we found that, but it was still closed. That wasn't what Pat wanted so he started banging on the door harder and harder till someone opened the door. They were a bit irate and started telling Pat forcefully that they were not open till later. Pat didn't go much on that and pulled the man forward to him and whispered something in his ear. I never knew what was said but the man appeared shocked and said he would open up for us and this he duly did. We entered and Pat ordered what appeared half the complete menu and also a couple of bottles of champagne. He plied the two girls he had with him with more Bucks Fizzes and started to give a song. Pat was terrific company but had a wicked side to him as well.

After a short time in there, two large Americans came in and Pat couldn't help but take the micky out of them. I thought he was very rude at times and prepared to strike if they did take offence against Pat. I would have none of that, after all he was only having a laugh and it was the booze that made it more of a challenge to him to get the Yankees at it and God he did that alright, but in a funny way. Nothing was meant by it and knowing Pat it was only a joke to him and no malice at all. When we finished and then ready to venture into the dog track Pat went up to the two Americans and said sorry he was only joking and paid for their complete bill then added a bottle of champagne on the bill and paid that as well. He was such a genuine person and great company.

We went to the track. Pat backed the dog with all books then watched him piss up, draw his money which was a lot of money, gave out a big laugh then proceed to the exit still happy as Larry. When we got outside I told him we had to get back to our house and as the road was very tricky to drive on, where it had so many twists and turns in it, we decided to not have any more drink and just head back as best we could. I gave Pat a kiss on the cheek and told him we would be moving back to England due to Toni's dad's condition. Pat was shocked and said I can't do that. He had tears in his eyes. He said he would miss me so much then he said, and this was a thing that stuck in my mind to this day, that was if I had any trouble in England give him a ring and he would send a helicopter and there was no doubt in my mind knowing Pat that he meant every word of it.

We cuddled again and left for our car and he went with his girls and a driver to his one, shaken by my words of saying we were moving back to England but knowing he had to accept it.

Chapter 43

Once when Toni was flying home I took Johnny Cockland with me to drop her off at the airport in Cork. She had a Walkman in those days and as she was going through to board she kissed me and put her earphones in from the Walkman and went on to the aircraft. Me and John carried on and had a drink in a few pubs on our way back home. After a few days with her parents she came back to Ireland and I picked her up with John. She came through to the lounge with her earphones in again and we took her on home. After a few days John came to our house and told us he was going to England and had booked a flight to Manchester and asked if I would take him to the airport. I agreed to do this and he said to Toni that he got the ear plugs but couldn't get any with wires. We had a job to contain ourselves, he never knew anything about a Walkman so thought Toni just put ear plugs in for the flight, not knowing any different regards the wires. He was so dry as he had led a very sheltered life, so was as green as grass with life in general and would take anything for gospel. We dropped him at Cork airport and waved him goodbye. He had our phone number in case he needed it and was like a little kid bounding to the plane to board. What he would do in England we had no idea, after all he had never been anywhere other than his village. How would he cope? We hadn't a clue how he would go in England, but fair play to him he booked and arranged to go all on his own.

We got back from dropping him off and were still puzzled what made him fly to England – we would never know. After a few days had passed we got a phone call. It was the Salvation Army. They had Johnny in one of their hostels and he had no money on him and couldn't handle the hustle and bustle of a big city like Manchester. They said they would get him a flight ticket back to Cork but would I send them the money for the flight as they needed that for the needy. I agreed to send them the money and had it transferred to their account, then was told they would ring me with the flight details and would I meet him at Cork airport when he got there. I agreed to this and would wait for a call later with the details and to assure him I would be there to meet him off the flight to take him home. He was glad to see us waiting for him off his flight and we had a drink on the way back to the village. In every bar he told them he had been to England and had been in the army. It was so funny. How could I mention it was the Salvation Army? All he remembered was the 'army' bit so I left it at that and took him on home to his village.

We were now ready after a few more weeks to pack the van with our furniture and belongings. A friend came over with a separate van to take our greyhounds back home. It was quite emotional closing the door for the last time and making our way back to Rosslare for the ferry to Pembroke dock then on home to Portsmouth. Looking back, we had some great times in Ireland and bred some great greyhounds. All our litters were open class so we knew then it was the rearing that makes a good pup. It's a hard thing to do if you're also running a racing kennel, as well as a rearing one, they do not seem to go together fully.

Back in England we soon obtained a house, it was next door to Toni's sister so in the same road as her parents. This I thought was a good idea as Toni was still concerned about her dad after the scare with his heart. We built some kennels in the back garden of the house, taking up some of Toni's sister's garden as well. They were nice-sized kennels and built to the greyhound organisation's specification that was to comply with the governing body, the NGRC in those days. Our dogs were now housed properly and it was a pleasure to see them all happy. We then applied for our training licence, being as we had trained in Ireland this should be a formality. The forms were sent off and I had a couple of good references from Portsmouth Greyhound stadium. It took a while to get a reply back from the board, that said our application had been denied, no explanation, nothing. So Toni rang the NGRC as she was the applicant and asked why she had been refused. All they told her was that they do not have to give a reason. I was used to being blocked whatever I tried to do as people were scared of me, only as they never knew me and so went by hearsay, but why Toni? She hadn't even had a parking ticket.

So there we were, a kennel of dogs that we couldn't run, without a licence being granted by the powers that be. I knew then they were a piss-poor organisation. Listening to others and not giving her a chance. Still we were told by the trainers' rep Paddy Milligan to try again, which is precisely what Toni did. So we gave it a short while then sent in another application form. In the meantime, I said to her we will have to flap the dogs just to keep them on the go and reasonably fit. I used to race at Aldershot flap years ago but on examination found out that was closed. Next stop would be Glastonbury, a nice maintained flap but about one hundred miles from our house. Still if that was where we could run, so be it, the trip had to be done. We trialled a few in and was told they would be on the card as soon as he could arrange it by the racing manager. What we had to do now was phone up his number in the week and he would inform us when we would be down to run. A primitive way to go about things, but what else could we do? The dogs could at least be kept on the go so not going out of condition. Anything went at that track so we were always getting winners. The only thing was we couldn't get a decent bet on, £20 max, so we soon stopped betting at the track as I was always having a ruck with whoever, seeing how jealousy had crept in to our being at the track. In fairness, most of the people there were feeders not trainers so I could understand they couldn't see how we could turn up and keep getting winners.

One day Toni rang for our entries to the racing manager and he told her that a lot of the trainers, so called, had complained to him that we were getting too many winners. He would even, though short of dogs, have to only run our dogs about once a fortnight just to keep the moaners happy as the track had to keep running and a lot had refused to run against us. What a carry on that was! So every time we ran I seemed to get annoyed with someone, how I never punched them was a godsend. We ran there for a while, as we were restricted to the track, but instead of us ringing to ask about our runner the manager rang us instead to tell us basically when we were on. We were still visiting Portsmouth stadium as I had to watch greyhounds running no matter what. One night Toni's brother Les asked to use my car as he had to deliver something. He was a quiet and inoffensive person who would do anyone a favour, so I said yes, he could use the motor but he would have to drop us off at the dog track and pick us up again about 10.30 after the last race. We could have a good drink now, knowing I never had to drive home as Les would pick us up. Sure enough just about 10.30 Les turned up to pick us up and drop us home. I told him he could keep the car and return it in the morning. He was very grateful for that and he showed it on his face, a gleam appeared as he wanted it again the next day. We got in the car and Les said he could see we had a good drink and asked if we had had a good night. I told him yes, had a few winners so the night had cost me nothing. In fact, I had shown a profit and that is always a good outcome at any track.

Les was a good steady driver and we proceeded on home. When we got to the old Southdown bus depot at Hilsea a man in the car next to us was blowing his horn and making gestures to Les that he was a wanker. Now I was in the front seat and I can honestly say Les had done nothing untoward, yet here was a chap calling Les a wanker and using his hands to make a point of this. I told Les to cut him up and pull him over. I even pulled the steering wheel round to stop the chap driving. I jumped out fuming. What's up with you, you prick? And that's when I saw the back window was quite a way down and a big dog with a massive head was barking at me, his mouth was frothed up and he was going ballistic. Then the driver of the car said to me "Fuck off or I'll let the dog out!" This made me even more wild so I answered him saying "You won't have to let him out, I'll get in!" So I grabbed the hound by his neck and bit his nose through. There was blood squirting out all over his car. I was still shaking his head, my teeth firmly attached to the dog's nose. He was just screeching out louder and louder and in great pain by now, then I said to the pillock driving, now it's your turn. He shit himself and put his foot to the floor so fast he had a wheel spin and shot off up the road with the mad dog still screaming in the back. When I got back to my car, Les looked shocked and said, "I do not believe what I have just seen, you are mad Tungatt" and laughed then off we went for home. He still brings it up to this day. "I was there," he would tell me "Remember, but I still couldn't and would never believe what I have just seen." I told him, "Les, when my head goes I see nothing, just a grey mist that comes over me" and that I could quite easily kill someone and not realise till I calmed down. The rage just takes over me and I had to agree with him I am a mad man when I'm in that mood.

We got another refusal of our training license, yet again. No explanation given, this made me so mad, I felt like going to their offices and spanking everyone in there. Who do they think they are? Looking back they were so lucky, I found a solution to their rudeness and never resorted to violence with them as they wouldn't have liked to see me in one of my violent moods. I would have walked through their office doors, even if locked they would have been smashed in, at least they wouldn't treat anyone else like they did Toni as they would have been in no fit state to walk let alone go to work in their offices I was that mad with them.

Chapter 44

With no licence I had to do something as looking at the dogs getting older on their beds was by now doing my head in. I had to do something, so I went back calling. Working with a good mate, Ian Ward. He had a van and used to drop me off to work round the doors, it was good of him. I was doing this one day when an estate car was on the driveway of a house I had billed. I could see the tax was well out of date so I knocked on the door and started to talk about the estate on the drive. Apparently, the woman who answered the door was separated from her husband and it was his car. As the chatting went on I asked her how much she would take for her ex-husbands car, I could do with one for work so agreed a price. Later that day Ian dropped me back to the house and I paid for the car and drove it back home. The thing about it was it was a green motor and I had it in my head that green cars were unlucky and still believe that to this day, but it came cheap enough so to work with it I would go.

I had some very good days earning with the car and one day I had to take a dog to meet a man who I had sold him to at Swindon greyhound stadium. After all he was no good being left on his bed getting old when he could be on a track running what he was born to do. I drove the estate car with the dog in the back to Swindon stadium, had a deal in the car park, handed the dog over and then me and Toni made our way back home. We were on the A34 and on the south way towards Portsmouth, the fuel light came on and another engine light was showing on the dashboard. I pulled into the last petroleum station just before you get to the steep rise section of the A34. It was then the light came on again on the dash, there was clearly something amiss. The heater gauge came on as well and a knocking sound started. All I could do was hope and pray I could make the hill section and into a new service station at the top of the hill on the same side of the road we were travelling. Now the noise was getting louder and all the dashlights were on, the car started to shudder and then stopped. I was fuming, head was totally gone by now. I jumped out of the car and said to Toni get out and we will have to walk. I was in such a temper I slammed the door and we proceeded to walk up the main A34 towards the service station. We had only got a couple of hundred yards when the car blew up, just as if a bomb had gone off and the car was ablaze. How glad I was then that my temper had made me leave the car and not just sit there pondering what to do next. If we had we would have been burnt to a cinder along with the car. We carried on walking when a car pulled up. They said they had seen the car ablaze and asked if we were going to the services. I said we were but there was only room in their motor for one more passenger to squeeze in. I said Toni can go and after they pulled away I told her I would get the next lift and meet her in the services. I hadn't gone far when another car stopped explaining they had seen the car ablaze and asked if I was alright, then agreed to take me to the services.

On arrival, I thanked them no end and started to look for Toni. She went by me in the services in the back of a police car. I ducked down near a bank by the petrol pumps and watched the squad car go by with Toni still in the back. They had in fact circled the service area obviously looking for whoever Toni was with and then took her back to the burnt-out car. Toni said it was completely burnt out and the bonnet had bent up and gone through the windscreen with the force of the blast. All Toni told the police was that she was hitchhiking and got a lift from a man who she never knew who dropped her off near the services. Toni said even the tyres were burnt completely away, the fire was that intense, so another lucky escape. My temper had saved me again, but what made the experience worse was that I had just filled the car tank up to the brim, so had helped the blaze along. Lucky Ian I would say.

We were still having no joy obtaining our licence to train greyhounds from the NGRC board but now my head was working on the whys this wasn't getting passed. We were at Clonmel coursing meeting, a function we went to every year. This is when I got hold of an Irishman and explained it all to him. That was it, he started to get signatures from all the crowd at the meeting, we must have had 1,500 in the end and they would be sent to the board. Something had to be done with that amount of backing. Then I got talking to the trainers' representative Paddy Milligan. He couldn't understand their reluctance and took up our case. Then one night I was drinking with a Freddie Warrel, a lovely man and a gentleman. He was very influential in the greyhound world, and told me he would be on the case also, and would find out who had the block in for us or should I say me, as Toni had no enemies. He also said the worst one on the board then was an Archie Newhouse. He called him shit-house. That made me laugh as he knew I would see the funny side of it. He said leave it with him and he would find out who was stopping Toni getting her licence.

We got back home after the national meeting and sent all the signatures we had obtained from Ireland and were now waiting for Freddie to do his bit along with Paddy. Sure enough we got a letter from Freddie not long after he got back. He took all the board out for a meal, he used to put it down to his firm so it made no difference to him how many went along, the tax man paid. Well he said in the letter, look at your references and then a bit was Tipp-exed out and it carried on that's where your troubles lie. So I used a razor blade and scratched off the Tipp-exed bit and it said Portsmouth, so that's where your trouble lies. Then it all made sense. One of our references was Bill Frances, the manager at Portsmouth stadium. Now I knew the bastard and all I did for him I was his minder for years, how could he do that to us? I used to knock anyone out who upset him at the track and answered his call whenever in trouble anywhere in the town. Right now, I knew so much about him he would be out on his ear I would make sure of that. I'd had Toni in tears every time she had a drink saying it's my fault and I couldn't argue after all she had done nothing wrong in her life so she was correct it was me. I would soon rectify that. I got hold of the NGRC board and told them all about the pig Frances. He would put bent tickets in for everything spent on the track, inflating the price tenfold. How did I know? So I told them all, he was after all a piss-hole, doing what he did to us. Living in glasshouses came to mind. He put grossly inflated receipts in to the GRA like painting the stadium every so often, ten times the price charged. How did I know this? Because it was my relations who painted it so I knew. Then there was the time he had the old tote building painted. He told me just to get the scaffolding put round it to have access for painting, it was quoted at £10,000 – astronomical in those days – so I told him I would get it painted and they would do it off a ladder. He couldn't believe a man would go that high off a ladder and lean out to paint it. Well I got a three-large-sectional-adjustable ladder, a man to do it who I would pay in his hand, got the paint from the dockyard, two 45 gallon drums which would be mixed together and used and being ex-government paint it was very durable. The ladder was extended up the building and the man proceeded to use a roller off the ladder till the job was complete. Frances couldn't believe it how the man did it all that way up, and off a ladder it shocked him. When it was done I paid the painter out and France's gave me £500 but put a bill in for £15,000 he told me. Did I get any more? Not a cat in hells chance of that.

His best friend when he came to Portsmouth was my best friend Derek Rees. He used to know him from West Ham greyhound stadium and when Frances told him he was coming to Portsmouth, Derek picked him up at the railway station with his push bike and put him up so he knew Frances inside out. He told me when he was racing manager in the beginning of his reign at the track he used to hold the times on trials and then make a race up whereby the dog had to get a run so would always win. Derek often put the money on for him, little but often was his motto, that way the bookies wouldn't scream too much as they never tumbled what was going on. He used to do it so often in the end he would end the fiddling times in a three or five, that way he could remember the trials that were well in his favour, then another time in case he was tumbled he used to change the end trial number of the fiddled trials to say two and four. The money was soon rolling in for him and he was a naturally greedy man.

Now he was in a position to buy a flat and this he did and was sitting pretty, no one was there to question his integrity. He got with a girl and soon had a child. One day he was out with my friend Derek and got very drunk, then he started to cry. Derek asked him what was the trouble and he said how he had killed his child. "What?" Derek said. Then he explained he never meant to do it and that it was an accident. Apparently the child would not stop crying and he lost it then put a pillow over the child's face to stop the noise, but it was then the baby stopped breathing and when Derek quizzed him over this he clammed up, but Derek enlightened me on this and said he couldn't look at Frances again in the same light.

Then one day I was running along the seafront promenade and a friend of Frances' who knew me pulled up for a chat. It was a Sunday morning, and he told me how he used to take money off Frances playing golf as he was useless at it but thought he was good. Then as the conversation went on he told me how Frances told him when they were out drinking that he had a fiver on every winner and every forecast for himself, then he went on to explain how he did this. Apparently, the tote operator at the stadium, would open the tote up with his key after the result and punch in a fiver on the winner and the forecast, so he was making a fortune out of this scam. That's how one day he asked me while we were drinking in his middle bar at the track – that's the bar where he had his own optics up so all profits would be going in his pocket – to watch his back and I followed him round the back of the old tote building where his office was and it was a very dark area at night. I waited outside while he went in. He returned clutching a white bag and shuffled with me following him to the main gate where his car was parked. He opened the boot and placed the bag into it, then closed it again. We made our way to his middle bar and on the way he said there's 40,000 there, they would kill you for that. It would be ten times that amount nowadays, so what was he getting out of the track he was fiddling everything, even to the extent of having a large gin bottle up on the optics and everyone who offered him a drink, even doubles, they were in fact buying him water as that is what his bottle was filled with. And Toni's mate told her that as she worked in the bar for ages so was told before the bar was open.

When the NGRC knew this they came out to us on a Sunday morning asking us if we would sign a form saying they had looked into it and were happy with the result. Toni said no, unless we had our training licence. The head steward of the NGRC in those days was Frank Menville, an ex-trainer, so that is why Frances had him refusing our licence.

It was so corrupt, but it was as I say on a Sunday he visited our house. They must have been desperate to put a lid on what I knew. They left just after their form was sighed and we got our licence within a week and Frances had signed his resignation note, and fucking good job the pig. He came on a bike and ended his time there with a million-pound house, yet no one challenged him over his income. He must have helped the GRA going skint but ended up losing his firms pension, his firm's car and his considerable income.

Chapter 45

One day Toni and me met a man called Jerry Fox. He told us he was considered a successful businessman. He had a hotel, a factory making furniture and a Rolls Royce, a chauffeur. One day he went with his family to a posh restaurant for his birthday, yet there was Frances in there with two girls spending more than him, and he said how can a racing manager be spending more than him, it just can't happen was his conclusion! But it was happening, he was amazed. He crossed us and his life was finished, he couldn't go anywhere as I would get a phone call no matter where he was in Portsmouth and it was only what he deserved, he was scum of the highest order. I wished him dead every day, having seen Toni crying over that pig and to think I helped him no end one day he was in the club in Eastney, quite near his house and I got a call. He was there so made my way there, he saw me and ran nearly collapsing on the way. It wasn't I would hit him, it was just to keep the prick on his toes, yes that was big Frances the piss-hole who was now a little waster back in the hole he climbed out of.

One day when he went away on holiday he arranged for someone to come to the track and give me a hiding. That's what I was told afterwards. Anyway, I beat the shit out of him and when Frances came back he reported me to the governing body and I got a £500 fine. That's what Frances was like, he wanted something done, it never happened, so he got me done another way. And to think I let him still live in Portsmouth, that was a big mistake, as I could have made him squirm more than I did. To think they thought he was good for the GRA, yet he was robbing them blind. He should have been locked up for what he did and had the key thrown away. I just hope he had a terrible death for that is what he deserved and who never knew him only through the track thought he was a lovely man I can assure them everything he did was for his benefit no one else's, he was truly a selfish man of the highest order.

Chapter 46

Looking back on it I have been very lucky regards not getting seriously injured in car mishaps. Once I was driving on the old Cork road to Dublin when I saw a dangerous bend ahead sign. Being as I was nearly on top of it, it was hard to take and drive safely. The consequence was, I started to swerve and slide on the apex of the bend and totally lost control. I lost control and was now left to the elements. The car was slipping and sliding wherever the road took me; when I came to a halt I was amazed to see that I had come to a stop between two gate posts. The gate was luckily left open, if it hadn't I would have been squashed to a pulp no doubt about it, with the speed I was travelling and the impacted thrust I would have had.

After the initial shock I got out, composed myself and carried on to Dublin, none the worse for wear. Another time I was travelling back from Glastonbury after racing two dogs and travelling at 70 or 80 miles an hour, it was raining very hard while we were driving on the main road down south. I started to aquaplane, as we hit a flooded part of the road. It must have been three feet plus deep. We were just gliding in the flooded water with no control of the car, add to that it was pitch black.

Me and Toni were bricking ourselves, we suddenly shuddered to a halt and then the engine stalled and wouldn't start again due to the water getting into the engine. Toni got out letting water run into the car so I shouted to her to shut the door to stop the water flooding the car and putting the dogs in danger. It was so dark and still pissing down with rain we were well and truly stuck. I could see us getting flooded out and having to carry the greyhounds to safety. It was then a miracle happened. An old fashioned Land Rover stopped, a high wheeled one. The chap driving asked if he could help us out. I couldn't believe it, he even had a tow bar and tow rope, we connected it to our estate car and he pulled us out of the flood and continued to drag us until the engine had dried out and started to fire again. We got out of the river type area and onto a road that was now just wet. Our engine was now running as normal so I pressed my horn and the driver of the Land Rover pulled over and unhitched us. I asked him if I owed him anything and he said no he was glad he could help and we were indebted to him no end. The odds of that happening were a million to one, beings the state of the weather, pitch black condition and with no houses anywhere near us. When out of the blue a guardian angel came from nowhere to give us all the help we required to put us back with the dogs on to the road.

Home wet and dishevelled but happy now knowing all was well with us and the dogs, thank god for that.

There was a trainer at Portsmouth greyhound track that we got very friendly with John Copplestone, a lovely man and one you could really have a laugh with. He said one day that he was going on holiday, with his local pub he used in Botley, just up the road from his house. Apparently the landlord, a Ray Angel, was putting a trip together leaving the Dolphin pub by bus, travelling to the airport and booking us into a apartment block in Tenerife. The price quoted was what I would call cheap so I asked Toni if she would like to book in with the pub crowd and have a holiday with the Dolphin regulars.

She said she would love to, as we knew a lot that were going anyway, as we would often meet Copplestone in there for a drink. The day soon came and John was there with his wife Janet, a very nice couple and there were, quite a few couples in the group. Ray's friend Jack had a pub just up the road from his bar and he came with his wife as well. There was a good happy crowd of us and just the people you would want to have a holiday with.

There were laughs aplenty when we were waiting to leave and I knew the holiday would be a good experience and one we wouldn't forget in a hurry. When we arrived our apartment area was alright, it was like an hotel but opened up into apartments as you went through the entrance to the back, and the main reception. We were asked to deposit our passports in the reception where they would be kept in a safe until we booked out.

We made our way to the apartment we were given, they were all piss artists so in no time we were all changed and left for the nearest bar. There was a nice drinking strip, quite close to where we stayed so no trouble walking there. A place we found was a pub called the Golden Gloves and the landlord was always playing the old boxing fights on a screen, some real old classics and the crack in there was brilliant. It seemed like an old boxing meeting point, as a few boxing types were in there, most of the time. Apparently it was once owned by the London boxer JL Gardner and there was a book there you could sign. It was a who's who of most sports, even the greyhound Derby winners owner was in there Terry Duggan.

It was nice to look at all the ones who had filled the book in. Some big names had obviously visited the Golden Gloves bar and the landlord was a nice conversationalist who could converse on any subject especially sport. One day he told us there was a boxing ring put up as a laugh; where women could have a go at each other. We decided to venture there to have a look at any matches made. They were offering £25 for a fight between two ladies but this would be doubled if one did it topless. Me and Copplestone got Toni to have a go but she didn't seem keen at the time, but we got her wound up and relented but she still never said why she didn't want to do it.

Then when she was getting in the ring she said she was breaking her neck for a piss that was the reason, as she loved a fight in them days. Me and John Copplestone kept on at Toni to go topless and John said you got no tit anyway.

She only weighed 6-8 in them days and topless was £50, a nice sum. We gloved her up and the fight was on. The girl in the other corner hit Toni straight in the face and after she told us that was when she pissed herself a bit, but it spurred her on and she pummelled the other girl till she gave in. Toni's hand was raised and she took her gloves off then was handed £50. "very handy." she said.

We were all out having a good drink, a few of us anyway, John and Janet, had gone home as Janet wasn't feeling that good. So Jack his wife, Ray his wife and me and Toni carried on drinking. The drinks were really flowing ,it was now well into the early hours and we were all having a sing song and generally having a great time but soon it was time to head back to our apartments.

We were all merry singing and having a good loud laugh. We entered our complex when the man on the desk started to tell us all to shut up and keep quiet. He was rude with it, saying the English were pigs and saying it out loud. We carried on shouting back "you Spanish gits" and obviously making a lot of noise. While heading into the rear area where our apartments were, the guard who must have been asleep in the back, came rushing towards us waving his baton. He struck me on the shoulder and I knocked him down. He rolled over and struck Toni with his truncheon, very hard on her ankle, she went down, I was helping her up when the guard grabbed her and put a gun to her head. That was it, I hit him so hard he was knocked clean out so we went back to our rooms.

There was a lot of commotion going on and it was clearly the police, who were called in the complex. There was a holiday rep who also made her way to our apartments. About six of us, three couples in one apartment. We heard the police outside. I took a knife out of a drawer in the kitchen, saying to them all, "they will shoot us, there's no law as such here so we should take a couple with us." The women all started to scream "No we will all get locked up!". So I put the knife back and they opened the door which was now getting knocked very hard. The police and the rep were waiting. We had no idea what was getting said but the rep told us we were getting taken to the station to take our details. After a while she told us we had to report to the police in the morning, as it was now late. We were released and told we had to bring our passports with us as well in the morning. The rep said she would come with us as our interpreter and told us it would be better as we knew exactly what we would be charged with.

I couldn't sleep so was ready early after just a couple of hours shut-eye. I had a shower, dressed smart and prepared to go with the rep and Ray. I thought they would throw the book at us, as when I knocked the guard out Ray and Jack were kicking him while he was on the floor. I never agreed with that but it would make no difference as it had happened so couldn't be changed. The rep went with us to the reception so as we could get our passports out of the safe. Then we made our way to the police station. On arrival our passports were handed over and the police chief started to give us a right earfull. In a way we couldn't understand, then the guard who got knocked out came into the station. He had a really big shiner and his eye was closed with the bruise; it looked painful. I could imagine what the police chief was thinking, how we had hit one of his own kind, terrible was the only thing he could be thinking. The chief then started opening our passports. I have no idea what made me say what I said next. The chief said, "Signor, these stamps in your passport why so many?" Then with no thought at all I said, "diplomat." It just came out. He then shut the passport, looking shocked and started to make a gesture, about a pile of what ever and then said while using his hands, that what ever it was it would get to the top then get put to the bottom again. I was lost so asked the rep. She told us there were so many cases to come to court that when this one came to the top of the pile it would be put back down to the bottom so could take two years to come to court.

I had said the right thing. He knew all about the word diplomat so was under the assumption I was one. He was putting me off from charging the guard, then it was starting to make sense, it was cleared up, but then Toni chirped ,"what's a diplomat?" I told her to shut up she could have put the block in unknowingly. The chief shook my hand after seemingly being pleased, I wasn't going to make a case against the guard, according to the rep interpreter, as she understood what was said to the letter. She did tell us afterwards she had never heard anything like it before and probably would never hear the likes of it again.

When we were on holiday there we met an ex-boxer called Ricky Porter and his wife Angie. They were lovely and a real laugh. Ricky used to run a pub in Swindon called the County Ground and also had another guest house. We continued to meet up and it was a pleasure to have a conversation with him and his wife. I was later to meet up with him in England and promote a couple of boxing shows with him, and we still keep in contact to this day.

I even tried to get him in his boxing manager roll to sign my nephew who had won five British titles as an amateur and had won about a hundred bouts against only three losses.

He would have been a champion. Rocky Roy Tungatt was his name but after Ricky took him under his wing, even letting him stay in his guest in Swindon for nothing, he messed up big time and Ricky reluctantly had to let him go. I was gutted for Ricky and Roy, he would have made a fortune off that I have no doubt. He was a champion that got away.

Chapter 47

We had only just got back to England when we moved into Toni's mum and dad's house till we had sorted a permanent place to live. Her parents were great and let us house our dogs as well. We took up all the sheds in the garden but her parents never objected at all, they were great parents and couldn't do enough for anyone. They certainly were old school in that department – help and be helped was the name of the game in their time

   We hadn't been back too many days, when I bumped into an old friend of mine, Bob, whom everyone knew as Laughing Bob. This was due to the screaming laugh he would shout out at anything that would be deemed funny to him. I knew him well from the days we drank in the Black Dog public house. He was a barman in there and a good one at that. He had a computer brain when remembering all the orders he had shouted at him and they were large ones as a lot of dealers and travellers used it at weekends. How he did it was beyond me, rounds could easily come to 50 pounds a time a fortune in those days. Numerous different drinks would be ordered so his mind had to be very sharp and he was backed up by the landlord, my very good mate Brian Bromley. Yes they were a great team and the bar ran like clockwork, round after round would be sorted with great efficiency.

   Bob brought it up about our trip we had while holidaying with him and his girlfriend Chris, he booked me and Toni on a holiday to Spain Chris had sorted out a deal that was unbelievable, for just £108 per person we would get a coach to Lydd airport which was in Ashford Kent, then fly to Spain and board another coach to our hotel in Blanes Spain for this ten-day holiday. I thought this was a price no one could turn down, Chris certainly knew how to bag a bargain. The time soon came round and Brian had a stand in barman while we were away but just how he could handle the rounds as Bob could, it would be a sight for sore eyes. He couldn't slot into the shock of handling such large rounds with Bob's precision. Just like that all I knew was it would be a shock to get such large orders thrown at you with no pre warning given. Bob never worried, he was off on holiday and his laughs were getting louder by the day, deafening at some points but funny with it.

   When we boarded the coach there were a couple on there already with two children, the younger one about five never stopped crying and the whole of the coach was complaining about the child. I thought for the minimal price we were paying you couldn't complain but I also understood the other passengers, you couldn't close your eyes for one minute without the baby's crying penetrating your brain. So a sleep was out of the question but I did try and calm some of the passengers down saying this was such a cheap holiday you couldn't justly argue about a baby crying. The parents of the child did apologise saying they couldn't stop the child from crying but never went into detail. Mind then I had taken enough and said you shouldn't have brought him if he was uncontrollable. All the passengers were tired so needed a bit of shut-eye. It had now become a big hindrance to any thoughts of some shut-eye, even when we had a stop to go to the toilet the child wouldn't stop crying. It was mind blowing really.

When we arrived at our hotel we were all knackered with no sleep or rest, it had taken its toll. All the passengers were still going on about the noisy child whose crying was relentless. I said to Bob and Chris we should go to our rooms get showered and changed then meet in the bar, as if we laid down, I was sure we would oversleep and waste part of our ten days. A day would have past before the fun could begin and the holiday got into full swing. I never wanted that to happen. We were in the bar area, changed and ready to hit the town. There were quite a few in there and I ordered the drinks when Bob and Chris came in. The television was on but it was what appeared to be a German channel. I said to a few of the guests if they wanted that on as most in the hotel were English. They said they wanted another channel on but pointing to a very large German said he won't let them turn it over. So I went to the set and turned the channel over. The German shouted out something in German and proceeded to turn the telly back over. I couldn't understand that as there were only a couple of Germans in the bar area and it was nearly a completely English establishment, guest wise. So all I did was get up and turn it back over to the English channel. The German went off his head and started shouting abuse at me or that's the impression I got as I didn't understand German. I never mucked about and punched him, sending him sprawling to the floor. He was shaking like a large jelly and out cold when the twitching stopped. I just took it in my stride and approached the screen to make sure the side was left on an English one for all the other guests in the hotel. What a shock I got when all the bar area started clapping me. Apparently the German had been a big bully for the past week he was in the hotel and had scared most of the English guests to such an extent that no one would challenge him. All they could do was watch the German channel that the big bully wanted on and not any English ones. He was a sizeable bully who used his size and mouth to frighten all the English in the hotel, but that never came into my plans. He had to come second to me no matter how hard he thought he was. He wouldn't worry me and was welcome to try his luck with me whenever he fancied having a go. There would only be one result and it wouldn't be in his favour.

Now everyone in the bar was offering to buy us a drink and you could see the relief on their faces. He must have been terrorising them all, the big useless prick. I stood near him waiting for him to rise in case he fancied having a go back but he got up still wobbly and made his way out of the bar area and up to his room. That was the last I saw of him as he moved out after that. Everyone was so happy now we had come to their aid and Bob loved it – his laugh got louder and louder but in a nice way, bless him.

From that point on and for the rest of our holiday there was always a drink put in for us and we enjoyed the company of all the guests, they were so grateful. The child from the coach was still crying after two days and everyone was complaining about it. Then the next day it became very quiet and not a sign of the crying. It was then on enquiring that I learned he had gone to the hospital with his parents, he must have been bad which would account for the continued crying. When the parents came back to the hotel I asked if we were going to have a peaceful night now with no crying. I was flabbergasted to learn that he had passed away and they told me they knew he would pass but wished to give him his last holiday as there was no cure for his illness.

I never went into it in depth but felt terrible, I kept having a go at the parents not knowing the full extent of the boy's sickness. All I felt was disgust at myself not asking why the child wouldn't stop crying. Obviously it was a thing the parents had no control over and I was gutted for getting on to the parents, God rest his soul.

We carried on with the holiday and I must say Bob and Chris were great company and we had a laugh everyday. A bar we used in the town was run by an ex-professional footballer. He used to play for a top Spanish club and put something on everyday for us, either to eat or entertainment. He was a scream, when he had a drink, and spoke perfect English. Even jokes he told us were funny; he said he would get a lot from the holidaymakers and he remembered most of them. I added to his repertoire by adding a lot of my jokes to his and in those days I could go on for ages telling joke after joke yes we had some great nights and days in his bar.

The landlord asked me what I did for a living. I told him buying and selling, mostly gold and silver but also antiques and said it was very interesting going round the doors nor knowing what I would get. It was just like having a bet, not assured of a deal or not, so the gamble was there a wage or nothing at the end of a day's work. He understood and agreed not knowing was the buzz, it could be very good or next to nothing and he liked the idea. Then he mentioned that he had lent someone some money on some old coins but he had not come back to pay him, so he still had the coins. I said I would look at them and he went to get them. They turned out to be five pesetas bits, about the size of a old crown piece and Victorian age wise 1870s onwards. I knew by the weight of them they would be about an ounce each. In those days they would only be pure silver. So I knew if I bought them I had to earn, going by how much an ounce of silver was. The landlord had no idea how much they would come to. to. So I bid him in the balls and he agreed to sell me them, after all he would sooner have money he knew he could use than just some old silver coins. I don't think he even knew they were silver. I convinced him they were just base metal and of no value, that was my job and I knew it inside out and when I paid him I knew that me and Toni had a free holiday lovely jubberly.

One night we had a really good laugh and Bob was in full cry with his loud laughing; plus the drinks were flowing and I could see Toni, being so young in those day, had began to get quite drunk. Then she started to argue about nothing really, just became argumentative. As the drink took hold of her I dragged her out of the bar and said we were going home. Bob knew I had copped and him with Chris left saying they would see us back at the hotel. As I was dragging her to the hotel as she had no idea where she was, two brave minded chaps came up to me trying to tell me how to treat a girl. Not knowing she was drunk and not capable of getting back to the hotel they got heavy handed with me but I told them to piss off or get hurt.

They thought that was funny, being there was two of them, and proceeded to try and get Toni off me. I had enough of this and whacked the two of them one after the other, sending them to the floor and asleep. I then carried on getting Toni back to the hotel. If she had not been drunk, on seeing me dispatch those two louts with the minimum of fuss, she may not have been with me till this day. At least when we did get married she knew the bad side of me as well as the good one. We got back to the hotel with no more upsets and continued to have another week of fun and laughter, plus sun and beach weather before the time came to return home and all this was brought back to me when I saw Bob again after all those years when returning to Portsmouth.

Chapter 48

About 37 years ago my then boxing manager Jack Bishop mentioned to me he had a connection in Thailand who asked for him to send a boxer there. He would receive a free holiday for six weeks, free flights, free hotel, keep full board, and expenses as required, also a reasonable purse, the temptation was there and he gave me the phone number and venue. The place was Pattaya. It was a boxing bar called Roses Bar. I was really thinking of taking up Jack's offer when my leg had the hiccup with the fight I had at the stables. Bugger, what an offer, I thought. Holiday paid for in full and a sizeable purse. Anyway, I had kept the address of the place in Thailand and the man's phone number, not intentionally thinking of going now as my agility had taken a big knock, but the place I had looked up appeared to be a nice place to visit should I fancy a historic and memorable holiday destination.

Well now I was with Toni I thought it would be nice to see Thailand after all, and what I had read about the place seemed to be a good holiday place untapped. I went into Bantry West Cork near our village where we lived in Ireland and asked if they could book us two flights to Thailand. We were to go via Amsterdam so the travel time would be over 24 hours, a long time to be travelling, but the pictures I had looked at made the place look inviting, so yes two tickets please and me and Toni would be going to Thailand. Would we like it? I couldn't say but let's give it a go, after all we only had to go the once, if we never liked the country who would know until we did visit the place. It was a puzzling scenario but one I was prepared to give a go. The travel company was Kuoni. They were specialists in exotic venues and had given us a lot of brochures on Thailand to look at to prepare us for the holiday. Toni packed our cases and put in jumpers and coats for the night time, then off to the airport and ready for our flight. We changed at Dublin from Cork first, then on to Amsterdam. Change again for our flight to Bangkok. The whole trip took about 26 hours with the stops on the way. I have trouble sleeping so to say I was knackered when we arrived would be an understatement. When we landed in Bangkok they unloaded our luggage onto the tarmac where we all had to determine our cases and carry them to the buses provided to take us to the airport terminal. What I did notice was the very large dragonfly-like creatures that were flying around making you duck to avoid and not let them fly into you, not a nice thing to experience. Toni was very jumpy every time one flew near her, but they were avoided and we boarded the coach then got taken into the terminal entrance with our cases to get processed and have our passports stamped, letting us proceed to the transport that would be taking us to Pattaya.

My! Wasn't it hot! Even though it was dark the heat just hit you, a very dry heat. And to think Toni had packed all our coats and jumpers thinking it would be cold at night so they would be needed, yet here we were in the evening and sweating with the humidity plus heat. After about a three-hour drive we arrived at our hotel in Pattaya, the Orchid Lodge right on Beach Road, a lovely hotel. Then when we were taken to our room, on the bed was an orchid. A nice gesture and a welcome note with it.

Our holiday was terrific and it was fun every night and beach every day. Mind, in those days the beach was not very nice but we used it to meet people and enjoy the sun so the outlook of the beach itself never came into it. Every day we seemed to meet someone new and the laughter was second to none. All day we would stay on the beach with the sandwiches the hotel prepared for us and the drinks could be obtained everywhere along the beach stretch. Every night we would walk along the beach and to the bar area of Pattaya as it was just getting built up then so the actual drinking bars were limited in those days, not as now there are thousands of them all over Pattaya, so you're spoiled for choice. We would be returning every year after that first time, but with fewer coats and jumpers as there is no way they would be required.

We soon got in with some regulars over the years and there used to be a load of right villains who used to meet up for regular get-togethers. A lot of them could not go back to England as they were on the trot, and had been living in Pattaya for years. It was great, the stories that would come out were unbelievable but the banter was really good, and Sunday was the main get-together day so you would look forward to that.

One day years ago, Toni and I were looking at some paintings that an artist had displayed in his shop window and blow me there was one of a great friend who I mentioned as the one who held the wager on the fight I had where my leg became injured – Harry Madgwick! How could that happen 6,000 miles from Portsmouth? Yet there we were staring at a painting of the great Harry. You couldn't have planned that. I asked the painter who had got the painting done, was Harry here? No that couldn't happen, could it? He pointed to a chap sitting at a bar off soi eight. He was alone so we made our way to meet him. His name was Robert Graham, he used to be the landlord of a pub in Portsea called the Invincible, near The Hard. I had seen him before in Portsmouth, but never really knew him that well. We soon were in conversation and he was a very nice chap to talk to and it came out that Toni's dad used to go in his bar in Portsea as he worked close to it in the dockyard. Also being a keen cricket follower, Bob knew Toni's dad well, even been to a few games with him. That made our chat even more intense, talking about Toni's dad Les and he agreed he was a terrific person with no harm in him at all and one who was very well read about cricket so knew all there was to know about the game, so did Bob here when we talked about it. He told us he used to just go to Bangkok but decided on advice from one of his customers in the bar to venture down to Pattaya to make a change and to see the better night life where he wouldn't be taken on so much. Plus in those days you could meet some very interesting people with no hustle, just a relaxing holiday in Pattaya and the villains there were very good company plus the crack was brilliant.

We had been going there a good few years when we walked passed a bar called U2 Bar. I asked Toni if we should go in and have a drink, her words to me were "No, he is shifty looking." we walked passed and had a drink further up. All the bars in that area were now a good laugh and the girls were nice and sociable, always having a game with the customers. Most of the men you would meet there would have what I called the Pattaya head, whereby they would be talking to you yet seem not to take any notice, instead keeping their eyes on the girls. Some get smitten by them and end up one way skint, they even say, trying to convince you, my girl isn't a bar girl they work in a restaurant or something like that. Why, I have no idea, they are what you would call working girls. Mind, you can feel sorry for them as there is no social money there, they have to earn their own money, so when someone runs them down me and Toni get so annoyed, after all they are only earning a living so don't deserve to be treated badly.

We got talking to a chap who seemed caught up in the system so kept forking out money, when I talked to him about it he explained he had won a nice amount of money and was separated from his wife and so was out to enjoy himself. He also told me he was going to meet his two daughters at the airport as he had paid for their airfares and was going to give them a good holiday. Next time we saw him he was with the daughters – they were stunners. Anyway, he told me they were only there for a week so he was making sure they had a good holiday and would show them all the sites he could. Then he told me he had booked a trip to the elephant park and they would see some places on the way back to Pattaya. I never saw him again so wondered what had become of him and his girls. Then the shock came. Apparently, his girls had laid on the ground as is common practice to let the elephants walk over them for luck. Well one was stood on so crushed and when the elephant was spooked he swung his head around, spearing the other sister with his tusk through her body. She was rushed to hospital, but a few days later it filtered back to us she had also died. The man we had been conversing with must have been in total shock. There he was giving his two beautiful daughters a holiday of a lifetime and loses them both, that must haunt him till this day if he is still alive himself. How is that for luck, God bless them all.

I used to visit the boxing ring there most nights. It was Roses boxing bar as I said. Well we got to know a lot of people in the bar, being there nearly every night. Soon the topic came to boxing as we were watching, so I went over to the boss of the bar and said I would challenge their best. The only thing I stipulated was that it was purely boxing, not as was their art, kickboxing, seeing as I had the injury to my leg so couldn't afford to get it injured again. But I loved a fight so it was the most feasible thing to do, I would fight anyone they selected for me. Apparently the one who ran the place matched me with the Pattaya champion. I had no worries about that as long as there was no kicking. This was agreed and the match was on. The manager was going to make sure he earned well out of it so he had big boards written out, 'English versus Thai big fight is on this Saturday'.

I was game and knew my potential. I couldn't see a little Thai would have enough power to worry me. I only had trainers with me so had to box in them. The Saturday came around so quick, or so it seemed, all I could do to get a bit fit was to swim and shadow box, but I felt fit enough to do myself justice, so got ready and went to Roses Bar.

The place was packed to the gunnels, even the Thais had turned up to see their champ. I got in the ring and they gave me a couple of seconds. Mind Toni was in my corner as well so I felt well at home. My opponent entered and the crowd went wild, both sides were going ecstatic and the cries were at fever pitch. I went to the centre of the ring and was given my instructions by the ref, but I never understood a word of what he was saying. The thing that did stick in my mind though was how small my opponent was. I knew then I couldn't hit him with my full force as he could get killed if I truly connected. Anyway, the bell sounded and the fight was on. He was so small compared to me and when we were in a clinch he seemed so much weaker than me so I just danced around for a while, pulling my punch every time he was open for a good whack. The crowd were going wild, yet I never had a sweat, he was so easy to hit. Mind he was probably brilliant with his kicks and he couldn't use them so that must have been a big hindrance to him.

I played around with him for a couple of rounds then when I returned to my corner a Thai was there who could speak good English. He said I should hit him hard. He could obviously see I was pulling my punches. I told him he would get hurt if I caught him, but this never deterred him. He told me not to worry about that, I should just hit him hard. Well I needed no better invitation and went out for the next round with the idea of just clipping him. It was then I walked into a straight right hand, it landed square on my nose which was now giving a trickle of blood. That was it, I retaliated and gave him an almighty whack with my left hand. The poor Thai went six foot into the air and travelled right across the ring. He bounced on the ring floor and was out cold, there appeared to be no life in him. I thought he was dead. I leaned down to Toni and said the calaboose for me, he's dead.

The crowd, not realising what had happened, was going mad and chants of "England, England!" were ringing out. All this did was make me more apprehensive. I would be put in prison having killed a Thai, that was one thing I was sure of or in my mind I was. His corner started throwing cold water over him and another one was banging his head on the floor. What was he doing? It wasn't sinking in, there was a dead man lying there, yet they were hitting his head on the floor and still throwing cold water over him, even putting ice in a bucket to make it a lot colder. I was still shocked. Then he just jumped up, started shaking his head about and approached me, lifting my hand up and calling out "Champion! Champion!" The crowd were still going wild and I could now join in the celebrations, knowing my opponent was up and appearing well, yet the way he went over this was a godsend. I had thought he was dead and every indication he had given out one had to presume that would be the outcome. How glad I was to see him jump up and then raise my hand, I could only praise him.

For a while after that we were recognised as champs. We even used to get the police pulling up and giving us a lift back to our hotel, no matter what part of Pattaya we were in. We were now visiting two or three times every year and got to know all the locals, it was great. I was getting respect everywhere there and the holidays were great. We even got to know the owner of the U2 bar, the one Toni said looked shifty. He was Bob, a great fellow, and one we are still great friends with to this day. There was a hotel a lot of the villains used to drink and hang out in called the Prince Hotel. The owner was said to be the King's illegitimate son, but how true that was is debatable, but that was what a lot of the English villains were led to believe. One day I was drinking with the boss as he was called and he took to me straight away. He could drink red label whisky like no other Thai I have ever seen. One day we were drinking and he said, "Come Ian, we drink in my bars." He had the front of his hotel done out in separate bars and had them all let out to different people, many of them English. There were about 15 to 20 bars along the complete front of his hotel. He said again, "Come with me, we drink in my bars, no money for you." I took that to mean I wouldn't be having to pay. We started at the first bar and he would just sign a chit that the bar produced to him before we moved to the next one. His minder came with us, but never drank and he was packing that was a bit of concern, but you couldn't help but like the boss. He had a charm about him and everyone, no matter where we went, would show out to him as if he was royalty, so who was I to challenge their signs.

We got to the last bar of his complex when he started to row with the girl behind the bar and even hit her on the head. What that was for, I had no idea, but the boss was with me so he was right in my eyes. Then three English who were drinking at the bar started. The boss's minder started to withdraw his gun, there was no need for that so I knocked one out, pushed the minder and the boss behind me and knocked the other one out, as he was about to hit the boss with a metal table. Then I moved towards the third one and he ran away. The boss was laughing, he thought it was so funny, then the two I had knocked out got up and disappeared into the line of bars in front of us, never to be seen again. We returned to the boss's bar and continued to drink. The boss kept laughing, he had enjoyed the night and the amount of drink he had consumed made him want his bed. He said, "Good night" and proceeded up to his apartment on the top floor of the hotel. The lift went directly to his floor, then you saw all his staff rejoice as he had left the hotel to go to bed, so wouldn't go on at anyone, they were all beaming. From that day, the boss loved me and even used to let me stay at his hotel free whenever I was in Pattaya. They were the good days. It's not the same there now, it has become over populated and I would say for the worse.

The boss had a fallout with another big noise in Pattaya and apparently had been threatened. You had to see what happened to believe it. Me and the boss were sitting at a table in his Prince Hotel and one table was surrounded with the army, another with the special boat crew, another with like the Thai SAS and the navy were all around another table, all there to protect the boss. Apparently, it was over money and the boss said to me if he had the money it was costing for all the protection, he could pay any money they said he owed, then he laughed and said crazy, but with the Thais it's losing face, that is the biggest thing for any Thai – it's frowned upon to lose face, so that is why the boss was surrounded with the protection. He mustn't lose face.

Another time we were in the boss's bar when a man sitting there named Bow, who was a hitman, got annoyed and started pistol whipping someone sitting at a table. Bow was a lovely man who had an upmarket restaurant and bar in Bangkok which he got from his ill-gotten gains. The police came as it was reported and took him into the station. I said to the boss you got to get Bow out and he said not today, if I leave him overnight it will be cheaper to get him out. That was the humour of the boss, a really funny man, and sure enough the next day Bow was out and back with us.

I was getting a gold watch repaired once and the man who was doing it started to muck me around, putting it off and not telling me when I could collect it. I told the boss as the watch was bought for me by Toni and he had a word with Bow. The next day I was in the boss's bar and he was waving his arm around. I never saw it at first, so he waved his hand. That's when I looked – he had my watch on his wrist. Bow had gone and got it back for me. There was no mucking about with Bow, he was the business. Later on they told me he went to do a hit job and got shot. I was shocked as he was a nice man and one you could easily get on with and to think he got killed just up the road from Pattaya, not where you would expect near his restaurant in Bangkok.

One day I was walking back to the boss's bar three parts to the wind when a motorbike went past me at about 60 miles an hour, flying down the small road. It would certainly have killed me if it had hit me, it was that close. I had to do something about it. A person I got on well with was Micky's bar, the Elephant and Castle was his pub and it was just around the corner from soi eight. I used to go in there in the early hours when on my own. Mick was a very funny bloke and nice to have a chat with in the early hours. He could make you cry laughing. Well one day I told him how close I came to getting killed and told him I would get the boss to get sleeping policemen put in the road to save anyone getting killed. They used to speed down that road it was crazy. Mick bet me I wouldn't ever get them put in. It was so nice after a few years of working on the boss I got them put in, it made the road so much safer at night. It was a hard task and Mick knew that, but he underestimated my influence. The thing is the roads with sleeping policemen in those days were known as police roads and usually owned by the police who even to this day run the toilets. In the groups of bars who have shared toilets this is a very profitable earner for them. I got the humps put in but it took a few years, but the boss told me it had to have three very prominent business people in the soi to sign to get it done. I couldn't wait to tell Mick I had arranged to have the humps put in and they were now there. He knew as he was on the corner of the square but still couldn't believe I could get it done and that was down to the boss.

Chapter 49

We were again in Thailand. Toni and I talked about having a baby. I could understand her wanting one, after all she had to put up with my past children why shouldn't she have one of her own? I couldn't give a good answer why she shouldn't. She said when we returned to England she would go to the doctor and check if all was well with her and if it was possible for us to have our own child. She went and saw the doctor and he said it was probably a good idea and should stop her painful period pains. There was a big worry the doctor pointed out that being she had been on the pill for so many years it would conceivably take a while to fall pregnant. How wrong could he be, this was Christmas time she left the pill alone and in the January while in Ireland she fell pregnant it was that quick. That's when the doctor explained I must be very fertile and that this could be attributed to me not smoking plus being a fit person. He said all this was a big plus. Toni never cared how it had come about but was glad we were now to have our own child, she was so happy at that. When she was carrying, she carried on helping me with racing our greyhounds and came to every track with me even when she was becoming rather large in the belly.

Once we were training a dog at Romford it collided with the inside fence and had a bad cut to his side. The fur on his coat had got caught up on the inside gate post and was stripped back off his body. This looked terrible but Toni ran to the dog's aid and caused a reaction to her pregnancy to such an extent it appeared to start the birth off at least four weeks earlier than it should have. Romford, fair play to them, took the dog over with their vet who took it to the surgery which was quite close by. There he would stay until he had recovered enough to return to our kennels. The good thing was that Romford picked the bill up and that was substantial, so not a price the owner would have wanted to pay. After all, the gate on the track had a protruding bolt that had caught our dog on his side ripping his coat off and also his own natural coat, stripping it right back so it had to be reattached to him. Then there was the convalescing, so over a week he would have to stay at the surgery. All me and Toni could do was return home and await a phone call to pick him up. On our way home Toni was clearly in pain from her pregnancy, the shock and strain of restraining the dog had taken its toll on her. We had to go straight to the doctors when back home and make sure all was well with her carrying. I was a bit worried as the pain she was in couldn't be normal and in fact would induce her early or that was my worry.

Sure enough, Toni's pain grew worse so much so that me and Toni's mum took her straight to St Mary's Hospital where she was admitted. I stayed waiting with Noreen, Toni's mum, and the noise Toni was making was unbelievable. She called the poor doctor every word that she knew – not very pleasant so hear, but that was Toni. The doctor told us we could go home and await a phone call as she wouldn't be having the baby that night and he assured us as he had all the qualifications and had delivered loads of babies. So leaving Toni there, her mum and I went on home. I dropped mum off and went on home, I hadn't been in that long when the phone went – it was the hospital. Toni had a little girl so what did the so-called expert doctor know? Clearly Toni knew more than him. So I proceeded to the hospital with Toni's mum to see the little one. The little girl was placed into an incubator. Being six weeks early there was a big risk for her safety and to be honest I didn't think she would pull through, as she also had jaundice, a blood disorder and one that would be very hard for a small and weak baby to overcome being she was only the weight of two bags of sugar or four pounds. That's why I couldn't see her pulling through. This stopped me getting too involved with the little mite, after all it was hard enough to have this going on in your mind, let alone thinking of the possible outcome and the way it would hit Toni – she would be devastated of that I was sure.

I kept going to the hospital and they wouldn't let Toni and the baby come out. Apparently she would put on a fraction then lose it during the night and until the baby kept a bit of weight gained during the day on during the night she would not be allowed home. All I could do was drink and wait, Toni was hysterical at times, asking why the baby would not keep the few ounces she gained during the day on at night. This is when I had a brainwave. Was she like me, I thought, and would sweat at any rise in temperature?

So I told Toni to leave a window open slightly at night. This was to my mind a way to keep the temperature down in her room so as not to sweat off any ounces gained. And after about four weeks in hospital my hunch had worked and her weight gain stayed on, so now the staff nurse, after having a meeting with her managers, had decided she and Toni could go home.

I picked her up and I couldn't believe how small the baby was. She had to have dollies' clothes on as that was all that would fit her, she was so small bless her. Mind, it was still hard to see the little one coming through all this turmoil unscathed, but come through she did. The fight that she had in her was so strong and it was a bit of a miracle she lived through it all. Toni told me she wanted to call the baby girl Sidney but the nurses had got so attached to her during her four-week stay in the newborn baby unit at St Mary's hospital decided she was too good looking to be called that and called her Rosie. So that is how her name was decided upon and now it shows what a good choice it was.

Chapter 50

When Rosie was home you could see she had a protruding belly button. We were told it had to stay as it was until she reached the age of between 18 months and two years old. It was very unsightly and stuck out about one and a half to two inches from her belly. Still there appeared to be no pain for her so wait we had to do. When she reached 18 months a letter came telling us she would be required to go to Southampton Hospital on a Saturday morning at eight o'clock. This meant an early start from Portsmouth, but one that had to be done. When we got to the hospital department we were assigned to, it was strange, after all it was a Saturday morning early. Staff wise there should have been a limited crew present, but on the point of staff there seemed a flood of them on duty, crazy but there was at the time an argument going on with the unions with regards staffing, so getting in on the act they had extra staff at weekends. This would benefit staff and porters from the extra overtime agreement, a liberty really so many booked in when they weren't needed. Still nothing to do with us, just glad Rosie was now here to get her belly button sorted, after all it had been an unsightly burden on her for the past 18 months.

We took her to a room assigned to us and Toni left leaving me and Rosie. I had to sign a form agreeing to the operation before they could continue. The thing that stuck in my mind about it all was that I had to hold my daughter's hand and they asked me to hold the mask on her face until she passed out. While I watched her go to sleep all different things flashed before me, was I in fact letting them kill my daughter? It was very emotional and I couldn't get my head around it as me and Rosie had become so close and that didn't help the situation. There were a couple of tears in my eyes. All I could do now was wait in the adjoining room for Rosie to come out of the operating theatre. It wasn't that long, but seemed ages. I found myself pacing up and down. There were staff everywhere trying to reassure me it would be all OK in the end and Rosie would benefit from the operation, after all she couldn't go on with a belly button sticking out it was so unsightly and I knew this deep down, but it wasn't a nice experience I was going through. It was like having a fight with one's hands tied.

All was well with the operation and she came out and placed in a separate room to come back round in time. Toni came in now and waited with me while our little girl came back to us and adjusted to life again. It was so nice to see her open her eyes and appear to be none the worse for the experience. Toni and I were so grateful with the outcome. After a short while they told us we could go home with Rosie as the operation had been a success, but that we had to not take her out of the house for a few days so she could recuperate. We hadn't been home that long when Rosie needed some food. I sat on the bed and fed her. After a short while Rosie seemed to go a reddish colour and became hot to the touch, then she retched and brought up all her food I gave her, then started crying. What was wrong with her? I couldn't fathom out what it was, but it did seem that the hospital had discharged her too quickly so anything could have gone wrong. Rosie was now burning up and getting redder. I asked Toni to get me a thermometer I kept downstairs and on applying it to Rosie the reading was high. Seeing as Rosie was still under the newborn baby unit, I rang them and asked them for advice on Rosie's condition. I told them I had taken her temperature and it appeared high. They said get her to the hospital straight away, there was no time to wait for an ambulance, it would or could be crucial. Panic had now set in and I rushed her to the car to make a dash to St Mary's hospital where she was born. I had totally lost it by now and put my foot down while heading to the hospital, which was about five miles from our house. I remember flashing my lights and blasting my horn, this was a life or death situation I was in. According to the hospital there was no time to lose, she had to get there for treatment. I remember getting to a roundabout at Cosham and there was a queue going into it. I did the unthinkable and went round it the opposite way, still blasting my horn and flashing my headlights. I just had to get to the hospital, then when I got to Kingston Crescent there was a line of cars in front of me but I just went on the pavement on the other side of the road, fully expecting to get pulled up by the police, after all I was going passed the police station on the pavement and on the wrong side of the road. I had to get pulled up, but I had the perfect excuse and also the emergency number of the newborn baby unit on me so they could check the details I would give them.

Surprisingly I never got stopped and got to the hospital in record time. Rosie was, like me, born lucky or I was hoping that was the case, but as yet I was still not sure of the outcome. I carried her into the hospital running and Toni was in hot pursuit, we were frantic. They decided the best thing to do was give her antibiotics and she was put on a drip straight away. She looked terrible and was getting redder.

Toni had to go home to look after the dogs and I stayed with Rosie, my decision would end up a lifesaver. I stayed the night and shared a bed with Rosie. She was just lying there appearing to be just a weak dolly. I couldn't believe this was happening, all I could do was cuddle her and pray she came through the night, but was very tired and couldn't eat as all she was doing was bringing any food I had fed her up. The doctors came to see me in the morning and told me Rosie had septicaemia. This must have come from the operation she had in Southampton. Could they have let her out too early? That was my first thought, but all we had to do now was wait and see if the treatment would get Rosie better. After a few hours and numerous drips her condition seemed to stay as it was. When we first came in there was no improvement at all, then there was another shock. Two nuns from the Catholic Church came in to bless Rosie. God was this it? Was my little baby going to die? No it couldn't happen, after all we had made it to the hospital and that was the main thing. To get on top of her complications was now the priority. Were the nuns there to give her the last rites? No, I wouldn't have that, she had to come back and be OK. Again, this is where the luck came in again. I stayed another night with her and was woken up all through the night so a nurse could give her regular injections of antibiotics, then about five in the morning the nurse came in again, but this time I told her not to give her the injection. She told me that the doctor said she must have them. I said she is my child and I do not want her to have any more of them. Then I explained that every time she had the injection she had a reaction and started to sweat and go scarlet, there was clearly something that was happening to her when she had the injection, it was clearly her body rejecting this. I only knew this as I had stayed with her all the time, so saw the reactions first hand and where I had animals all my life I knew when a body was rejecting a medication and this was the case in this instance. With this a doctor came to see me to ask about my concerns with regards the injections. He asked me if I was allergic to penicillin. I said no, then he asked if Toni was allergic to the same and again I told him no. He said well the odds of Rosie being allergic to penicillin was near enough nil, but he would try another antibiotic but one that didn't include penicillin. I agreed to this so the doctor prescribed this. The result was amazing. After just one injection she seemed to improve, all I could think of was how lucky it was I stayed with Rosie so saw first hand what was happening to her after each injection. This would indicate that she could have died and nearly did if I wasn't present at all times and stayed the night with her. This ended up a couple of nights and thank God I decided to stay with her. Yes, thank God for the outcome. She was now getting better rapidly, the antibiotics were working and we were soon able to go home.

On the way I decided to call into my mother's house. I had not told her of Rosie's trouble, not wanting to worry her too much, then a shock came out. Mum told me I was allergic to penicillin as a young boy – this was a thing I was not aware of so perhaps I should had told Mum in the beginning and she would have told me all this. Still we came through it and I was so glad Rosie responded to treatment, this was a godsend.

Chapter 51

When Rosie seemed back to normal, we got a call from the boss in Thailand asking how Rosie was and he seemed relieved with the answer I gave him regards her now being back to normal. He said we deserved a break so he invited us to stay in his hotel in Pattaya as then we could recuperate and get over the trauma we had been through. Toni said she would stay with Rosie to be on the safe side as the shock of nearly losing our little baby was too much for her. Where as I had been there in hospital with Rosie and that was a good job seeing as I saw first hand that she had a reaction to penicillin and so I was able to point this out to the doctors who were treating her, which may have contributed to saving her life as they changed the medication she was on and the outcome was clear to see in no time. God bless them all and thanks to the wonderful NHS, our daughter was now back to normal and full of beans.

Toni said I should go and see the boss as he was so good to keep in touch while worrying about Rosie, a brilliant gesture. I booked a flight and was soon on my way to Bangkok. The boss told me he would have me met at the airport so I let him know my flight number and ETA and he said no worries, he would be there in his hotel to meet me when I reached Pattaya. The biggest shock was to come. When I came through the arrival gate there was a police officer standing there holding up a sign. It had my name on it. My first reaction was what had I done wrong? But that was soon dismissed when he told me the boss had sent him to collect me and take me to his hotel. Talk about VIP treatment, this was the bee's knees! I felt a big noise, for once a police officer was here to be at my beck and call. He pushed my trolley with luggage on to the car park where his squad car was parked. He placed the luggage in his boot and drove to Pattaya where the boss met me at his hotel. He got my luggage taken to a room and we sat down for a drink and a catch up on all that had gone on while I was away. He was shocked when he heard the full story of Rosie and how she had the last rites given to her while in hospital, she came so close to passing away. This makes you appreciate life and the boss made sure the drinks kept flowing as he came to terms with what I had let him know about Rosie's near miss, thank God.

With the jet lag and tiredness now hitting me I soon knew I had a good drink and the boss could see that so he summoned a member of staff to bring my room key and show me to my room. I told him I would see him in the morning and went, showered then crashed out for the night. Next day I rang Toni and told her I had arrived OK and the boss had sent her his best. A friend we have there had a bar called U2 bar, I used to take stuff over for him that he couldn't get there or not the same as here. Mainly he loved English cheese and I would take a lot of that out for him. Tinned beans over there were like snot in a tin, not the same as our real baked beans. Bob the friend and bar owner loved whatever I brought out for him, the trouble being the weight I was allowed in my luggage. I had to watch that but as a rule I could take enough to help Bob out and satisfy his needs and I could see he was very grateful, no matter whatever it was.

I had been there a few nights and had meet a few young English lads in Bob's. They were new to Pattaya and asked me if I could show them around the area. This I agreed to, mind they were very noisy with the drink in them, but no worries I would look out for them. I took them to a few bars to show them around. One we went to was a busy bar which had a load of girls working there. They seemed in their element and became louder and louder with the drink in them and appeared to be showing off to the girls. One of the boys started to get out of order, thinking the girls had to fancy him over the other lads. I tried to tell him you're only a walking bank to them and there were no barriers regards money, longs as you are not rude to them, but he started shouting at the girls and becoming a bit of a pest. Then a tall minder came over to him trying to calm him down. There was a language barrier there and the young lad was the worse for wear so started being annoying to all the other lads. The bouncer who had had enough by now, drew his gun out of its holster then pointed it to the asshole who was still shouting out abuse. I moved in at that point and got hold of the lad, forcefully telling him to be careful because the guard would shoot him and think nothing of it so behave himself. The way I did this and the power I used to hold on to him made him pull back and listen. I even shocked him to make my point, that's when it appeared to sink in so when he had calmed down I took all the lads back to Bob's bar, then explained to him what had happened. He said no worries, he would educate them on the way to behave in Pattaya, so I went to meet the boss at his hotel and bars as he was brilliant company.

The boss told me the next day, come night he was having a party and get-together of a lot of Mafia and crime bosses and that he would love me to meet them. I agreed, saying I would definitely be there and that I did.

It started about three in the afternoon and the boss kept introducing me to top Mafia men and crime bosses. There was also a very big Thailand Buddhist monk there, all their minders, and there were a lot of them, were packing. Funny this would normally be scary, but for some strange reason I had no fear at all in me and the boss was very well respected by them all. There were plenty of eats and drinks there for all and there was mild music being played in the background, a lot of it classical which seemed to go down well with the mobs that were there. Most of them were clearly educated and spoke very good English. I had good conversations with a lot of them and it was very rewarding and educational. One was a big Columbian Mafia boss, the boss told me, and he took a shine to me and had deep chats with me. He wanted to know all about England and the party who were in power at the time. His minder never took his eyes off us, he was a very big crime boss so had to be watched at all times. Apparently, he told me there were many who would like to see him in a grave and his minder had to be present with him at all times and he also had others watching his back as well. Yet here I was with such a clearly powerful man but still fully at ease in his company and found him a very bright and educated man.

He asked me if there was a bar we could slip away to and have a good chat as there was something he wanted to tell me, then we would return to the party. I told him yes, a bar I used just over the road it was called the Sailor Bar. He said let's go and we made our way there, followed by his main minder with a few others following just behind. This made me feel important, but in a nice way. We entered the bar with his main man standing just off us, and his other men just hung around outside the bar area but within clear sight of whatever could go on so on call straight away should they be needed. He ordered the drinks, or his minder did, and they were brought to us at the table we sat at. This is when he told me something that would shock even me. He asked me if I bet on football. I said, no not really, then he asked if any of my friends backed football. To this I replied, yes some did. He told me it was his gang who would run the football this year in England, it was their turn, the Columbian Mafia turn. This was a thing that took its time to sink in, but then he went on to explain how all the main Mafia gangs of the world had different chances to run the show and that it was worth billions to the mobs. He then went on to say, tell your friends to back draws as that way bookies win, the mob wins, everyone wins. Not many people back a draw to that way we get a clear book. This I found shocking, but it was feasible as I watched a lot of football and when you think most of the players could put a ball on a dustbin lid, yet when you watched you could see they would put the ball ten or 20 feet wide or over the top it was beginning to make sense now. They were clearly under orders to play for a draw. He then went on to say you can get it wrong at times, like if there was a deflection or a rebound etc., but their aim was to go for a draw, that is why now when you know this you see the games that are fixed by the misses that happen. I'm just waiting for a whistle-blower to blow this all out in the open, that has got to happen. Anyway, our conversation went on for about an hour then it was time to return to the party and the boss.

When we got back, the boss asked me if it was all OK and I told him how interesting the Columbian was and that I could listen to him for hours. When the party ended early evening a lot of the minders and hit men you could tell were relieved, at least they would not be out in the open when away from the hotel so could relax. Well that was the impression I got.

The boss was clearly connected and I saw that first hand. Once when Toni and I were there he met us straight off the plane, he was on the actual gangway waving at us as we stepped off the plane. He led us straight through the passport control in the VIP area, we went through and had a VIP stamp placed in our passports. When we were through, the boss said how stupid we were at the carousel and waiting for our luggage, that's when he saw no matter how quick you get through you still have to wait for your luggage. We never had ours with us and had to wait for it to be placed on the carousel so we could collect it and proceed to the arrival area and out to the car park to get the car the boss had turned up in.

He took us then to a hotel where we showered and changed to meet him and he would take us out in Bangkok. Everywhere we went, everyone would be bowing to the boss, he was well respected no matter where it was we visited. One day he took us to the prince's palace, apparently when someone has been successful in life and business he would like to build a temple for his village people where he was born. First he has to get permission from the crown, but as the King was in hospital at the time it had to be up to the crown prince, and apparently it was the boss who would take the person wanting the temple to meet the prince and as we were with him we would go along as well. When we got to the gate of the palace house the guard who knew the boss was welcoming him with open arms. He was apparently the prince's number one bodyguard, you could see he was as fit as a flea with not an ounce of fat on him and he was the one who led us to the prince's house which was also his place of work.

The boss went in with the one who wanted to build a temple and we followed close behind. We sat down and were given special tea for luck and the boss went to meet the prince. On his return the number one bodyguard talked to the boss and he said he had arranged to meet him later that night and we left. That evening the boss came to our hotel and picked us up to go out to eat. He was with his wife Sa. She was a lovely person and one we knew well from the hotel in Pattaya, which she seemed to run for the boss. After we had eaten, the boss took us to a nice area with some upmarket bars, this is when the bodyguard met us and we had a nice drink and a laugh with him. Mind, he never drank, only had a soft drink.

As the night wore on, dancing started in the bar we were in and the bodyguard danced with Toni. He was a good laugh and spoke some English, enough to understand him and enjoy his company. The next day we returned to Pattaya and the boss's hotel to finish off our holiday and I told U2 Bob all about our experiences with the boss in Bangkok and the good time he had given us.

We have had so many good times in Pattaya it seems like our second home and we have so many people there it does seem like that now. One trip while drinking around the bars a chap who was on his own started to talk to us. We had seen him a few times in the past but now he seemed to want to talk more and he was soon letting his heart out to Toni, saying he was all mixed up. Apparently, he didn't know if he was straight or gay and Toni gave him the time of day and he loved it. She said if you do not know by now then something is wrong as it's in your genes, but he was going on and on about his mixed-up life and that his mother had told him he would have to find that out on his own, it's not a thing someone can tell you about so the ball was in his court so to speak. His name was George and seemed a nice enough fella, but Toni said you will have to try and find out one night and that it was up to him. He thanked her for listening, brought us a drink and went off into the night.

The next night we were sitting at a bar and George came and sat down next to us. He said, "Good news I went with a lady-boy last night and loved it! I must be gay!" were his words. We had to contain ourselves for fear of laughing out loud. Apparently, he had even rang his mum at four in the morning British time to tell her. He seemed so happy and brought us both a drink again. Toni was claimed now and he couldn't stop talking to her about it all and going on just like a woman. There was a group playing in the bar and they beckoned me to the stage to sing, so I left Toni talking to George, relieved really as I couldn't get my head around George ringing his mum at that time of the morning waking her up to tell her what he should have already known. Anyway, after a few songs a tall chap I watched walk passed the bar and I heard Toni shout "Leave him alone!" and apparently he had smacked George round the face and started calling him names. I had no idea what was going on but stopped singing and went to Toni and George's aid, when I got to the chap I saw he was about six five tall and had a Kung-Fu top on. I always believe anyone that displays something like that are normally bullshitters, but you never knew. Anyway, I squared up to him and hit him so hard he wobbled and all but went over. I moved into put him away when all the motorbike taxi boys whom I knew well jumped on me and said, "No pup pa!" and held me so as to stop me from knocking him over and out. The chap straightened himself up and walked up the road, I knew I wouldn't be seeing him again as we were flying home in the morning and couldn't afford to get in trouble in case we missed our flight by being in the monkey house.

I had no worries as the boss would come to my aid and get me out, but it still wasn't something I wanted to go through so we stayed by the pool till we were about to get our taxi to the airport which would be picking us up after we had showered and packed our clothes, a thing that Toni has always done to perfection. So it amounted to me finishing my swim, showering and off in the taxi to the airport.

Chapter 52

We hadn't been home that long when Toni's dad had a stroke [and] recovered from it. Apparently, he had a bleed on the brain as well [and] came out of it, he collapsed on the Monday and passed away on the Th[ursday]. The worst of it was that I had booked my flight back to Thailand so would [miss] the funeral and that wasn't a thing I was proud of, but Toni knew I was so up[set] as she was, so never minded me not being there, after all he was such a love[d] and respected man it was best I wasn't there.

After Toni's dad had passed I felt obligated to look after her mum and as she used to look after Rosie when we went on holiday I thought it was only right that we all went on holiday together, knowing mum would love Thailand and this is a thing we did for many years. All the four of us would go and mum was soon looking forward to her next holiday as a family. After each one she couldn't wait to go again.

One trip while we were there with mum and Rosie they went to have a massage and we waited in a bar just opposite as a good massage usually took about one hour. After they came back Noreen, Toni's mum, said while massaging her the masseur said you have problem there and pointed to her stomach area. She said, "No there's no problem." "Well you go to doctor when you home and ask for tests, I think you have problem." Noreen just laughed and took it as a joke, but I did tell her it's probably nothing but go to your doctor when you're home and tell him what she told you just to be on the safe side and she agreed with me. Yes, she would go to the doctor when we got home.

When we got back Noreen got an appointment with her doctor who sent her straight for a full blood test. It came back not good – she had pancreatic cancer, but they would try and treat it and maybe we had caught it early enough, said her doctor. She had regular tests and chemotherapy, but after about two years she had to come to terms with there being no cure and sadly she passed away, bless her. We miss her so much even till this day.

We started going back to Thailand and still do, it's 30 odd years now and the good thing is you know what you are getting there and we always have a brilliant relaxing holiday.

About four years ago Toni and I were there and a good friend who is in the book already and used to go to school with me called Don Price, he met us for a drink and we had a run around visiting numerous bars. Then he suggested we went to a little bar he used now and then as you could have a sing-song and often you would get singers up who would give a song for the crack. So we made our way to the bar and it appeared to be a nice quiet bar, but yes there was entertainment on and we sat down ready to finish the evening off and have a drink.

...re long and I remembered the bar, me and Toni had
...w times and enjoyed ourselves. There was a Thai
... and no disrespect to her but she sounded terrible and
...ut fair play to her she tried and it takes some bottle to get
...a go. We were trying to not laugh at the singer and that was
...was very bad. We looked at each other, me and Don, and decided
...t there, enjoy our drinks and take it all in, not taking the piss at all.
...when an English fellow came over to us and started to row with us. I
...to calm him down and told him it's having a go, that's the main thing,
...how well she sings. But the more I tried to calm him, the more he went
... He was calling us all different names and the more I tried to calm the
...ituation the more he became brave, thinking we were frightened of him. I
gave him as long as I could and Don warned him to go away before it was too
late. He thought we were just scared of him, yet that was far from the truth
and I knew that, but he wouldn't shut up. Then I just got up, hit him so hard
he went a few feet in the air and travelled right across the bar landing on his
back. I headed towards him, but Don said, "He's had enough, Ian, leave it."
This I did and looking at the chap who had now gingerly risen to his feet, I
could see his nose was broken and spread across his face at right angles and
was bleeding badly. We left and went to another bar and I was trying to forget
the incident, after all we didn't need it after a good night out and up till then
a good holiday. You always seem to get a dickhead, but when you look at it
mine and Don's age is well into our pension age so he was clearly a bully and
that is one thing I will not tolerate, after all you can't help getting old, it's a
thing we all hope we reach.

Chapter 53

I was drinking in Portchester. Toni was a bit worried, knowing how fiery I could get and may find myself getting wound up by a young fool, who didn't know me. I could retaliate and get locked up and that was the last thing she wanted. To this she would have no worries, as my reputation had proceeded me and I was welcomed in the local club and bar in the precinct. In the club, I found out that my good friend Brian Bromley was a barman and he knew me well from his time as landlord in the Black Dog. This at the time was my local and as stated before a real rough bar to drink in.

Brian knew everyone in the area, so soon marked their cards with regards my ability to look after myself. In all the years I have used the club, I have only got really annoyed three times and that is brilliant for me. It might be my age calming me down or that's what I put it down to.

I often drink with Martin who is a Porchie boy through and through, but good company. I found myself often drinking with Martin in all-day sessions, but we have never had a cross word with each other so I put him in a good class drinking wise and one that can handle his drink.

I also drink now and then with Ray Rogers. He is an ex- Portsea boy and as such was a natural person to get on with, and me and Toni would often go out with him and his wife Tracy. Also Dan and Pam Adams we used to meet up with and venture into town having a run around. They are lovely people and Ray would let me use his own private gym which he has built in his back garden. It's fitted out perfect for keeping fit and has a few punch bags, so I could go on them.

One day we were sitting in the Red Lion Bar in the precinct having a quiet drink when Martin's nephew came in full of drink. He is Keiron, normally a good boy who often drank with me in the Red. This day he was heavy and kept on about me hitting him, saying he could take a punch. I tried to laugh it off as he was only a youngster, but no he wanted me to punch him to show me how he could take a punch; again I tried to ignore him but he was having none of that and went on and on about it.

I was trying to have a good chat with Ray and he was keeping on, well that was it. I wound up and punched him up the body. He went flying over two tables and was out on the floor holding his stomach. He was also gasping for breath. He got up after a time and went into the toilet.

I thought I had hurt him badly. I apologised to Ray and followed him in there to see just how hurt he was. It transpired that the punch had made him sick and he was doing it down the toilet. I warned him he should know when to shut up, drink or no drink, and this I think sunk in.

When I returned to Ray he said he had asked for it, and there was nothing I could do about it. Even so I should have ignored him, which I did until my fur went up. I just had to lash out. Mind it was only one punch that did the damage and I never followed up, as I felt sorry for him. He now enjoys a drink with me and says he has learnt when to shut up,

I should be calm at my age but I still get fools upsetting me. Across the road from us a couple moved in. They were selling drugs and everyone knew this in the road. People were at their door at all hours. Apparently, they were giving evidence against a gang from Oldham and were in the protection plan, as their statements were crucial for a conviction of the gang. You would have thought they would have kept a low profile, but not on your nelly. The girl Becky was a pest who never stopped when on the gear. She would come home and argue with her chap till all the road knew about it; a proper pest apparently. They had been moved to a couple of different addresses in Portsmouth by the police, as they were important to a case they had put together. One day she came home quite late and I heard a loud crash and I looked out of the window and saw her running away from our house. She had put a rock through my van window, the cow.

I was out of our house like a shot, following Toni who was first to approach her. We had our slippers on and to grip was a job, but we had to make the best of it. Toni slipped and fell between two posts but while she was trying to get up the little pygmy jumped on her back and was banging her head from side to side on the posts. Toni shouted, "Let me get up and I'll beat you!" But no, the little Becky wouldn't get off her back. So Toni had no way of getting away to have a fight with her and she knew that. So no way was she letting her up. I moved in and picked her up like a rag doll and she started screaming "Help! Help!" the little pig. Then her chap appeared and sprang at me while I was on the grass verge. As I tried to punch him I found myself slipping on the grass in my slippers. We got in a clinch, more for me to stand up, but again no grip. Then he began biting my cheek. Right you want to play that game, I thought and proceeded to bite the end of his nose off, I spat it away from us so the earwigs could eat it. Then every time he looked at his face he would remember he upset me, the prick.

226

The police were called and I was taken to the hospital to sort out the ripped piece of my cheek which was hanging down and bleeding quite badly. All I could say to the police was that I have had worse, learning to eat with a knife and fork, which brought a few laughs.

I never stayed too long in the hospital as I became restless thinking what if they would go across the road and start on Toni when she was there on her own. No I had to get back, so discharged myself and made my way back home just to be on the safe side. I rang Toni to tell her I was on my way back and if the outside was clear could she come and pick me up, and told her the way I would be walking. She soon appeared and told me the troublemakers had gone in the ambulance to the hospital. You can't trust grasses and even worse are junkie grasses. They don't even know themselves what they are going to say, nothing short of scumbags.

The next day I saw her pull up outside her house. I wanted to know when she was going to pay for my smashed van window, so approached her. When she saw me and screamed out "Police! Police! Help! Help! He's going to kill me!" Yes, a proper pig she was. After a while I went to their house and knocked on the door, but nobody came, so I began banging it harder and harder. Then I shouted I would break the door down. Then after a short while the door was opened by a woman who told me they were up the hospital and all she was doing was looking after the children. I told her to tell them I would be back later. After a short while two police officers came and knocked on our door.

We opened it and they came in. They told us the couple had made a complaint against us and they had come to follow it up. Toni had dark glasses on so I told her to take them off and show the officers the state of her face. They couldn't believe the state of her, both her eyes were black where she was banged from one post that she got stuck between and the other. They did look bad. They felt sorry for her, but had to follow up a complaint. After the interview, they asked us to go to the police station the next day, then this would be followed up.

We went to the main police station the next day and after they took our statements we were bailed to appear back at the station in a month's time, what a waste of money that was. Just shows you how they look after grasses, we should have been the ones to bring charges, not the other way round. After all, we were in our house after coming back from racing the dogs when we got our van window smashed in, yet here we were getting seemingly charged with an offence that was not our fault. Pigs again protecting their own grasses. Terrible when you think about it.

I couldn't put up with them living across the road from us knowing I would cop if I came home with a drink in me and they were to jeer at me. I would jump their fence and smack them both, clearly not a good thing to do. And it would result in me getting locked up again. I had to divulge a plan to get them moved out to be on the safe side.

I knew who to approach. I had done some charity work for the then Lord Mayor Jim Patey. He would be the one to sort it out, or at least that was my plan. I went to his house and I was met by his wife Joy. I explained it to her from the beginning to the end of the trouble. She seemed quite sympathetic towards me then said she would have a word with Jim when he got home.

I thanked her and found her a lovely woman to converse with and was sure she would explain it all to her husband so he knew the story in full when I went back to see him. She told me when the best time to find him at home and I would return then. When I met Jim he told me Joy had told him all about the trouble I had and that he had some of his councillors trying to sort out a place to put the troublemakers. Apparently, they had been in a couple of other places in the city and had started there as well so they were well-known to the council who would try and move them on as soon as they could. Within a couple of weeks Jim had arranged for them to be moved out and the plan was completed. We wouldn't have to see them again. Mind they were returning to sell their drugs for a while afterwards, but that soon faded out also.

Chapter 54

I had got to know a friend of Martin in Porchester. He was Steven Sindall, a lovely laid back fellow and a good laugh. He used the Red Lion so I would see him most days. I had a good drink with him one day in the Red and was about to leave. I rang Toni to pick me up and she was on her way. I stood outside the Red waiting for my lift home, when I saw Steve in an argument with a chap. They had told me he used to be in the services, I knew him by sight. Anyway, it was getting heated and as Steve had bad legs and very bad gout, I thought I should try and defuse the situation. I told the chap to shut up as Steve was an invalid and couldn't defend himself. He came back at me asking what it had to do with me. I told him he was a friend so get off and leave it. This he wasn't going to do. Then I saw Toni pull up at the adjoining bus stop. I thought, what am I arguing for and whacked him, knocking him out. My Rosie was in the car with Toni and came over to get me away, but just then I saw the chap having a fit. I had to get out of there. I looked up and saw a large camera beaming straight at us, my first thought was that I had done it now. Steve told me he had a friend who worked in the office where all the films went to and that he could get the film destroyed. I said that's handy, Steve, get working on that then mate.

He then went on to say he had never seen anyone hit that hard. I said it's a gift. Steve then got into Toni's car. As we were about to pull away I saw an ambulance with its lights and siren going pulling up behind us. Again, I was so lucky. Mind he was only a youngster compared with me but that wouldn't have mattered to the old bill when they heard my name mentioned. But I got away and heard no more about it. I'm really trying to keep out of trouble with regard to the fighting game, but seem to attract it like flies around honey. Just last year I got a phone call from a friend called Bibby who asked if I knew an Andy Handcock. I said yes, he was a local thief and a pest to all in the area. He went on to say that his van had been broken into and all his tools had been taken, thousands of pounds worth in value and that the person seen was in fact Andy, and that if he could get them back he wouldn't get the police involved.

I said leave it to me and I would go and see him. This I did, well I went to his house where he was living with his mum just around the corner from us. I knocked on the door and his mum answered and invited me in. I told her what had happened but not to worry as if the ones who owned the tools got them back there would be no police involved. I even left my phone number and told her to give it to Andy and asked him to ring me, then left it at that waiting for him to call me. It was about half past six at night and we had just settled down with a can of cider when the door was nearly knocked off its hinges. There was a lot of shouting and I got up, rushed to the door and opened it. There was Andy spurting his mouth off saying something like I never burgled your house and blurting on and on clearly on drugs and God knows whatever else.

I said if you did my house I would cut his throat, but he was now in a right state and saying get out, here I'll give you what for, the prick he's only just 40 and going on at me, the pillock. He thought I was too old to have a go at him, bullying really. What a shock he was in for. Bear in mind he is about six four to six six, a bean pole with it, and there's me nearly 70, the prick. Anyway, let's have it then, but hang on I never gave it a second thought. I only had them stupid slippers on again so no grip or floppy feet! He rushed at me and was like an octopus, all arms and legs, he was all over me so all I could do was bring uppercuts into play. Every time I hit him he shook, he was trying the same on me, but with not the same force. I kept bringing my uppercuts up and he was rocked with every one. I was now enjoying it and he had a battle on his hands. I knew that I got a few nicks on my face as well but then I managed to get a couple of strides away from him then lined up his body. I hit him one side of his ribs then the other side. He was winded and moved away then started running up the road shouting abuse while he was going.

That's it, I was not letting him get away with coming round my house so I went indoors, changed into my trainers and took a hammer, put it in the back of my trousers and ran as best I could round to his mum's house. On getting there he went into the side entrance and bolted the side gate behind him, stopping me getting him. I was jumping, trying to hit him on the head with the hammer. All I managed to do was break the broom in bits. With that, a person I know who lived in our road, Dave, came running there with Toni. He never mucked about and just kicked the door in, not a thing I could do with my new knee now fitted, but he was a diamond. Apparently, Dave had a row with him before and wanted to give him a hiding but his mother didn't want to see it. So I said, come on Dave he's had it now mate, and we made our way back home. He was due in court the next day, but apparently as I was told he had broken ribs so never went. They tell me he got lifted for not appearing in court and ended up being sentenced to three and a half years, that's the best place for him as he is an habitual thief so they should throw the key away,

I got barred from the Red Lion a couple of years ago and never went back. It has helped me as I was in there most days and I would be drinking up to 20 pints some days, not clever, but that was what I was up to drinking, killing myself really. Claire the landlady knows they are selling drugs in there and it is a drug den so not a nice place to be seen in. The quicker the brewery straightens the place up by getting rid of them, the quicker the trade will return.

She is no good, as a friend of mine who has known her for years, so very well, has marked my card about her. The bar will go down and down till she has gone, and they're still in and out of the toilets taking the stuff. That's enough to put anyone off from going in there, the smell is pungent.

We are now putting more time into running our dogs and getting a lot more winners as you only get out what you put in and now it's a great deal as time shows that. Funny how times change, they say different people can have a fight in Portsmouth but good job I'm not still young, they would have been taken to the cleaners.

A lot of people look at me and have no idea how hard I was. Fighting then was a pleasure, not gangs and knives as it is today. The only thing that worries me is that I may use a weapon or gun if anyone tries it on with me at my age, as there is still no fear in me, but let's hope I soon grow old gracefully but this is only a thing I will know when it happens.

As most Pompey people know Toni and myself have spent most of our lives around greyhounds and we have had some great greyhounds over the years. Our prefix on the dogs we own and breed is *Silverview*. We arrived at that name when we lived in Ireland. A friend of ours brought a greyhound over to us, one that was running in England and even broke a couple of track records. His name was Skelligs Silver. We were going to stand him at stud with us. My friend Peter Richardson, transporter then, drove over with him to our place in Ireland. We had a long drive up to our bungalow and while sitting outside enjoying a drink we heard a van coming up the drive. It was Peter bring Silver to us. Peter shouted out, "Stay where you are! I'll open the gate!" He came walking in with Silver.

At the time we were going through all the possible names we could use as a permanent prefix. That's when it hit me. Here was Silver being walked up the drive and I was looking at the view, and in the back ground was Dunmanus Bay. Fantastic site and it all came together, that was our prefix. Silver the dog and a fantastic view, bingo – *Silverview* that was it. Our perfect prefix and we have used the name ever since. Then all our dogs from that day began with it.

A few years ago we came in touch with a Irishman called Dan Collins. He had a great brood bitch and we had a dog or two out of her past litters. These were all very good dogs and he had let us know he had bred the bitch again. Her name was Owens Rover and she had all the litter sold bar three bitches. Anyway we were sitting in our front room having a few ciders and Toni said how about me buying you a pup out of Owens Rover as a present. I said it was up to her as the mother had a brilliant record of throwing fast pups so there was a good chance it would be a fast pup, but we never dreamed of what would follow.

Toni rang Dan and asked about buying a pup. As the conversation went on Dan talked her into buying a pair of pups and he would rear them on and they agreed a price plus the cost per week to rear. They agreed and the deal had been completed. We had two brilliantly bred bitch pups. Toni put the phone down and we carried on talking about what we had hoped we had just got hold of and sat there drinking more cider. After a few more drinks had gone down I said to Toni there's only one more bitch left of Rover's litter. So we agreed she should ring Dan up again and sort a price out for the last pup. This she did and brought the last one with the proviso that he reared the three on; so would get the cost of that paid to him every month. After about 11 months of paying for the cost of rearing, Dan gave us a ring. He had carried the bitches to the schooling track and as they went so well, an on-looker asked if he could buy them and he relayed this to us saying we could name our price and have a healthy profit on our outlay. I said to Toni they sound good then and to refuse the offer. Let's see what we have got when they come over. Then we arranged for the transporter to deliver the three bitches to us. When we had them, we galloped them up our field a few times and you could see they were all special.

Now it would be off to the schooling track, that is a private one you could visit to try your pups out with no shouting or anyone putting babies off. They flew round and you could tell they were in fact special pups. We named them Silverview Pinky, Perky and Spot. Terry and Barry O'Sulivan whose private track we had started them off at, said how great they thought they were and that they were as we had thought very special pups, and that we should take them to a registered track now as they would be very fast pups. Terry said to me as much as I like to take your money, and as you had to pay for the trials we gave them, they were very good pups so needed no more trials at his track.

We took them next to Wimbledon stadium, the premier track and the home of the Derby. The first time was an eye opener, the second was a brilliant sight to see, they had broken the 29-second barrier, a landmark that was only achieved by extra special dogs. To think these were only 15 months old. Perk had done a flying time for her age of 28–84, unbelievable for her age and with limited experience. Yes we had very good pups on our hands.

Their first race was an open one at Wimbledon but their lack of experience caught them out. In the meantime, Toni's mum Noreen was getting very weak with the cancer she had and we knew under the circumstances we could not run around the country with them for fear of having the call mum needed us. That is when we decided they had to go to a trainer who could give them the best of care and could run them around to the tracks that would suit them, these being mostly in the midlands and north of England.

We entered them for a race at Nottingham where we would meet a good friend of ours and probably the best trainer ever. We agreed he would have Perky first, then followed by Pinky. Little did we know these would give us the best times and joy we had ever achieved with all our time in greyhound racing. Perky was to win the Oaks by over six lengths and the next year due to Perky getting injured Pinky came to the four and also made the Oaks final the following year. This was so far the top of the tree with regards bitches' races. Perky also before injury won the select stakes and reached the Monmore Gold Cup final. This was to be her last race, after only 28 races our dream was over with her. She had given us unbelievable pleasure and the three great bitches are still living with us and will do until their lives end. God gave us these three great bitches and memories that will never leave us, brilliant.

I have trained some great bitches over the years and Perky
is as good as I have ever had

Charlie Lister OBE
Winner of a record seven Greyhound Derbys

Afterword

It was April 2011 when my niece phoned me. She said, "How are you, uncle?" I told her fine. Then she said, "You'd better sit down."

That's when she told me that a daughter I never knew had been in touch with her on a media site. I never knew about sites in those days. It appears that the girl I was going with from the dog track, Sheila, who left to get away from the dogs for a while, was in fact having my child. This was a blow to me as I never had a clue she was pregnant, but she returned to Reading to have the baby and kept that to herself so never let the trainer she worked for know anything about it. We were soon in touch. She is called Clair and I went to meet her.

It was gutting as I had been no part of her life till she found me. We now keep in touch and I have been to her place and she stayed with us in Portsmouth for a while. She is a hard-working girl and has a boy called Billy. That's another child that I have. Talk about luck you have to have that. I was trying to find my daughter who was taken to Australia to live and I had not seen her since she was seven and every time I met anyone from Australia in Thailand I would talk about her, telling them her name was Julie and asking the best way to find a lost one in Australia.

There were a lot of different suggestions given to me and a lot that I had pursued, but the big breakthrough came when I got a computer. I put in 'Australia' and the name 'Julie Ann'. Hundreds came up and I went through them, slowly clicking on the ones that appeared to cover the age that Julie would now be. I sent an email to one and they got back in a couple of days stating that she was sorry but that it wasn't her, but she told me she would give the details to a group of people who got a lot of pleasure reuniting lost families. She was apparently part of this group. Luck seemed with me again. I gave her all the details and she said she would put it to her friends and help me find my lost daughter. I thanked her by mail and waited for her reply. This is where it went into stagnant mode and I never heard from her for about six months. All I thought was, another messer.

I had come across a lot of them over the years from looking for Julie, so back to the drawing board, but first I would send an email to the lady who was last onto me.

I got an email straight back saying she was terribly sorry but her husband had been very bad and had in fact now passed away, so she would give her time to me now. She sent me an email with four email addresses on it. I looked at them and just picked one and clicked on it. A questionnaire dropped down and I filled it in with all the details that I had of Julie – date of birth, name when left England, area I last knew of (that was what the Salvation Army had given me namely Adelaide). I sent these off and an email was returned to me which they asked me to sign. This stated that I would stop letting anyone who may be looking for Julie or who I had given permission to help me find her to stop this and leave it to this organisation to do all the searching for me.

It transpired that I was in touch with a long lost family firm who, as in England made a show of their arranged meetings with long lost families and I had to sign and agree to giving all the rights to them should they be successful. Then a lady asked me to go on a FaceTime site where she would interview me I suppose to see how I came across for their show. I connected with her at the time and we both agreed to and sat through the interview, she seemed very pleased with me and told me she would send me an email when she had more to tell me. A few weeks had passed when she got in touch again telling me they had found her, but she did not want to appear on the programme. But she did agree to me having her email address, so the lady gave me this and I was now over the moon. My first born, I have found her at last! After all these years, 42 years to be precise. By now it was 2015 and I was so chuffed just knowing she was alive and well, we have been communicating ever since and we have even made the trip to Australia to see her. She is married to a nice man, John, and has two children, Luke and Bianca, who are now 22 years and 20 years old. It seems now my life is complete, and now I have this book to tell all and sundry, of my life to date.

God bless all that have made this possible.

IAN WALTER TUNGATT

"I was talking to Toni's brother Mark, the other day, he reminded me of the time myself, Mark, brother Les, brother, Peter Cave, Danny Curzons all staying in my guest house, went to see a world championship fight of Colin Jones. It was held in the Birmingham exhibition centre. When we arrived there was nowhere you could get any food as it was a new venue then. We asked where we could get something to eat and was informed the nearest place was a hotel but that it was a bit pricey. We were hungry by now after the trip there, so had no option but to venture to the hotel. There was a buffet-type meal layout under a hot plate but first we would go to the bar area for a drink. I said I would pay for the drinks and meals as they only had a small income. While I was queuing up the man in front of us was ordering a largish order and when it came for him to pay he said, "Johnson room 103." The waiter came back with the bill and he signed it. Since as it was quite a big bill I took notice. Then proceeded to order and pay for our drinks. After we had finished them we made our way to the dining area and helped ourselves to the buffet which was laid out and you had a large selection to chose from. After the meal I asked a waitress for our bill and thought I would have a game. When the bill was presented to me, I said "Johnson room 103" she went away to the main desk then came back for me to sign the docket. I never thought I could do it as it started off as a laugh but to my amazement they had accepted my details. I scribbled a signature and said to the waitress I'll order breakfast as I wanted two boiled eggs with mine. She said that would be no problem then we made our way to the toilet. On the way to them we passed an open door which was the kitchen and the back door was open, to allow steam and alike to disperse away from the kitchen. Now the joke had gone too far and we had to get out of the hotel but still being prepared to pay should we get stopped. So we proceeded to go away from the hotel and into the car park, then drove off. We couldn't stop laughing, what a result we had. We went to watch the fight and drove home. When we were talking the next day it appeared nearly all of us had caught food poisoning – that would teach us. The hotel had the last laugh."

IWT

A PORTSMOUTH LIVING LEGEND

IAN TUNGATT